PRAISE FOR
WHAT MAKES SAMMY RUN?

"This is the greatest, fastest, wildest, most timeless collection of celebrity journalism ever!"   —E. Jean Carroll, author and columnist

"Alex Belth, with his keen, keen eye, has brought a 20th century art form—the celebrity profile—into the 21st century. This is a brilliant collection. And it proves that the '60s and '70s were, without a doubt, the apogee of American journalism."
—Lili Anolik, contributing editor at *Vanity Fair* and author of the forthcoming *Didion and Babitz*

"Longform lovers: Time-travel back to the glorious days of unfettered access and infinite word counts with this engrossing collection of classic profiles. Often, the journalist is as notable as the subject— Nora Ephron on Helen Gurley Brown, patron saint of mouseburgers everywhere; Rex Reed on booze-swilling, ball-busting screen siren Ava Gardner. Many of the profiles feel definitive: a Mary McCarthy deep dive that's both unsparing and anointing, sessions with Warren Beatty that manage to peel back the enigmatic layers, a master contextualizing of Truman Capote post-La Côte Basque In an era of quick-and-dirty clickbait, *What Makes Sammy Jr. Run?*—with invaluable intros and postscripts—is the pleasure-read we need now."
—Lucy Kaylin, Editorial Director, Hearst Magazines

"*What Makes Sammy Jr. Run?* pulses with life, the subjects' and the authors' hearts sometimes beating in synch and sometimes in contretemps. As an anthology of celebrity journalism from the 1960s and 1970s, it is a vivid survey of the literary possibilities of the celebrity profile, from a time when magazines were powerful and there were only half as many lawyers."
—Lucy Sante, author of
I *Heard Her Call My Name: A Memoir of Transition*

"The smartest pieces you will ever read about the most captivating celebrities and cultural rascals in our collective memory. The New Journalism at its most most."

—Terry McDonell, former editor of Esquire, author of
The Accidental Life: An Editor's Notes on Writing and Writers

"The celebrity profile, when taken seriously by a non-fiction master like the ones included in this book, is a uniquely American art form that opens windows into the national mood, identity, dreams and insecurities. These stories are as essential to understanding America as Route 66, Norman Rockwell and cable TV."

—Wright Thompson, author of The Cost of These Dreams:
Sports Stories and Other Serious Business

MORE BOOKS FROM THE SAGER GROUP

The Stacks Reader Series

The Cheerleaders: A True Story by E. Jean Carroll

An American Family: A True Story by Daniel Voll

Flesh and Blood: A True Story by Peter Richmond

An Accidental Martyr: A True Story by Chip Brown

Death of a Playmate: A True Story by Teresa Carpenter

The Detective: And Other True Stories by Walt Harrington

Soldiers in the Army of God: A True Story by Daniel Voll

Original Gangster: A True Story by Paul Solotaroff

The Dreamer Deceiver: A True Story by Ivan Solotaroff

*Mary in the Lavender Pumps: A True Story about Love,
Murder and Gender Identity* by Joyce Wadler

*Not Guilty by Reason of Afghanistan:
And Other True Stories*
by John H. Richardson

The Strange and Mysterious Death of Mrs. Jerry Lee Lewis
by Richard Ben Cramer

Love and Death in Vermont by Marguerite Del Giudice

Growing up Stoned by Elizabeth Kaye

General Interest

*The Stories We Tell: Classic True Tales
by America's Greatest Women Journalists*

*New Stories We Tell: True Tales
by America's New Generation of Great Women Journalists*

Newswomen: Twenty-Five Years of Front-Page Journalism

Next Wave: America's New Generation of Literary Journalists

The Devil & John Holmes: And Other True Stories by Mike Sager

Lifeboat No. 8: Surviving the Titanic by Elizabeth Kaye

Hunting Marlon Brando: A True Story by Mike Sager

Notes from the Road: A Filmmaker's Journey through American Music
by Robert Mugge

The Living and the Dead by Brian Mockenhaupt

See our entire collection @ TheSagerGroup.net

WHAT MAKES SAMMY JR. RUN?

CLASSIC CELEBRITY JOURNALISM
VOLUME - 1
1960s and 1970s

EDITED BY ALEX BELTH

What Makes Sammy Jr. Run?
Classic Celebrity Journalism Volume 1 (1960s and 1970s)

Edited by Alex Belth

Cover design and Interior design by Siori Kitajima, PatternBased.com

Cataloging-in-Publication data for this book
is available from the Library of Congress.

ISBN-13:
eBook: 978-1-958861-23-3
Paperback: 978-1-958861-24-0
Hardcover: 978-1-958861-38-7

Published by The Sager Group LLC
(TheSagerGroup.net)

WHAT MAKES SAMMY JR. RUN?

CLASSIC CELEBRITY JOURNALISM

VOLUME - 1
1960s and 1970s

EDITED BY **ALEX BELTH**

WITH A FOREWORD BY **JOYCE WADLER**

For Emily Joy

PUBLISHER'S NOTE

These stories include words, attitudes, and sensibilities about gender, race, body image, socioeconomic class, and politics that reflect the time and place in which they were written, researched, and published. Some elements may be potentially triggering to modern readers. The stories have been left in their original form as befits historical writings.

"History is not the past, but a map of the past, drawn from a particular point of view, to be useful to the modern traveler."—*Henry H. Glassie*

CONTENTS

FOREWORD
BY JOYCE WADLER

Every now and then somebody chases me down to talk to their journalism class about writing profiles and since this gives me the opportunity to get to a young reporter before some editor does, draining every ounce of creative juice and originality and delight out of their bodies and leaving them an empty, beaten, health insurance dependent shell, much like myself, I usually say yes.

Kiddies, I say, essential to getting a subject to spill their guts is establishing trust. One does this in many ways: showing interest in what interests the subject, feigning sincerity, mastering a range of words and sounds along the lines of "Wow! No! You don't say! That is so interesting! Oooh! Aaaah!" It may seem daunting, I say, but if you have ever been on a blind date with a person who appears mostly dead but you want to sleep with anyway, faking sincerity is a skill you already possess. You've feigned orgasm? You are ready for a career in journalism.

True, I was not always aware of all this as I traipsed gaily out into my journalism career. Nobody told me to save questions involving murder raps or marital tensions for last, which is why you once could have seen me sprinting down the halls of the Plaza as the son of a New York politician screamed, "I PISS on *The Washington Post*" or being frozen out by the crew on a sailing ship in New Zealand where they were doing a remake of *Mutiny on the Bounty*, because the star had a screaming fit about that bitch from New York. Actually, he was alleged to have used a much uglier word than bitch. No, no, don't ask who it was. I couldn't possibly tell you. Oh, all right, Mel Gibson. On the plus side, he wasn't anti-Semitic.

Eventually, however, I got the knack of the interview. If I was talking to the guy who got shot out of the cannon at the circus, I slipped into the cannon to get the feel. (Dumb, dumb, dumb. Had the thing fired it could have cut me in two.) If the subject was an animal trainer, I rode the elephant. (Bonus reportorial tip: Always be extra nice to the elephants. A human hates you; the worst you will suffer is a screaming phone call from the publicist. The elephant hates you; you will be a headline in the *Daily News*.)

So, when I had an assignment some years back to go up to Woodstock, NY, to interview Levon Helm, the drummer and vocalist of The Band who died in 2012, I was confident I was ready. I had grown up not far from Woodstock in the mid-1960s where The Band's members had hung out, I knew their music, I knew which Band member had killed himself and which had died of an overdose.

My interest was Helm's financial problems. Both Helm and the Band's organist, Garth Hudson, had almost lost their homes because of tax troubles. I had interviewed Hudson a week before I went to talk to Helm and the fact that I still remained in the business was proof of just how desperate I was for health insurance. Hudson didn't answer questions for several minutes or at all and, when he did, he replied in what I shall generously describe as parables. I am paraphrasing here, but it went something like this.

Me: Garth, you almost lost your house, but at the last minute someone bailed you out. You must be feeling pretty good about this.

A long pause during which life is discovered on Mars; an ice age threatens Woodstock, getting as far as West Shokan, then withdraws; I die and, having learned nothing from my previous life, am reborn as a feature writer.

Hudson: Well, I'll tell ya. I play a lot better with my left hand now than I did seven years ago.

Interviewing him was one miserable slog. Happily, I was accompanied by a photographer, Chris Maynard, a man of few words, though not so few as Hudson, and when Hudson left us for a spell, he made one of those corkscrew motions at the side of his head you learn in second grade, then spoke the three little words a reporter cannot hear often enough when an interview has gone south.

"It's not you," he said.

A week later I drove back up to the country to interview Levon, who was married and living in a barn-like house in Woodstock. He'd had a bout of throat cancer a year or two earlier but he was as chatty as Hudson was withdrawn. He talked about losing his money to drugs; about the record companies he felt had cheated him; about his former bandmate Robbie Robertson, the one decent businessman in the group as far as I could see, who was living in Los Angeles, scoring movies, who Levon felt had ripped him off too.

It was a humid August day and at one point Levon suggested I kick off my shoes and take a walk to his lake. Naturally—*take an interest in their interests*—I did. It was a nice enough lake, but very buggy, so after a little "Oooh, aaah, great lake, sweet property, gee whiz, trees and everything?" I cut it short. It wasn't until two hours after I had left Levon's that I realized that I was scratching my legs not because of bugs, but because of poison ivy. Within 48 hours they were covered with great oozing sores. It took a course of oral antibiotics to clear them up, but I was so grateful that Levon had been a great talker I didn't hold it against him, even when I learned someone else had gotten a wicked case of poison ivy on his land so he had to have known it was there.

About a week later, I was heading up to Woodstock again and since I had a few more questions for Levon, I made an appointment to drop in and see him again. He came out to meet me, wearing only a pair of faded, navy blue underpants. The name on the band was Calvin Klein. You notice things like that when a guy is wearing only his underwear. Also that even in rock 'n' roll, time takes a toll.

Levon said nothing about why he was dressed only in underpants and not wishing to be uncool with a guy who had played with Bob Dylan I did not bring it up. It certainly wasn't a seduction move, there was none of that vibe about it, his wife was in the house, and the '60s were over. We sat in his screened-in porch, stacked with crates of empty Coca-Cola bottles, and discussed heroin and getting ripped off and I thought about the gorilla in the middle of the room and what a wuss I was being and finally, as casually as I could, I asked Levon what I still feel was one of the most penetrating questions of my career. I wish *60 Minutes* had been there to capture it.

"Levon," I said, "Why are you doing this interview in your underwear?"

His answer didn't rise to the same level. It also didn't make any sense, considering we were sitting in a screened in porch: His doctor had told him it would be good for his health to get some sun, he said.

But giving the matter much thought, later, I decided that as so often is the case, the subject's words were not as relevant as his actions. The man had felt comfortable enough with me to do an interview in his underwear. I had established trust.

INTRODUCTION
BY ALEX BELTH

"There is, far as I can see, no reason to do a story on me. Most of what I have to say you couldn't print anyway. Most movie stars are not interesting, so to sell papers and magazines in the fading publications field, a writer has to end up writing his ass off to make somebody look more interesting than he really is, right? What it all boils down to is publicity because somebody's got some movie to sell, right? What do I need with publicity? You want to see me driving up and down the Sunset Strip in my car picking up girls, right? Well, you don't think I'd be stupid enough to let you see that side of me, do you?"—Warren Beatty, Esquire *1967*

"Hi diddle-de-dee. An actor's life for me."—Robert Mitchum, Penthouse *1974*

For more than a hundred years, we've made celebrity worship a national pastime without ever calling it as much. With their beauty, ability, and fame, celebrities charm us, and we yearn to know if that charm extends to their daily lives. We want to know everything about them.

In the third decade of the twenty-first century, it's hard to imagine a major star divulging their private lives to ... a *writer*. If a celebrity wants to document their life, they'll produce a documentary or docuseries or fictional movie or podcast. They won't leave it to a magazine, because why would they? But during the 1960s and '70s, the balance of power tilted in the other direction. Magazines, even low budget start-ups, had the freedom to publish nuanced, intimate, and occasionally revealing stories. Writers weren't invincible but they had freedom to write what they wanted, and a magazine could publish a critical piece without fear of damaging relationships with actors and agents and PR teams. It was a time of provocation where the results could be damning or exposing.

The happy result for us readers is a trove of lively, interesting reportage that is both entertaining and historically intriguing. The writers in this anthology, in a range of styles, all put us *right there* in the room with the entertainers and artists who are grappling, in some way or another, with their fame. What it means to have it, sustain it, and lose it.

There were notable magazine articles on celebrities before, of course; *The New Yorker* started doing their "Profiles" in the 1920s and occasionally wrote about a celebrity such as silent movie star Rudolf Valentino. However, during the golden age of the Hollywood studio system, from the 1920s through the '40s—which coincided with a golden age of magazines—movie stars were protected, which meant magazine articles weren't especially in-depth or candid. "In the old days the Hollywood press had real power," Joan Crawford said in a 1973 interview, "yet they could be so—well, discreet is a nice word ... I mean, they had to know something about what went on between me and Clark [Gable], and me and a few other men, but they kept quiet .... There was such a thing as a gentleman of the press."

Lillian Ross's 1950 *New Yorker* magazine portrait of Ernest Hemingway, and then her masterful examination of film director John Huston in *Picture*, detailing the making of Huston's 1951 film, *The Red Badge of Courage*, set the tone for smart, sharp, observational reporting. Truman Capote's 1957 *New Yorker* profile of Marlon Brando, "The Duke in His Domain," was the smartest and sharpest of all. Warned against being left alone with Capote, Brando ignored the advice and suffered the consequence: The piece had the inevitable, casual cruelty of a cat torturing a mouse. "Most actors are such children," Capote later told his friend, the novelist John Knowles. "Brando could have sued me over that interview and collected."

One of the early celebrity profilers, Helen Lawrenson became famous in 1936 when she wrote "Latins Are Lousy Lovers." Published in *Esquire* under an anonymous byline, the essay—meant to be a comic debunking of Latin machismo—instead created a scandal. Cuban officials confiscated copies of the issue of *Esquire* and jailed eight newsdealers. Much to Lawrenson's horror, the phrase "Latins are lousy lovers" became part of the American lexicon—most people were familiar with the line without knowing where it came from.

In 1958, she recalled, "I don't suppose that I have gone to a party in thirty years without having someone come up to me, sooner or later, in the course of the festivities, and announce with a bright gleam in his eye, 'Say, I understand you're the girl who wrote that piece!' There is never any doubt what piece he means because the next thing is, inevitably, 'Tell me, how did you ever come to do it?' If the man is a Latin, he is eager to leap into the arena and avenge his national honor. If he is a non-Latin, he regards me skittishly and is afraid to spend much time with me, lest he wake up some fine morning to find that he, too, has been immortalized in print."

By the '50s, primarily in the pages of *Esquire*, Lawrenson became known as a go-to profiler of celebrities, from Marlene Dietrich to Errol Flynn, writing not so much with innovation but bookworm smarts, sexual frankness, keen observation, and self-deprecating appeal. Elsewhere, at *Time* magazine, Brad Darrach delivered stylish, often confidential portraits of A-list stars—Frank Sinatra, Marilyn Monroe, and Elizabeth Taylor among them. Darrach succeeded the great James Agee as *Time*'s movie critic, and also wrote about books for years, while finding his groove writing profiles in the style of *Time* stories, all of them masterpieces of compression.

Thomas B. Morgan, a young magazine editor, quit a cushy job at *Look* magazine in 1957 to write fiction and spent the next couple of years working on a pair of novels that went unpublished. Hoping to make some money, he turned to magazines as a freelancer. His first assignment, on the entertainer Sammy Davis Jr, came from Clay Felker, a rising young editor at *Esquire* later known as one of journalism's power brokers during his run at *New York* magazine. Morgan assimilated what he'd learned as a novelist. His profile of Davis Jr., he later recalled, "came out virtually as a short story, using dialogue, atmosphere, and character development ... I plan more novels, but

I no longer tell myself that journalism is a preliminary before the main event."

Meanwhile, successful fiction writers such as Norman Mailer and Truman Capote dove into journalism with zeal and facility. Capote went so far as to straight-facedly invent a new category—the nonfiction novel—with his true crime saga, In *Cold Blood*.

While it's tempting to picture the '60s as a golden age of magazine journalism—think of all those incredible *Harper's Bazaar* and *Esquire* covers—the reality was less rosy. Sure, a few legacy brands, *Esquire*, *Harper's*, and *Cosmopolitan*, enjoyed revitalizations, but by the early '70s, many long-standing titles—*Collier's*, *Life*, *The Saturday Evening Post*—pillars of magazine's golden age, folded. Still, even if the industry was forever in flux, and TV continued its ascent as the dominant form of media, magazines *were* at the center of cultural conversation. Scrappy start-ups like *Ramparts*, *Rolling Stone*, and *New York* found their audience; and at publications from *Harper's* to *The Village Voice* to *Playboy*, a new, less rigid brand of writing, best known as "New Journalism," flourished.

The term "New Journalism" is most associated with Tom Wolfe—who came to regret it, as did many of the people labeled "New Journalists." At its worst, most cartoonish, New Journalism came to connote style over substance, and taking great liberties with the facts. But fabrication did not define the movement, which was all right there in Gay Talese's 1962 *Esquire* profile of retired heavyweight champion Joe Louis. It's this piece that Wolfe credited as a model, using the elements of a novelist's toolbox that Morgan discussed. Crucially, magazines offered more space and more freedom to writers than newspapers could—at times, a single article would take up an entire magazine issue. And, as was the case with Mailer, columnist Jimmy Breslin, or journalist Hunter S. Thompson—the authors themselves became a character in their own stories. Others, like Talese, Joan Didion, or O'Connell Driscoll, took a more third-person, voyeuristic approach, with the writer receding into the background, the "eye" of a documentarian's camera.

There was nothing "new" about any of this. But hey, in the '60s, hype carried the day. In fact, New Journalism proved the exception not the rule; I don't think anyone would mistake Lawrenson or Helen Dudar or Anne Taylor Fleming for a "New Journalist." No matter the label, the best journalism is rooted in great reporting. Talese called it "the art of hanging out."

"I'm one of those who believe that reporting is an art form," he once said, "or should be pursued as an art form. You can do anything with it." Even write a story about a subject that won't grant you an audience, which is what happened when Talese tried, unsuccessfully, to interview Frank Sinatra in late 1965; the result, "Frank Sinatra Has a Cold," a brilliant depiction of the atmosphere and people around Sinatra, is one of the most celebrated magazine stories ever written. Its perceived failure—not getting Sinatra to talk—turned out to be a blessing. The piece is also a reminder of the limitations of a writer's clout, particularly when it came to access, which even in the '60s did not come easily. "Gay Talese came out here and got hot under the collar because it took him three weeks to see Frank Sinatra," Guy McElwaine, Beatty's press agent told Rex Reed. "Hell, Mia Farrow [Sinatra's then wife] doesn't even see Sinatra until the lights go out."

Other reporters had better luck, like Doon Arbus, a young reporter from New York who was able to convince James Brown and his entourage to let her to go along on a music tour of the South, at a time when a young White woman traveling with a group of Black people could be scandalous. Sara Davidson got plenty of cooperation from Jacqueline Susann when the author was at the height of her success as a publishing phenomenon. Then there's "Jerry Lewis, Birthday Boy," a massive 1974 *Playboy* profile by Driscoll. The complete opposite of Talese's Sinatra tale, Lewis allowed the 21-year-old USC student to hang out with him up close in Los Angeles, Miami, and Germany. Lewis had previously had a circumspect, almost cagey attitude toward the American press. How did he let his guard down enough to let this kid reporter see so much? When Driscoll handed the story in, his editor at *Playboy* said, "I hope you have notes because we're going to get sued." But a lawsuit never came. The piece both made Driscoll's career and marked him as someone who saw too much and thus couldn't be trusted. Never again would he enjoy that kind of access.

A few pieces in this anthology created a stir when first published, like Barbara Goldstein's 1967 *New York* article on Viva, one of Andy Warhol's superstars. "A lot of horrible things have happened to me," Viva later said, "but I would consider that the worst." Robert Ward's juicy 1977 *Sport* profile of Reggie Jackson reignited a tabloid storm for Jackson with the New York Yankees for which the baseball player never forgave Ward. Darrach's *Penthouse* profile left Robert Mitchum's family mortified. A year later, in a 1973 *Rolling Stone* article, Mitchum's twenty-year-old daughter conceded that Darrach's piece was a "fairly accurate story"—though hardly a fair one. "The thing is," she said, "it was all so *private*."

This isn't a compendium of the most controversial celebrity profiles ever written. If it were, we would have included Reed's 1967 dismantling of Beatty in *Esquire* ("Will the Real Warren Beatty Please Shut Up?") instead of selecting Lawrenson's sympathetic, and perhaps more accurate, portrait.

You'll find plenty of writerly "voice" in these pieces—witness the tour de force that is Brock Brower's lead in to his profile of writer and critic Mary McCarthy, devoted to her smile (one of the characteristics of this era of journalism is an emphasis on physical descriptions, the kind of details considered offensive today). And you'll also see plenty of humor, such as Mark Jacobson's visit with movie star Pam Grier, which ends hilariously, albeit painfully for the author; or the lighthearted, almost meta-hijinks of Sally Quinn's lunch interview with Rudolf Nureyev. Quinn writes with sly humor about Nureyev's appeal as a sex object; he beams with pride as he successfully evades her questions. And then there's Albert Goldman's coffee shop comedy riffing with Philip Roth on the occasion of the publication of *Portnoy's Complaint*, the book that made Roth both a celebrity and a wealthy man.

What binds these stories is that they all touch on the nature of fame and the inner workings of the fame machine. They are presented in chronological order; the fact that there are consecutive pieces about the publishing industry is coincidental. The overall result is not meant to be definitive so much as representative. This isn't a collection of stories about celebrities whose fame transcends time, it's a collection of stories about what it meant to be a celebrity in the '60s and '70s. We've left out standards like "Frank Sinatra Has a Cold" by Talese and "Radical Chic" by Tom Wolfe, the "Sweet Home Alabama" and "Stairway to Heaven" of celebrity profiles—because, like Capote's Brando piece, they are heavily anthologized and easy to find. Instead, the aim here is for you to enjoy some names that you may not be familiar with. Or those you might know but not in this idiom—such as the inimitable Nora Ephron, who, decades before she became a famous filmmaker, was a kick-ass magazine writer. Rex Reed later joked that the celebrity interview was the lowest form of journalism, but the truth is, he was terrific at it, and his profiles from that era sparkle.

The bylines you find here are a gratifying mix of seasoned veterans such as Helen Dudar and Jacqueline Trescott, and short-timers like Anne Taylor Fleming and John Eskow. Lawrenson was in her seventies when she wrote about Beatty, and Darrach in his late fifties when he profiled Mitchum. But one remarkable aspect of this collection is the poise and restraint shown by the younger writers: Sara Davidson was twenty-seven when she wrote about Jacqueline Susann; Driscoll twenty-one when he got to Jerry Lewis, and Doon Arbus just twenty when she profiled James Brown. Each of their stories have a measured, even tone you don't immediately associate with a young writer.

Bear in mind the reporting standards of the era. Many of these reporters took notes, but not in front of their subjects, scribbling them on cocktail napkins in the bathroom instead. Tape recorders were cumbersome and not yet industry standard. Lillian Ross and Talese didn't use them at all. When Anne Taylor Fleming showed up at La Côte Basque for her first interview with Truman Capote, she placed her shoddy-looking tape recorder on the table. "Put that away," said Capote. "If you're going to be a good reporter all you have to do is listen." Taylor knew it was part of a game, a challenge. "He was putting me on notice," she remembers, "so, I learned to listen with all the fiber I had."

Just as Capote had put his finger on Brando twenty years before, Fleming's portrait of Capote, which ran in two-parts, in consecutive issues of *The New York Times Sunday Magazine*, presented the writer as a victim of his own lust for fame. By the '70s, Capote had squandered his immense talent, reduced to a caricature of himself, gossiping on TV talk shows. He underestimated Fleming, and while her piece lacks the acidic glee of "The Duke in His Domain," it stings all the same. Like Jerry Lewis, Capote was a star of yesteryear trying to make a dramatic comeback only to face his own dramatic failings.

Lauren Bacall, on the other hand, had a more grounded perspective. Captured with brisk, effortless precision by Helen Dudar—who, as a longtime reporter, struck many as a real-life version of Rosalind Russell in *His Girl Friday*—Bacall hadn't acted much in the '70s but was on the verge of publishing a memoir when Dudar interviewed her. The book, which Bacall wrote without a ghostwriter (though in collaboration with legendary book editor, Robert Gottlieb), not only became a bestseller but is regarded as one of the finest Hollywood autobiographies ever written. In their conversation, brief, courteous, and professional, Bacall is levelheaded about her life and celebrity. "I'm not desperate about it at all," said Bacall, a star at nineteen, whose fame would never burn as bright as it had when she'd been married to Humphry Bogart, who died in 1957. "I just don't want to waste my time," Bacall continued. "I don't want to give myself away. I don't want to go to cocktail parties anymore."

Bacall knew the steep price of fame, but, as the saying goes, the show must go on. "There were, after all, today and tomorrow to be faced," writes Dudar. "Besides, she knows very well it's not supposed to be easy."

—Alex Belth

THOMAS B. MORGAN

Before New Journalism emerged in the 1960s, Thomas B. Morgan (1926–2014), a magazine editor and frustrated novelist, applied the literary techniques of fiction to magazine profiles with dazzling results. During most of the '50s, Morgan worked as an editor at *Look* magazine where he polished his craft while contributing pieces to *Esquire*, *Holiday*, *Redbook*, *Cosmopolitan*, and *TV Guide*. He quit *Look* in 1957 to be a writer of serious fiction, penned two novels, neither published, and with a young family to consider, quickly returned to magazine work. The day after he finished his first novel, Morgan commiserated at lunch with Clay Felker, a rising young editor at *Esquire*. Felker mentioned that he'd seen the brilliant Sammy Davis Jr. on TV the night before and talked about how Davis had never been properly profiled. Morgan got the assignment and hung out with Davis nonstop for a week. "I earned Sammy's trust enough for him to open up to me about his life in a way that he hadn't to any reporter," Morgan recalled. "He spent the weekend fishing with me and my wife at our summer house in Long Island, and I earned his trust that way. I had the feeling that he had never had a friend who was a journalist before."

Morgan said the piece "came out virtually as a short story, using dialogue, atmosphere, and character development to explore Sammy's personality." It proved a winning formula in a string of profiles Morgan delivered to *Esquire* in the early '60s on figures as diverse as Roy Cohn, Teddy Kennedy, John Wayne, and Blaze Starr. Morgan did eventually publish a novel, *Snyder's Walk*, in 1987, though novelist would be a minor accomplishment in what proved a fascinating career: Morgan served as Adlai Stevenson's press aide in 1960, and later was press secretary for New York Mayor John Lindsay; he held executive positions at *New York* magazine, WNYC public radio, and the United Nations Association of the U.S.A. And quietly, Morgan helped pioneer, and master, the show business profile.—Alex Belth

WHAT MAKES SAMMY JR. RUN?

Esquire, 1959

In a typical ten-day period recently, Sammy Davis Jr. had this schedule: the final week of an eighteen-day engagement at the Copacabana (sixteen performances interspersed with general frolicking, a record date, television and radio interviews, and two visits with Cye Martin, his tailor); a one-night stand in Kansas City to receive an Americanism award from the American Legion; one night at home in Hollywood; and the opening night of a two-week date in Las Vegas at the Sands Hotel, the management of which has a contract with him for the next four years, eight weeks a year, at $25,000 per week. The schedule could have been extended. The day after closing in Vegas, Davis was due for three weeks in Hollywood at the Moulin Rouge, another nightclub with which he has a five-year, million-dollar deal, followed by two weeks in Australia, followed by an eastern tour. Photographer Burt Glinn and I, however, arbitrarily pursued Davis through that ten-day period. Since this short, skinny, one-eyed, broken-nosed, umber-colored singer-dancer-musician-actor-mimic may be, as Milton Berle has said, "the greatest entertainer in the world," and may even be, as Groucho Marx has decided, "better than Al Jolson, who could only sing," we wanted to find out what we could, naturally, about what makes Sammy Jr. run.

Like most men, Davis lives a life of quiet desperation. The only differences are that he has little privacy to live it in and that on the average of twice a night, thirty weeks a year, he must stand in a spotlight and be Sammy Davis Jr.—comic, sentimental, bursting with energy, and immensely talented—no matter how he feels inside. If he were an average performer, the challenge might not be so great.

"But you see," says Davis, "what I do is different. Most Negro performers work in a cubicle. They walk on, entertain, and sing twelve songs before they say good evening. They never make any personal contact with the audience. Long time ago, I knew I could only make it if I broke through this wall. I was convinced that a Negro boy could do comedy—you know the kind I mean. Not the yassuh, nossuh thing. I decided I could make it as a person, like Jolson or Danny Kaye made it. Well, to do that, you have to be honest with an audience. You got to have antennae and feel what they want. And you have to try to keep your personal feelings from interfering with your communication."

The Davis act has a basic structure—songs, impersonations, dancing, laced together with comic patter or sentimental chitchat. The structure never changes, yet every performance is different.

"The patter between songs," says Davis, "is something that can't be planned. You can't write it if you're going to be honest. I can vary the act at any minute with a signal to Morty Stevens, my conductor. I snap my fingers a certain way and he knows we are going to go into 'Let's Face the Music.' I tap my foot just so, and it's going to be 'Old Black Magic.' If you're honest, you can feel the right way to get to them every time. Otherwise, Dullsville, Ohio. I don't mean all good shows are alike, either. You've got three kinds of shows—a routine show, a fun show, and a performance show. The fun show is lots of tumult and laughs. The performance show is the one, like opening night, where you belt it all the way. What I do works because I am trying to be honest.

"You take most of the material in my act: aside from the songs, I don't do any bits that I didn't contribute to. I have a choreographer—Hal Loman—but we work out the dances together. Nothing fancy about my dancing. I like to make clear sounds with the taps. Bojangles—that's Bill Robinson, who taught me a lot—he used to say, 'Make it so the people can understand it.' That's what I try to do.

"Sometimes the impersonations get in the way. They blur your image with the people and you die as a performer without a distinction of your own. I used to do a song called 'Why Can't I Be Me?' That's the story of most of my life. Every guy wants to sound like himself. But I keep the impersonations in the act because the audience wants them. They're like a frame. The audience says, gee, that's his best stuff, what's he going to give us next?

"The big thing is understanding the songs and projecting them honestly. When I sing 'I Got Plenty o' Nuttin',' I think about a guy who is happy with his life. Doesn't make any difference how *I* feel. I think how *he* feels. When you have that, daddy, you don't need any tricks. All I want is they should like me—say this is a nice guy. Just let them give me one thing—applause—and I'm happy."

Nightclub audiences do curious things when Davis is on stage. For one, they are prone to give him standing ovations. For another, they tend to gasp out telling comments—telling about themselves as well as the performer. Early in his act, Davis comes on wearing a grey porkpie hat, black suit, black shirt, white tie, with a trench coat flung over his shoulder, a cigarette in one hand and a glass of whiskey-colored water in the other. He blows smoke into the microphone, sips the drink, and says, "My name is Frank Sinatra, I sing songs, and we got a few we'd like to lay on ya." Davis puts the drink on the piano, throws the trench coat on the floor, and begins "The Lady Is a Tramp." The audience always applauds wildly and somebody is certain to cry out: "My God, he even looks like Sinatra," or words to that effect. A broken-nosed Negro does not look much like Sinatra, even though the latter is no work of art himself, but the illusion of Davis's voice and visage and movements, plus the complete rapport which has been established between entertainer and entertainee, produces a kind of Sinatrian hallucination.

For the full sixty minutes of his act, Davis sustains this kind of communication. It could be defined as an atmosphere of colorlessness in which he not only makes the audience forget that he is a Negro, but also makes it forget that it is White. This is why one of his closing bits has a special irony that is all Davis. He is sitting on a stool in a circle of light. He has, it seems, almost sung himself out in an effort to entertain. His coat and tie are off. He takes a few deep breaths and suddenly he brightens. "What do you say?" he asks. "Let's all get in a cab and go up to my place!" For one goofy moment, nobody laughs. Here is the source of his power and also the reason for his private desperation. In the spotlight, he and they are colorless. In the real world, he is a colored man who has made it and yet can never make it all the way. When the applause finally comes, it is deafening. The performance drives to a rocking, exploding, belting finish, and Davis is gone. As someone once said, "The only thing that could follow that act is World War III."

Thus driving and thus driven, Sammy Davis made $1.2 million last year—over half from nightclubs and the rest from records, TV, and movies. When you say it slowly, it sounds like a lot of money, but his net is considerably less. Besides taxes (he's in the ninety percent bracket), he has eleven people on his payroll: valet, secretary, conductor-arranger, drummer, guitarist, office manager, typists (for answering fan mail), and various assistants; his overhead is $3,500 a week. His agent takes ten percent. And even though his father retired from the act in 1959, because of a heart attack, and his uncle, Will Mastin, moved over from dance manager to manager in 1958, he still splits what is left equally with them, and presents the act to the public as the Will Mastin Trio featuring Sammy Davis Jr.

The three-way split of the profits is unique in show business. Davis believes he must spend on the "millionaire" level, yet the contract with father and uncle provides him with a mere thirty-three percent, of which still another ten percent goes to a group of Chicago investors.

Davis has not saved much money nor has he put his earnings to work for him with any conspicuous success. He owns a piece of an unspectacular restaurant in Hollywood and has an interest in a line of sports shirts ("Creations by Sammy Davis Jr.") and a hand grip for cameras. He put money into some TV and movie properties. But mostly the money goes for living well, if not too wisely. It would be surprising if it went any other way.

Davis was born in Harlem, December 8, 1925. His mother, father, and uncle were all in show business. He went onstage before he was three in a theater in Columbus, Ohio. He did a talking act with Uncle Will when he was three-and-a-half. He appeared in a movie, *Rufus Jones for President*, made at Warner Brothers's Long Island studios, at age four. The next year, in the midst of singing "I'll Be Glad When You're Dead, You Rascal You" at the Republic Theatre in Manhattan, he was pulled off the stage by a member of the Gerry Society, which enforced child-labor laws in those days. Until he was eleven, he trouped with his uncle's fifteen-person vaudeville act. When the authorities became suspicious, his father put cork on his face, stuck a cigar in his mouth, and passed him off as a dancing midget. In 1936, the vaudeville act was disbanded and the Will Mastin Trio, a straight dancing act, was born. They danced in beer gardens and theaters all over the East, making as little as thirty dollars a week (for the trio) and spending part of the time on relief. Davis's education consisted of less than two years in school and a few lessons from a now-and-then tutor.

In 1943, Davis was drafted into the Army. He passed the Air Corps cadet tests, but Negroes with less than two years of college training were not being accepted. He was transferred to the Infantry, in which he took basic training in one of the earliest integrated units. Three times he was rejected for overseas duty because of an athletic heart. Toward the end of the war, he was transferred again, to Special Services. In camp shows, he developed as a singer and mimic. "What was more important," says Davis, "I met a sergeant by the name of Bill Williams who gave me about fifty books to read. He's really the guy who educated me."

After the war, with Davis's songs and impersonations added to the act, the trio's luck improved. They traveled six months with Mickey Rooney, who encouraged Davis to develop all of his talents instead of concentrating on just one. Frank Sinatra, whom Davis had first met in 1940, got them three weeks on his bill at the Capitol on Broadway in 1947. In spite of favorable reviews, nothing happened. They toured the West Coast with Jack Benny, through whose help they were booked into Ciro's, Hollywood, in 1951. Herman Hover, the owner of Ciro's, offered them $300 a week to open a show starring Janis Paige. The trio held out for $350. Finally, Arthur Silber, their agent, put up fifty dollars of his own for the first week, and the contract was signed. The act caught fire. By the second week, the Will Mastin Trio was costarred with the headliner. They moved on to a date at the Chez Paree in Chicago at $1,250 a week as headliners, and so they remained, garnering top billing wherever they played.

After twenty-three years, Davis had become an overnight sensation. In the eight years that followed, the trio went round and round on the nightclub circuit—New York, Miami, Chicago, Las Vegas, and Hollywood. Davis made eleven record albums for Decca Records. He took intermittent turns as a guest performer on TV—notably the *Comedy Hour* and *The Steve Allen Show*. He appeared in *Mr. Wonderful* on Broadway—a mediocre show that ran for a year because it was cheaper for Davis's growing audience to see him in a theater than in a nightclub. In Hollywood, he made *Anna Lucasta* and the spectacular *Porgy and Bess*. The money simply poured in.

"After that night in Ciro's," Davis recalls, "every day for three years I had a new chick—wine, women, and song. After the war, I'd been hungry and mad, baby. You couldn't work certain hotels because of the Negro bit. Certain headliners refused to go on with us because we stole the show. I was so hungry. I was trying to do everything. We used to do an hour-and-forty-minute show. I could do fifty impersonations. Play the drums. Play the trumpet. Play the bass fiddle. Play the piano. Dance. Sing. Tell jokes.

"Well, then we made it. It's the old story of the guy who doesn't have it and then gets it. He fluffs friends. He does a hundred things wrong. He *knows* he's doing wrong, see, but he can't stop.

"I bought twelve suits at a time—$175 a whack. I bought tailor-made shirts, cars—fast ones. Once I bought twenty-one pairs of shoes from Lefcourt in New York. All my life, I wanted to buy something in a store and not ask how much. I lost all sense of value. I had credit everywhere and just signed my name. Between 1951 and 1954, I must have blown $150,000. My head got *so big*. I wanted to pick up every check and pay every tip. The first time I was booked into the Copa in New York, I bought a pack of cigarettes and left the girl change from a twenty-dollar bill. I wanted to do that because once I went in there as a nobody and they put me on the side. I bought a Cadillac

El Dorado. I bought gold cigarette cases for everybody. I remembered when, for Christmas presents, my dad and uncle and I used to exchange a carton of cigarettes. Every day was like Christmas. I got snotty. Everybody I saw, it was, 'Hello, chickee. Love ya, baby. See you later.'

"It takes a terribly long time to learn how to be a success in show business. People flatter you all the time. You are *on* all the time. And if you're a Negro, you find yourself using your fame to make it socially. Let's face it. The biggest deals with the big moguls are made in a social way, around the pool, that sort of thing. If you're not there, well, you're not *there*. So I used to think the greatest thing in the world was to be invited to a movie star's house.

"Things got bad. One night in Vegas, I lost $39,000 playing blackjack. That's how bad it was. There's nobody who's got that much money to lose.

"I feel I've been changing. If a man doesn't change, he isn't one to swing with. But his friends stick by him while he's changing.

"November 19, 1954, I'm driving along with a buddy at eight in the morning near San Bernardino on the way to Hollywood. It was a beautiful, typical, happy California morning. A car pulled out of a blind drive and I hit it going fifty-five or sixty. The steering wheel hit me in the face. I got the car stopped and ran over to see if the lady in the other car was all right. She was, until she looked at me. She turned green. Then I felt my left eye. They took me to the hospital and Dr. Owen O'Connor and Dr. Frederick Hull removed the eye. If they hadn't done that, I might have gone blind in a month. I spent three, four days in total darkness. I began thinking about my faults. I was sure God had saved my life. That's when I began to change.

"I met a rabbi at a Jewish benefit in Las Vegas and got interested in Judaism. I found the faith gave me something I'd been missing— peace of mind—so I converted. When I am home, in Hollywood, I try to attend services whenever I can. For a long time, I was reluctant to go into a synagogue. I was afraid people would think I was trying to pull something. While we were working on *Porgy and Bess*, Sam Goldwyn thought I was kidding when I said I wanted to be excused for the High Holy Days. Then he had to believe me when I said I would take off anyway.

"I admit the Jewish thing has been a bit of a problem. It couldn't have been more of a problem if I'd have had my eyes fixed and become Japanese. But I think everyone has to find God his own way. Sometimes it takes something like the loss of an eye to get you thinking about it. Life is very confused and you need something. I accept the Jewish idea of God. As I see it, the difference is that the Christian religion preaches love thy neighbor and the Jewish religion preaches justice. I think justice is the big thing we need."

Davis has not been without a sense of humor about his religious conversion. During his nightclub act he is likely to say, "I could have starred in *The Defiant Ones*, but I lost the part when they found out I was Jewish," or "The Irish kept me out of the St. Patrick's Day Parade for *two* reasons." On the *Porgy and Bess* set he looked accusingly at German-speaking director Otto Preminger and said: "You made lamp shades out of my people." But the justice he seeks, of course, is the most elusive of human ideals. Instead, there is irony, which Sammy Davis runs from and into almost every day of his life.

During his stay in New York last spring, Davis's dressing room was a small, seedy, two-room suite on the third floor of the Hotel Fourteen, which adjoins the Copacabana. One night after his late show, the average crowd of thirty people was milling in the twelve-by-fifteen-foot living room. Among them were Sidney Poitier, the actor, and Archie Moore, the fighter; Fran Warren, the singer, and Althea Gibson, the tennis star; three plain-clothes cops ("just friends"), and a Mrs. Goldman and her daughter ("We're fans!") from Queens, Long Island, and twenty-or-so other people who were helping themselves to the liquor, watching TV, and fooling around with the expensive portable stereo rig on the mantel—yakking and puffing as though none of the satires on showbiz had ever been written.

Davis was in the bedroom, wearing a white terry cloth robe with a torn pocket and drinking bourbon-and-Coke from a sterling-silver goblet, which a friend had given him. With him were his valet, Murphy Bennett; his secretary, Dave Landfield, who looks a little like Rip Torn and is an aspiring actor; and a man from Hollywood, one

Abby Greshler, who seemed proudest of the fact that he originally brought Dean Martin and Jerry Lewis together as a team. Greshler was there to organize a movie vehicle for Davis based on Joey Adam's novel, *The Curtain Never Falls*, about a Broadway-Hollywood star and heel. As usual, Davis was conducting his business in a fishbowl. He has no secrets from his valet, his secretary, or from almost anyone else. In exchange, his employees are deeply attached to him. A guest once said to his valet: "Tell you what, Murphy, I'll kill Sammy, and you come work for me." Bennett replied: "If Sammy dies, I'll just have to go with him."

Davis was passionately convinced that *The Curtain Never Falls* with himself in the lead would be an important step forward for all Negro actors and entertainers.

"So the hero in the book is Jewish," he said. "We make him a Negro. It works, motivation and everything. Look, I want to make it as a movie actor. I always wanted to act, but what chance was there? I remember when the reviews came out for *Mr. Wonderful*—everyone was crying about the beating we took and I was walking on air because Brooks Atkinson said I was a believable actor. Atkinson said that. Or you take *Porgy and Bess*. Now I simply *had* to play Sportin' Life. I mean, he was me. I worked to get that part. My friends—Frank and all the rest—worked to get it for me. So one night after Sam Goldwyn saw me perform, he called me into his office and pointed his finger. 'You,' he said, 'you are Sportin' Life.' Let me tell you, I mean, playing that part was the gasser of my life."

"Well, this'll be great too," said Greshler.

"The way I see it, Abby, the movie positively can't preach. It's got to show it. Here's this hero. He knows there are only three ways a colored cat can make it: as a fighter, ballplayer, or entertainer. He's got to make it, see? I remember one time a guy asked me, 'How far you going to make it, Sammy?' and I said, 'I've got an agent, some material, and talent.' So the guy says, 'Yes, but you're colored.' And I said, 'I can beat all this.' Now this is what the hero in the movie wants. Only he's ready to renounce everything he is to make it. He's a character who's ashamed of his father, see? That's the way we'll do it. People have to believe it's honest."

"They will, Sammy, they will," said Greshler.

Davis and Greshler shook hands, resealing their contract, which would never be more formal than that until the money-talk began in Hollywood. Davis turned and walked into the living room to join his guests. In the crowd, he looked smaller than he seems on stage. He is about five foot six and weighs only 125 pounds. His hair, combed flat, is neither brown nor black, but somewhere in between. It is next to impossible to determine which eye is the blind one. He has a U-shaped scar across the bridge of his nose, which was broken in the 1954 accident. His face is thin, the jaw slightly underslung. As Bob Sylvester once said, he looks as though he had been hit in the face with a shovel.

Davis spied Sidney Poitier, who is husky and tall and reminds you of an unspoiled Belafonte who can also act.

"Sidney!" cried Davis. "I'm glad to see you, baby!"

Sidney Poitier embraced him, lifting him off his feet. The room, which had been shaking with noise, became quiet, except for some shooting on the TV and Tony Bennett, lisping on the stereo.

"Everybody's got to see it, baby," said Davis, turning to a clot of people on his blind side. "I mean, you have to see Sidney in *Raisin*. Only the end—a definite gas!"

Now Davis embraced Poitier, then backed away, bending over, shoulders hunched, hands dangling in a precise imitation of Poitier in *A Raisin in the Sun*, crying: "I'm thirty-five and what am I—I'm *nothing!*"

A girl laughed, "Oh, you're something, Sam, and you're only thirty-three," and everyone laughed with her.

"She's got to die," said Davis, pinching her cheek. "If she makes one more remark, death!"

The crowd began to thin out after a while. Poitier and Moore and many of the people that no one knew departed. Davis paused to say goodbye as each one left. At the door, he did a short bit with a girl who asked him how he was getting along with the head doctor. Davis has had some psychoanalysis, but he is rarely in Hollywood long enough to accomplish much.

"Well, I've had a little, baby," said Davis. "I'm still sick, but I understand it now, see what I mean? I told the doc I didn't want to understand myself, I just wanted to be better. So he says, what you got, a cold or something—what better?"

Then Davis kissed her cheek and sent her on her way. A hard core of a dozen cordial-to-very-close friends remained. Dave Landfield, the secretary, strapped on one of the two gun belts which had been hanging in the closet and practiced his fast draw.

"Not that way, Dave! Dave—God, I could draw faster with a pencil and paper," Davis said. "Get the thumb on the hammer, man, and do it all in one motion."

Over his bathrobe, Davis buckled on a gun belt holstering a single-action Colt .45 six-shooter. He tied the holster things above his knee. He drew the gun, twirled it three times over his trigger finger, and brought it down smartly into the holster. He drew again, very fast, cocking and dry-firing in a split second. Then he twirled the gun vertically, horizontally, over and back into the holster. (In Hollywood, Davis has a collection of thirty Western guns and, next to Mel Tormé, he is the fastest nonprofessional draw in town. Once I saw him hold a bottle at waist level, *throw* the bottle to the floor, and draw, cock, and shoot before it hit the carpet. "I love things Western," he says. "Morty, Dave, Arthur Silber, and I go to Phoenix and dress up in the tailor-made jeans and the tailor-made shirts, the cowboy hats, .45's on our hips and Winchesters in the saddle holsters. We ride out like cowboys and talk about the south forty, tip the hat back with the thumb, and chew on filter cigarettes.") Davis demonstrated the fast draw a few more times.

"You dig, baby?" asked Davis.

Landfield nodded and Davis retired to the bedroom to dress. As he hung up his gun belt, he said to me: "I'm crazy to make a Western. Can you imagine a colored Western—they'll never do it! But if they do, it'll be the first time they let the Indians win!"

From the Hotel Fourteen, Davis and the hard core of friends rode three cabs to the Hotel New Yorker. Davis was living there in the penthouse. (Going up in the elevator, I remembered a story I had once heard about Bert Williams, a great Negro song-and-dance-man of twenty-five years ago. When Williams played New York, he also rented a penthouse at a midtown hotel. The only difference was that his lease required him to enter and leave the hotel by the service elevator. One night, Eddie Cantor was riding up with Williams and asked him if it bothered him using the service elevator. "Mr. Cantor," Williams said, "the only thing that bothers me is not getting applause" A great deal of progress has been made since then, I thought, but there was still a strong trace of Williams in Sammy Davis Jr.) Parties of varying intensity were held every night at the penthouse during Davis's eighteen-day engagement at the Copacabana and this night was no exception. When Davis arrived, three Copa girls, a former owner of the Chez Paree in Chicago, Davis's lawyer, another one of Davis's assistants named John Hopkins, and the comedian, Jack Carter, and his date were waiting. Hopkins and Murphy Bennett tended bar. Landfield sent out for hamburgers and Davis turned up the stereo. The hamburgers arrived and talking stopped as the guests leaped to the feast. In a twinkling, the hamburgers were gone. Everyone got one, even the pretty girl reclining on the floor underneath an oak bench—everyone, that is, except Davis.

"It's a definite steal," he said, cheerfully, but for an instant he looked as though he would have liked a hamburger.

The party broke well after dawn. Only a few bitter-enders remained when Davis's father and stepmother came in from their room down the hall. They had flown to New York from Hollywood, where they live with Sammy Jr., for a vacation and to see him at the Copacabana.

"How's my baby?" asked Sam Sr., and kissed Sam Jr.

"I'm fine, Dad."

Davis stepped back to examine his father. The older man is taller and heavier and the family resemblance is faint. He wore a new suit.

"You're getting fat, Dad," said Davis.

"I'm going to get fat as I want to."

"Well, then, get into your old clothes. Nothing looks worse than a fat man in a Continental suit."

"See what kind of a boy I have," said Sam Sr., and the two men embraced, laughing.

To me, Sam Sr. said: "We have a fine house out there. We all live in it together—the wife and me, Sam's two sisters, grandmother, and

Sammy. A fine house, yes! Believe me, it's a kick for a man who was born on West 39th Street."

Sam Jr. was proud of the house too. It had been built by Judy Garland on the side of one of the Hollywood hills, just up the road from where Davis's friend, James Dean, used to live. Davis had bought the house a few years ago for a reported $75,000. Built on three levels, it provided an apartment for Davis's grandmother and more-or-less private quarters for the family of Sam Sr. The upper floor—living room, bedroom, terrace, and guest room—was Davis's domain, furnished with white rugs, mostly black furniture, and gigantic lamps. The terrace overlooked the inevitable swimming pool. The most unusual piece of furniture was Davis's bed, which was twice the size of the average double bed; otherwise, the house was ordinary-California-expensive without being lavish.

"It is a fine house," Davis said. "It means a lot to me. Someday, I'd like to arrange things so I can spend some time there."

Davis finally went to bed that morning at eight. He was up at noon in high spirits. After lunch at P.J. Clarke's with Dorothy Kilgallen, the columnist, he walked crosstown. Everywhere he went, people on the street spoke to him, a bus driver pulled over to the curb to shake his hand, and teenagers chased him for his autograph. A few days earlier he had been taking such a stroll on Seventh Avenue and had obliged a middle-aged lady with his signature. A crowd had formed and had followed him to the door of a haberdashery. From inside, he had seen a hundred noses pressed to the window. The crowd had grown, tying up traffic on the street. At last, an irate police sergeant had forced his way into the shop.

"Mr. Davis," the policeman had said, "you got a crowd outside."

"I didn't bring them," Davis had said.

"I'll call some more cops for you."

"No, I'll get out all right."

"How can you stand it?"

"I worked twenty years for this, sergeant. I can wait."

Now as he walked, Davis enjoyed the waves and glances of passersby again. "This sort of thing started a couple of years ago," he said to me. "All of a sudden, it was there. People knew *me*. Then

I was sure I'd made it." His high spirits lasted through a sloppy recording session at Decca studios late in the afternoon. He was not in good voice and, besides, the songs were not right for him. When Dave Landfield, the secretary, asked him, "What's next?" Davis said: "Well, Dave, baby, it's a definite leave from here in two-oh minutes, maybe even one-five, followed by a definite cab, which will speed me to Danny's Hide-a-Way for a little din-din. Then it will be another cab-ola to the Hotel Fourteen, that is, one-four. After that, chickee, it is a definite lay-down with closed eyes and Morpheus dropping little things in them for about forty winks, until I awake again, as myself—like refreshed—ready to go on. I mean, baby, is that clear?"

Davis laughed. When he is very happy, indeed, his talk often becomes a combination of hip, showbiz, jazz, and, of course, English. It is in-group lingo of the kind he shares with his Hollywood friends— Frank Sinatra, Dean Martin, Peter Lawford, Eddie Fisher, and Tony Curtis—who are members of a determinedly informal organization known as "the clan."

In about one-five, Davis said to me, "Let's split," which meant *leave*, and we rode a definite cab to Danny's Hide-a-Way, a midtown restaurant in which Davis frequently dined. He ate his one big meal of the day with gusto. At seven, I followed him to the hat-check counter where he retrieved his derby, cape, and umbrella. A teenage girl asked for his autograph. Davis signed a postcard for her. "Thank you, Sammy," she said.

"You're welcome," he said, walking toward the door.

A heavy-set blond man, waiting to get to the hat-check room, said: "That's very nice, but why don't you do that in the *street*—"

A car was waiting for Davis. He stood inconclusively on the sidewalk. He looked through the window into Danny's, trying to spot the man. Then he got into the car. By the time he arrived at the Hotel Fourteen, he was deeply hurt and enraged.

"What a Jackson!" he said.

"What's a Jackson?" I asked.

"A Jackson is some guy who calls a Negro 'Jackson' or 'Bo,'" he explained. "I'd like ten seconds with that rat!"

What can happen to Davis at any time, no matter how high he is flying, had happened.

Davis's early show was, in many subtle ways, below par. His timing was off. He did not kid with the audience. The beat of his songs was slower. It was not a happy show. Afterward, he returned to the dressing room, changed into the terry cloth robe, and lay on the couch. Mike Silver, the drummer who travels with him, sat in a chair with his sticks in his hands, watching TV. Murphy Bennett straightened the bedroom. Davis was almost as alone as he ever is.

"I've never, never tried to be anything but what I am," he said. "I am a Negro. I'm not ashamed. The Negro people can mark a cat lousy for that and they won't go to see him perform. Well, we have Negroes here every night. If you go hear a Negro and see some Negroes in the audience, then you know how they stand. They'll ignore a guy who's marked lousy, see? So, I've never been the kind of guy who was ashamed. See, it's a matter of dignity. That's what makes something like that Jackson so tough on you. One time I went on in San Francisco and a guy down in the front row says to another guy, 'I didn't know he was a nigger,' and walked out. It's tough to play against that. In the Army, the first time anybody called me a bad name, I cried—the tears! I had spent all my life with my dad and uncle. I was loved. I was Charlie-protected. But now, this is the thing that is always just around the corner. It's like you can't get into El Morocco because you're colored. See?"

Davis's second show that night was better than the first, but he still seemed chilled. About four a.m., accompanied by fifteen men and women, he went to a West Side nightclub. Legally, it was closing time, but the bartender gathered up bottles, mix, ice, and glasses and carried the makings into a large back room. Cecil Young and three-fourths of a Canadian jazz quartet were having a last drink before calling it a night. Like the patrons, the fourth member of the quartet—the bass fiddler—had already gone home. Seeing Davis, Cecil Young began telephoning around to find another fiddle player. When the man arrived, sleepy-eyed, the jam session began. Davis, Young, the Canadians, and the new man played wildly and wonderfully for ninety minutes. Davis sat in on drums, blew the trumpet, and sang scat with Cecil Young. When it was over, the hurt was out of his system.

During a break, Cecil Young had said to me: "Jazz isn't polite, son. Jazz is, pardon the expression, screw you. If you don't like it, well, that's all. But if you do like it, then I like you, dig? With jazz, you thumb your nose when they don't like you. You get the message out, daddy."

Davis picked up the check for his friends and the group moved over to his penthouse for the sunrise.

A few days later, Davis landed in Las Vegas after overnight stops in Kansas City and Hollywood. Murphy Bennett had arrived a day ahead of him and had set up the suite at the Sands Hotel which would be Davis's home for the next two weeks. The stereo was rigged and 250 records (from Davis's collection of 20,000) were stacked neatly in the bedroom. There was fresh ice in the ice bucket and the silver goblet had been polished. After the rehearsal and a steam bath, Davis settled on a couch in the living room to relax until it was time to dress for the opening.

Jack Entratter, manager of the Sands, telephoned to report that five hundred reservations had been turned down for the dinner show. A friend called to tell Davis that his wife, Loray White Davis, was in Las Vegas divorcing him. Davis had been married in 1958 and had separated from his wife in less than three months. During the separation, a settlement had been made, but this was the first Davis had heard of the Nevada divorce proceedings. He shrugged. It was all over long ago. Another friend called to give him the latest on the romance of his friend Eddie Fisher who, with Elizabeth Taylor, was exciting Las Vegas and the world at that time.

Davis sighed. "Vegas I like," he said. "I feel like I've come home. You know I've performed in this town like twenty-nine times. We used to come in here before we were anything and when there were only a couple of hotels. The Sands I like. I was offered $37,500 a week to go into another hotel, but I turned it down. Very low pressure here. Easy. You're not fighting the knives and forks. It builds, but the pace is slower. You're running all the time, and then it's nice to come down to the Vegas pace."

Davis called to Landfield, the secretary.

"Hey, baby, call up Keely (Smith) and Louis (Prima) and tell them we'll be over after our show tonight. And find out what the Count (Basie) is doing. We'll swing with him tonight. And chicks. Chicks, we need. Ah, it's like a vacation. You can tumult all night, sleep all day, get a little sun—sun, I need—play a little blackjack. Oh, fine!"

And he lay back on the couch, running.

Postscript:

"Nobody had ever written serious pieces about entertainers at the time," Thomas Morgan said in Marc Weingarten's stellar book about the New Journalism era, *The Gang That Wouldn't Write Straight.*

Morgan later said he had more "pure fun working on 'What Makes Sammy Jr. Run?' than any other story I have ever written."

"After this piece was published," Morgan writes in his excellent out-of-print anthology, *Self-Creations: 13 Impersonalities,* "Sammy Davis and I were bosom pals for several years. Whenever he was in New York or I was in Hollywood, we would spend some evenings together. I must have seen his nightclub act a hundred times. Then, one day, we decided that I should write a screen story for him. It would be based on an incident I had witnessed while researching a *Look* story on juvenile delinquency. We agreed on a price and I produced an eighty-page treatment. Davis liked it and, moreover, Frank Sinatra liked it. But the months slipped by and nothing came of it. Sammy couldn't pay me and as creditor and debtor, we could no longer be Sam and Big T."

BROCK BROWER

With a name befitting a matinee idol, Brock Brower (1931–2014) made all the right stops on his way to a career some snoots might have deemed beneath him. He graduated from Dartmouth, attended Harvard Law long enough to realize it wasn't for him, and picked up a coat of intellectual polish as a Rhodes scholar. A bright young man with those credentials could write his own ticket anywhere. What Brower wanted to write were stories for *Esquire*. And not just any stories. He wanted to write the kind of profiles that James Agee crafted before the dawn of the New Journalism, profiles that defined America and the people Brower and his wife, Ann, identified as "us." The first one Brower delivered, a deep dive into the psyche of Alger Hiss, the Cold War spy, earned him the cred that would last him the rest of his days at *Esquire*. His instinct, however, was to ramble as a freelancer.

Brock's work turned up in *Harper's*, *New York*, *The New York Times Magazine* and, most significantly, *Life*, where he backhanded Norman Mailer as "elegant and lippy ... and always just short" and turned a middle-of-the-book feature on Ted Kennedy into a cover story in the wake of the fatal drunk-driving incident at Chappaquiddick. Still, *Esquire* got the best out of Brower when it turned him loose on political heavyweights from Spiro Agnew to Eugene McCarthy. But they got off easy compared to Mary McCarthy, the author and icon of the literary intelligentsia, and all she did was smile. Of her toothy visage, Brower wrote: "She can smoke through it, argue through it, spill the beans through it, even *smile* through it." Then it was his turn to smile.—John Schulian

MARY McCARTHYISM

Esquire, 1962

ary McCarthy has the nicest smile. At the slightest social pressure, it springs open and automatically catches. She can hold it there—flicking its long, white upper blade of handsome, emphatic teeth this way, that way at every threatening conversational turn—for sometimes five, ten minutes at a stretch. Nothing cows it. She can smoke through it, argue through it, spill the beans through it, even smile through it. It has gotten way beyond being anything quite so straightforward as her Best Feature. As a child, she remembers resorting to it, as such, regularly, snapping it down protectively on her face like a rubber band, the orphan's sweet guise of lovableness. But that early defensiveness—like her faith, or her worry over bowleggedness—is something she long ago left behind in Seattle with the Sisters of the Sacred Heart. Since then, whether framed under the large hats, the "terrific hats" she was famous for during her more bohemian days in the Village, or aureoled by the severe, yet somewhat wispy bunning of the graying hair she favors now in the quieter days of her fourth husband, that smile has become a subtle emanation of the mind: the poised cutting edge on one of the most knifelike female intelligences that Vassar, the Trotskyite movement, *Partisan Review*, the authorship of ten books, or eight years of marriage to Edmund Wilson ever tempered. "When most people smile at you, you feel cheered up," one of the maimed once told Dwight Macdonald, "but when *Mary*

McCarthy smiles at you ... !" It comes out of nowhere seemingly, like a concealed weapon, and the only difference now over the old days is that while she still carries it on her, she doesn't use it *quite* so often, *quite* so outrageously. "Mary," they all say, "has mellowed."

For whom, after all, has she *recently* left for dead in the blood-stained alley behind *Partisan Review*, his intellect cut from ear to ear? Nobody really, unless you count England's leading dramatic critic, Kenneth Tynan—that "somewhat adenoidal spokesman-for-those-under-thirty" (?!)—caught naked and alone in the pages of his own newspaper, *The Observer*, such as Marat was caught by Charlotte Corday in his own bathtub. She began her recent review of selections from Tynan's critical output, a volume entitled *Curtains*, by asking, "Is the title of this collection a pun ('It's curtains for me, pal')?" and, quite typically, she pinked him mortally on his "positive" side. "On his 'positive' side, Tynan tends to write advertising copy ... . The worst I can say of Tynan is that I thought better of him when I began this book than when I finished it." (?!!!) Who would've thought the young man had so much blood in him?

It was so like her old self, that review, precisely the kind of outrage that has made the name Mary McCarthy feared throughout the intellectual badlands ever since she began her literary career back in the late '30s as a dramatic critic herself for *Partisan Review*. She has since gone on to win acclaim as a short story writer, a novelist, a really superb essayist, and "quite possibly the cleverest woman America has ever produced" (according to *Time*'s latest distribution of superlatives for book-jacket copy), but from the beginning, her most individual gift has clearly been for the quick wit and fell decision of a hanging judge supported by a devastating female scorn. "You don't so much review a play as draw up a crushing brief against it," Edmund Wilson once told her while he was courting her, and the same could be said for all things mortal—bad writing, weak principle, political error, moral or mental lapse, the pandering of modern communications, or just the rather shaggy beast in men—that have fallen under her basilisk eye. Even in her famous short stories, such as *The Man in the Brooks Brothers Shirt* or *Portrait of the Intellectual as a Yale Man*, or in her three novels, *The Oasis*, *The Groves of Academe*, and *A Charmed Life*, she is still really the advocate drawing up a harsh brief against something or, more likely, somebody reprehensible. Her fiction, according to Macdonald, is really "a series of reviews of people's performances," and sometimes these "reviews" have been so crushing as to make life itself smart. When Philip Rahv, editor of *Partisan Review* and her old friend, discovered what she'd done to him as "Will Taub" in her first novel, *The Oasis*, he all but sued Mary. "*That book! That book!*" he used to moan to his compatriots, and Tynan—now harrowed as a living man, not as a mere fiction—must be all the more anguished. She has undoubtedly one of the most dread critical minds around, and this—combined with her substantial literary talent, her Amazonian courage in battle, her independence, and that smile—have placed her at the head of a train of intellectually rebellious young women, who, a little like the maenads, follow her more than she perhaps realizes, or ever wished.

In fact, there is some hint—from her friend Elizabeth Hardwick, a much gentler lady with a book review—that, at age fifty and much past her own Village days, Mary finds a certain sadness now accompanies the unpleasant duty of ripping up a bright young man like Tynan in his intellectual prime. "I once said to Mary, thinking more of myself really, 'Isn't it *awful* to be in your forties and still find yourself attacking people? Wouldn't you rather just write nice things about people you enjoy reading?' And Mary said, 'Oh Lord yes, I know just what you mean. I don't want to do it. It's something for young people to do. *But they don't do it!*' "

And so *she* must—smiling through—though what was once a pleasure has now become a duty. Not long ago, while she was waiting to tape an *Open End*, David Susskind walked up to her and, out of the blue, with a certain foreseeable male vanity, asked bluntly, "Why are you always so *bitter*? That's what I don't understand." Mary looked truly surprised. "But I don't think I'm bitter!" She smiled hopefully in all directions. "Do *you*?"—asking anybody. She really could not understand how someone could mistake high standards for personal bitterness, and she struggled with the problem, almost fidgeting, just as another woman might struggle with the awkward situation of being far too tall for her escort. It's embarrassing, but a woman of intellect can't very well walk around mentally stooped over all the time. It's just too bad if some people are frightened off.

And indeed they are. A not uncommon reaction among many who read her is to count up the bodies in that alley behind *Partisan Review*—the Man in That Shirt ("No, he was *not* Wendell Willkie!"); the Yale Man (an ex-liberal, who, in real life, has now gone all the way over to William F. Buckley Jr.'s *National Review*); Dottie Who Made an Honest Woman of Herself, by following in the stony path of volte-face virtue and getting herself fitted for a diaphragm; several husbands, or pieces thereof, crammed into her novels like dismembered limbs into a Grand Central baggage locker; Simone de Beauvoir, inflated and punctured as "Mlle. Gulliver en Amérique" in *On the Contrary*, even old friends and lovers from *Partisan Review* itself—and then to conclude in horror, "But she's so *nasty!*"

But no, *not* nasty, insist her very loyal friends. Only incredibly honest. "Mary is almost physically incapable of saying anything she doesn't mean," says Miss Hardwick. "Almost *bodily*." Macdonald—who incidentally makes his own battered appearance in *The Oasis* as his former pacifist self, "Macdougal Macdermott"—says it's in fact an amusing sight to watch Mary straining *not* to say what she really thinks. "She's always going to be goring somebody's ox, and when she knows she shouldn't, she gets kind of fussed," he notes. "She's a lot like what the Bloomsbury Group must have been like. Woolf, Forster, Keynes, Strachey, they all put personal friendship very high up on the scale, but, above all else, they put telling the truth. Mary has this same aristocratic attitude. She's extremely loyal, but, at the same time, extremely scrupulous about the truth."

Either way, nasty or honest, this intense scrupulosity, even in the most incredible fixes—such as the one her heroine, Margaret Sargent, gets into with the Man in the Brooks Brothers Shirt, waking up in a Pullman Compartment, convinced Nothing Has Happened, and suddenly brushing against his naked, unfamiliar body—has become her personal celebrity. "Lots of women had taken up with a man on the train before—or at least they'd *thought* about doing it—but this was the first time anybody ever *wrote* about it," recalls Miss Hardwick. "I was absolutely bowled over by it." So were a great many others (though there was actually some sentiment among the *Partisan* editors against publishing the story on the grounds it was *journalism,* not fiction), and ever since it has been a case of Mary's influence reaching a little further outward with each new literary "shocker." No one book or story has ever done it for her as much as the cumulative effect of a scene here—the outlandish seduction in *A Charmed Life*—a character there—the anti-Semitic colonel in her story, *Artists in Uniform*—and an outrageous statement somewhere in between— that John Hersey's *Hiroshima* "made [the atom bomb] familiar and safe, and so, in the final sense, boring." Taken all together, they display a candor that might slip from any honest woman occasionally but never from one honest woman so often. The shock, in the end, is the constancy of her candor.

Yet she always manages to carry it off—the most scathing critical attack, or the most clinical sexual scene—with an uncanny ladylike primness. She would not seem so audacious were she not also so fastidious. Her style, for instance; if there is such a thing as dainty, Ciceronian English, that is what she writes. Even during her school days, "writing with a Latinate turn, compressed, analytic, and yet having a certain extravagance or oratorical flourish sounded in my ears like a natural, spoken language." On the other hand, what most people consider the "natural, spoken language" often woolies her. "I have a horror of slang," she says. "I couldn't say somebody was 'loaded,' for instance—unless I put it in quotation marks." Yet she can have her distrait Margaret Sargent wake up the morning after—hungover, mortified, in need of a bath, undoubtedly bruised in (quote) places (unquote)—and respond to her Pullman lover's "Kiss me" by frankly confessing, "I have to throw up."

What saves Margaret Sargent from being really besmirched by this experience is her inexperience. Margaret—like all the thinly disguised Mary McCarthy *personae*—is the innocent at the nadir. She is "absolutely bowled over by it" herself—*surely nothing worse than this could ever happen to her*—yet it does, continually, teaching the always humiliating but never learned lesson to the wide-eyed, Pollyannish Girl with the Safety Pin in her Panties that "a Fall is only a pratfall after all."

In fact, there is a kind of hidden lesson book in the scandal of her better stories. Here (O Mistress Mary!), here's how a girl takes up with a steel man on a train, keeps the Young Man and the Husband civil to each other, seduces a fellow left-wing editor, goes for a "fitting," acts the gay divorcée at a genial party, goes to an analyst, seduces her own ex-husband, decides on an abortion, and finally suffers remorse for all these things, great or small. Nor have these lessons been lost upon youth—any number of bright young things, edging closer to defloration and beyond, imagine they have learned about the world from her (cf., Radcliffe's turnout for "An Evening with Mary McCarthy") and Philip Roth probably paid this uncanny didacticism its ultimate left-handed compliment in *Goodbye, Columbus*. When Neil Klugman tries to encourage his girl, Brenda Patimkin, to get herself "fitted," Brenda glowers accusingly at him for his seemingly firsthand knowledge of the Margaret Sanger clinic:

> *"You've done this before?"*
> *"No," I said. "I just know. I read Mary McCarthy."*
> *"That's exactly right. That's just what I'd feel like, somebody out of her."*

The reference is to Dottie in a much scandal-mongered 1954 story that does for contraception what *Moby Dick* did for whaling, but that feeling—like "somebody out of *her*"—is much more universal. It applies broadly to any number of emotional predicaments in which young women, tripped up by their own shaky modernity, often find themselves, or fear to find themselves. Many an intelligent young lady has declared fiercely for her sexual freedom, for her right to her own mind, even for the challenge of a head-on competition with men, no quarter asked or given, in bed or out—just like "somebody out of *her*"—only to find herself disastrously undermined by feminine self-doubt, foolish shame, and a desperate need to be Told What To Do—equally like "somebody out of *her*." Mary has defined these contradictions almost too well, so exactly, in fact, that her hostile critics claim that what she has really defined, for all men to know, is the Modern American Bitch. But bitchiness is hardly a fair estimate of her critical, imperious, yet highly feminine sensibility.

What she is actually writing—when she's supposedly being "just bitchy"—is her own true and faithful account of the sexual politics of certain modern women (what other "lady politician" has dared?), and one wag has described the upshot of this side of her work as Mary-McCarthyism.

Perhaps it's even worse to call Mary an -ism, but she has given such a detailed record of her affairs, marriages, political leanings, and other follies—and, incidentally, arrogated to her own use so many of the trials she has caused others—that she really has become her own central idea. In that sense, despite her intellectualism, she really *does* think like a woman. In her early stories, and in her mock-heroic *My Confession*, for instance, she reduces the entire radical movement of the '30s to a vaguely amorous aspect of her own personality. *Defend Trotsky!* was the insistent sweet-nothing she whispered at assignations in Webster Hall, and "out dancing in a nightclub, tall, collegiate young Party members would press me to their shirt bosoms and tell me not to be silly, honey." As passionately involved as she once was in the old anti-Stalinist Left, she just can't help treating it as long-dead gossip of a slightly personal nature. Actually, she loves intellectual gossip—"Did you *hear* what Stravinsky did when he was at the White House for dinner?"—and she is constantly getting herself intellectually gossiped about. "Why is everybody always talking about her?" pleads one disgruntled listener. "Do you know I once knew more about Mary McCarthy and Philip Rahv than I knew about *myself*?"

Her novels and stories—her "reviews of people's performances"—are an extension of this gossip. "She's always writing *romans à clef*," complains one unfriendly critic, "and then handing you the clef." In *The Oasis*, she might as *well* have used the real names, her Utopian colony was so patently inhabited by all her old soulmates from the Europe-America Groups (organized to help refugee intellectuals in the '40s) and so raucous with their chivying, backbiting quarrels. It took years for some of the "characters" in *The Oasis* to speak to her again. In her later novels—*The Groves of Academe, A Charmed Life*—her tracings from life have been a little less exact, but then again, this only starts up an egregious guessing game about the composite figures. How much did she make up, and how much really is Edmund Wilson? By now, she has also begun to pop up in other people's novels. Certainly nothing she ever "did" to anybody in one of her books is quite as satirical as what Randall Jarrell, according to literary gossip, "did" to her in his book, *Pictures from an Institution*. How much did he make up, and how much is really Mary and her third husband, Bowden Broadwater?

But, despite all these recriminations, Mary believes this is how novels are. "Most novels are that way—filled with real people. Very little is invented," she says, and in a recent essay, *The Fact in Fiction*, she has written, "Even when it is most serious, the novel's characteristic tone is one of gossip and tittle-tattle ... if the breath of scandal has not touched it, the book is not a novel. That is the trouble with the art-novel (most of Virginia Woolf, for instance); it does not stoop to gossip." She readily stoops to gossip herself—or rather, as she puts it, "I am guilty of overexuberant analysis"—tattling on her "characters" as if they had a half-life somewhere between fact and fiction, which they do. Dottie, for instance, whom she left all alone on a park bench outside the birth-control clinic in 1954. Dottie is to be part of a novel called *The Group* about eight Vassar girls in search of Progress. But Mary became "too depressed by it." "The fates of these girls were going to be just too cruel for me to go on. I mean, to humanity—not just to the girls. I only took it up again this year." Yet, in real life, "Dottie isn't like that at all. That never happened to her. The incident is entirely fictional. I saw Dottie recently, and she hasn't changed a bit." Then who is Dottie? What is she? And Mary can contrive the most dreamlike exculpations to show that a "character" isn't really "somebody" after all. As she told Macdonald, the former husband in *A Charmed Life* "can't be" Edmund Wilson, because (1) the former husband is tall, and Wilson is short, and (2) the former husband writes *successful* plays, and even though Wilson has been a playwright, "everybody knows that Edmund never had a successful play in his life!" True, true, we must be reading things into it ... .

The qualifying breath of scandal then has touched her own books and "made them novels"—some would even say it's Mary herself who breathes into them the magic fire, like a she-dragon lying back in the lair of Invaded Privacies—but in all fairness, she has easily survived as much scandal as she has published. She would not make a very good subject for an art-novel; her life has been far too calamitous and outrageous. Orphaned at six, when an influenza epidemic took both her parents in 1918, she grew up in Minneapolis and Seattle with various grandparents and relatives, a bright, deprived, rebellious girl stifled by all the usual petty tyrannies, described in her most sensitive book, *Memories of a Catholic Girlhood*. First the Cruel Uncle—Uncle Myers, a pinchpenny household dictator, whose one book was *Uncle Remus*, and who beat her for such grave offenses as winning first prize in a statewide essay contest on "The Irish in American History." Then the Church—her spiritual heritage from her Irish father, eked out in the loneliness of convent schools. One day she decided to Lose Her Faith in an exhibitionistic bid for attention—her first *scandal*— but though fully prepared to Regain It at the dramatic moment, she suddenly found, after listening unconvinced to all five gray proofs of God's existence, that she really *had* lost it. It was typical of the kind of apostasy that has overtaken her at her worst moments. Like objects jump at some people, lapses fall upon her. Her one big moment in convent school, for instance, came when a Sister snapped at her in class, "You're just like Lord Byron, brilliant but unsound." Thrilled by this sinister tribute, she ran home to tell her Seattle grandfather, and he promptly telephoned the Mother Superior to demand, scandalized, "what right one of her Sisters had to associate his innocent granddaughter with that degenerate blackguard, Lord Byron." To her mortification, the remark was coldly withdrawn on Monday, but it remains the classic example of the kind of dubious accolade that has been thrust upon her all her life, as if she simply could not win praise without having to take part of it in scandal.

Her four marriages, for instance. The scandal falls so patly against her, and she gets no sympathy, only excellent notices. She reacts by claiming—as she once did to her brother, the actor Kevin McCarthy, in a moment of marital despair—that no two people should be *allowed* to stay married for more than seven years, unless they could prove in court that they *should*. Her own marriages have lasted three years (1933–1936) to the late Harold Johnsrud, an actor, who, "too young for character parts and too bald for juveniles," was suited only to play blind men in "the portentous and equivocal atmosphere of left-wing drama"; eight years (1938–1946) to Wilson, the impediment apparently being that "my mind was so totally different from Edmund's"; fifteen years (1946–1961) to Bowden Broadwater, a quiet reading period that has been aptly described as "a rest for Mary"; and more than a year now (1961) to her present husband, James West, a State Department official, whom she met in Poland on a lecture tour and married after mutual divorces, much bad press, and considerable coolness issuing from the American Embassy. It has been an emotional collision course, no question, but Mary has survived it with her dignity intact because, as her close friend and intellectual companion, Hannah Arendt, points out, "it has by no means been calculated … . With Mary, it happens like a thunderbolt. She's not at all reflective about it." She just—as past husbands have sadly discovered—ups and walks out.

Yet, during the time she *has* been married, she has tried very hard to be the good wife. She really is a determined homemaker, to such an elaborate extent that some of her more jaded dinner guests—looking around at the embroidered samplers hanging on the walls of the Broadwater apartment in praise of Our Home—have thought she *must* be kidding. But no, she does everything well, except sweep. "I cannot sweep. I hate sweeping. And I don't know how to use a vacuum cleaner." She is also an excellent French cook. "I know you hear that about a lot of women," her brother says, "but Mary really *is*." Hannah thinks there is "something of a peasant" in Mary, but there is much more likely something still of the orphan. Mary has never been any good at being alone, and she instinctively nests as a hedge against that anxiety. "Mary must feel she can come home, *always*," Hannah notes, "and there must always be somebody there to tell *all* about it."

She has sometimes had to establish a home for herself under very trying circumstances. The tumult and the shouting from her marriage to Wilson has yet to subside completely in the gentle dells of Stamford, Connecticut. Its one totally happy issue is their son, Reuel Kimball Wilson, Mary's only child, "a marvelous boy," who, according to Hannah, has discovered "he can have the best of *both* worlds." "I tried to make him a lawyer," says Mary. "But I see now—though he would have made an admirable judge—he would've made a poor lawyer. He always had such a balanced mind." (Mary still remembers some of the rhadamanthine judgments he passed as a schoolboy on Man & Ideas, e.g., "I think slavery is a good idea, but quite mean," or on Macdonald's postwar struggle with his political conscience, "I think Dwight is trying to give up progressiveness, but it's too late.") Reuel, now twenty-three and still much his father's son, has chosen instead the study of language. "He's really brilliant at it too," says Mary. "Of course his father was a whiz at languages, but Reuel can actually *speak* them."

Despite the eventual rupture, however, she owes Wilson a large literary debt and freely admits it. It was not so much a question of influence—Mary stubbornly denies anybody's influence, including Wilson's, on her own thinking, though "I believe he *did* cure me of liking Aldous Huxley, if I wasn't over it already"—as a matter of encouragement. "He's extremely generous toward any young talent he believes is really there." He originally asked to meet her when she was only twenty-eight, because he very much admired the Theater Chronicle she was writing for *Partisan*, now part of her book, *Sights and Spectacles*. He very soon, however, started her off on an entirely new literary direction. "We'd been married about a week, and he said, 'I think you've got a talent for writing short stories.' So he put me off in the one free room we had at Stamford with a typewriter and shut the door. I wrote *Cruel and Barbarous Treatment* straight off, almost without blotting a line." This was the first of Margaret Sargent's misadventures—and pretty much a candid recounting of the prelude to one of her own divorces. She wrote five more of these stories—including briefs against the Yale Man, and the Man in That Shirt—and in 1942 they were loosely collected as *The Company She Keeps*, a book that has since become the *vade mecum* of Mary McCarthyism.

"Edmund always tried to make things easy for me—getting me help during the war when we had Reuel, and when help was really hard to find—so that I could go on with the writing." But at the same time, his own work naturally dominated. "Edmund gets his whole household involved in whatever he's doing. He tends to lecture rather than to converse, and he'll lecture all through dinner—even all through lunch, if he happens to come out for lunch." Mary overlapped mainly with Wilson's Marxist-Pacifist period, though, since she was something of a sympathizer herself, this wasn't half as trying on her patience as a briefer but more intense Walt Disney period. "I nearly went out of my mind. I can't stand Walt Disney, and he couldn't get enough of it." Obviously they split over much more than the Seven Dwarfs, but it does give some idea of how abruptly they could come to loggerheads. In fact, Mary's final exit from Wilson's domicile was another of those pratfall Falls that later appeared in one of her novelizations of life. But in her own words before the judge:

"We had about eighteen people at the party. Everybody had gone home and I was washing dishes. I asked him if he would empty the garbage. He said, 'Empty it yourself.' I started carrying out two large cans of garbage.

"As I went through the screen door, he made an ironical bow, repeating, 'Empty it yourself.' I slapped him—not terribly hard—went out and emptied the cans, then went upstairs. He called me and I came down. He got up from the sofa and took a terrible swing and hit me in the face and all over. He said: 'You think you're unhappy with me. Well, I'll give you something to be unhappy about.' I ran out of the house and jumped into my car."

But if that is Mary seen at nadir, she must also be seen at zenith, where, truly, she appears as the handsome, nervously controlled, various woman of intellect who has had the courage to make all her gifts answer in the absence of any one single compelling talent. "With Mary, work is constant," says a friend. Despite all her tergiversations, "she will always come back to the typewriter." In the last twelve years, she has published eight books—two novels; a brilliant collection of essays that speak out, *On the Contrary*; a retrospective volume of theater criticism; a book of short stories; the touching and widely read memoir of her Catholic girlhood; and two noble if somewhat *Les Guides Bleus* attempts at art history, *The Stones of Florence* and *Venice Observed*. This would be an impressive enough output for any writer, but during the same period, and with equal flair, Mary started several other ventures that make her seem only the more indomitable for all their feminine muddle and quixotic failure. During the McCarthy period, specifically, she was so personally disturbed over the course things were taking that she tried (1) to become a lawyer, and (2) to start a national magazine.

"It began with the defeat of Stevenson in 1952. I was terribly worked up about the Constitutional aspects of the McCarthy business, and it seemed that the judiciary—not even the lawyers, really—were the only ones who stood firm. The legal profession obviously needed some reforestation. Lawyers had gotten to be people who had a license to practice hairdressing. So I thought maybe I ought to know more about it, and in 1952 I conceived the ridiculous idea of going to Harvard Law School. I was all set to take the tests (but really I was too old, I couldn't have retained the material) when it occurred to me it was ridiculous, I could do just as well at C.C.N.Y. or N.Y.U. I was just being snobbish about Harvard.

"So I finally called an old friend, Judge Biggs, of the Pennsylvania Circuit Court, and he told me, don't do anything until I'd talked to him. So he came down in his white Jaguar, with his wife and a box of cigars, for a weekend, and I'm afraid he talked me out of it.

"But the press and the magazines were so terrible that then I felt maybe the thing to do was to start a new magazine. It was to be Dwight, and Dick Rovere, and Hannah, and myself, but I was the one who really wanted to do it. I was the one who was going to be editor, the one who got out the magazine. It was going to be more middle-of-the-road than *Politics*"—Macdonald's defunct pacifist "little magazine"— "with a reasonable circulation." It had a terrible name. *Critic*. Which is bad.

"I had a fantastic time. I learned more about politics, trying to raise money for that magazine, than I ever ... *all* the Democrats, *all* of them were interested in *bigness*. Which, of course, was just what we were fighting. The only people who were really willing to put up the money were all *Republicans*, people who were interested in the arts. I'd gotten myself stuck with the idea of a $100,000 budget, and *I* got it up to $55,000 and I ran out of money. By June, I was destitute."

So it all came to naught and yet it is so very much the sort of thing—the Intellectual Fray, the Exploded Hope, the Niggardliness of Political Virtue, the Hypocrisy of Commitment—upon which her own literary imagination turns, that it's as if she'd been aware precisely of the point at which her own literary imagination turns. It's as if she'd been aware precisely of the point at which the book had to stop. "I probably *could* have raised all that money. I was impatient, partly," she says. "On the one hand, I have a desire to be an activist, and on the other hand, *I don't*." And it seems only just that the one good deed to come out of all this activity should be the settling of an old literary quarrel that really began in one of her earlier books.

"Hannah convinced me that the magazine had to have Philip Rahv. So I finally got up my courage and telephoned him. He still wanted me to say I was sorry, and I still wasn't going to say I was, but I finally invited him to a long peace luncheon at the Charles. When we came out of the restaurant, all smiles, one of the PR gang saw us and actually *blanched*."

So that at least was over, and indeed many of her old antagonists speak of Mary with a much more forgiving air these days. Her fast friendship with Hannah Arendt, for instance, is built over the buried ruins of one of Mary's worst outrages. They first met during the early '40s, at Rahv's insistence, and as a result of that one evening alone, "I cut Mary for six years." It all started when Mary, indulging the full frivolity of her *enfant terrible* role, said she really felt sorry for Hitler, he didn't know what was happening to him, he expected the Jews to love him. "She was being so deliberately naughty," recalls Hannah. "I counted to one hundred and twenty to let Rahv—who is not the greatest hero of the age—say something to her, and when he didn't, it was just too much. I had to do something about it." Mary remembers "a sense of explosion in the room," and Hannah was gone. "I was horror-struck. I continued to admire her—on the principle that you must not adjust your attitude toward someone on the basis of his or her attitude toward you. But I didn't *dare* speak to her." Then, slowly over the next six years, they found that on any number of public questions they always ended up on the same side, and "usually alone." Gradually, they drew closer, both actually in need of each other's comradeship. "It is very difficult for women intellectuals to have women friends," says Hannah. "You need someone to face the problem with you of how to be regarded as a woman." By now, they've traveled several times in Europe together, Hannah very much in the lead, and done such things as invade the predominantly male Christian Gauss Seminars in Princeton "like two troopers." "Mary is someone I could ask to give my seminar on Machiavelli, for instance, when I couldn't." Like many others, she seems willing to accept a certain eternal childishness in Mary, now that Mary has grown more serious-minded. "But she will always be getting into impossible situations. She is always the child who sees no emperor's clothes, and of course this means she is expecting the most gorgeous clothes. In the sophisticated circles Mary travels, this is dynamite."

But, in Mary's case, it's easy to make too much of the child playing with dynamite and miss the womanly dignity with which she *chooses* to be outspoken. "You know what my favorite quotation is?" says Margaret Sargent, just before her Fall. "It's from Chaucer. Criseyde says it, 'I am myn owene woman, well at ese.' "Mary, at fifty, is a lot wiser than her *persona* at twenty-and-some, but that doesn't mean that she has ever left off being her own woman. If anything, maturity has deepened her sense of intellectual independence, her bravado, her penchant for risk. "I am my own woman, well at ease"—and one startling aspect of her present fame, a mark of her rather special position among other famous and intellectual women—is that she has accomplished it all *without a man*.

Not that there haven't been men in her life. But as her own woman, she has never been bracketed with a man in the way that most other outstanding women have been, even in their eminence. Eleanor Roosevelt is *Mrs.* Roosevelt, Clare Boothe Luce may be playwright, Congresswoman, and ambassador, but she is still very much regarded as *Mrs.* Luce. Jackie Kennedy is charming, intelligent, and lovely, but really as the President's wife. And even Simone de Beauvoir, despite her own outspoken championship of the Second Sex, is still the unwed existentialist bride of Jean Paul Sartre. But Mary is definitely *Miss* McCarthy, even though she may be in private life Mrs. Bowden Broadwater, or Mrs. James West. Even looking back on her most famous marriage, it's absurd to think of her as the ex-Mrs. Edmund Wilson. She simply cannot be bracketed, in her own particular excellence, with even that overawing presence in American letters.

Yet she is still, as the publisher, Roger Straus, points out, "a real dame." A difficult dame perhaps, but still a real one. In fact, she has an insistent femininity, and claims "a horror of career girls. The girls who are theatrical agents, or in publishing, or the kind of woman who tells anecdotes, or who uses slang." She has all a woman's foibles. She loves clothes—"too much," she says and shops Hattie Carnegie's for those "young" outfits that are expensively "right" for a cocktail party or a dressy afternoon. One of her prized possessions is a lovely diamond-and-silver brooch, given to her by her present husband as a wedding present: an intricate piece of Polish jewelry that she likes because it is "so old-fashioned." She loves to entertain in style—and to take charge of the party. Recently, for an occasion at her brother Kevin's house in Dobbs Ferry, she cooked up a *cassoulet Toulouse* that took three geese, fifteen pounds of beans, three days, an eleven-page recipe, every pot in the house in the absence of a medieval cauldron and served eighty-five people. After dinner, there was a program of theatricals, scenes written by such guests as Robert Lowell and Niccolo Tucci, and enacted by such guests as E.G. Marshall and Zero Mostel. "I said to Kevin, 'Don't you think we ought to build a stage?' but Kevin didn't think we ought to build a stage."

"She's very gay," says Miss Hardwick. "She doesn't believe in dreariness." And eternally, exasperatingly, despite her own caustic intellect, "she believes in Love." Macdonald is positively awed by it. "Anybody can see—and I don't mean she's offensive about—that she's *madly* in love with this new husband."

Perhaps this is what makes her, among intellectual women today, finally a unique case. For the tensions she creates around herself, it's necessary to go back to Madame de Staël and Récamier; no woman, in our complex, yet businesslike society, is supposed to consider them worth her while any longer. They may have been fine for George Sand, but nobody wants to get that involved, what with just normal female anxiety being what it is today. Have an affair, make a marriage, raise a child, write a novel, marry again, study art history, join the bar, start a magazine, join intellectual discussions, cook well, Attack the Center, Attack Tynan, entertain, gossip, Smile—do any several of these things, but for pity's sake don't try to be the Renaissance Woman!

Yet, despite all the criticism of her conduct—the many slurs on her femininity and the attacks on her work—there is a secret admiration for her candor, her audacity, and her stupendous try for the woman's moon. "She's one of the few people who never backs away," says her brother. "When I'm outspoken, I manage to make enemies. But when Mary's outspoken, people are convinced." *I am myn owene woman, wel at ese.* And once the Man in That Shirt understood the Middle English, he looked at her with "bald admiration."

"Golly," he said, "you are, at that!"

Postscript:

"It started with James Agee," Brock Brower told his friend, the writer Dan Wakefield. Not only did Agee write beautifully terse movie reviews for *Time* and *The Nation*, he also wrote a loving tribute on the golden age of silent movie comedy, as well as a fantastic portrait of John Huston ("Undirectable Director") for *Life*. "The idea was in the air and everyone I know was thinking this way too."

In his friendly memoir, *New York in the Fifties*, Wakefield explains, "Whether it started with Agee or the columns of Murray Kempton, or was given a new orgasmic pump by Norman Mailer's 'The White Negro,' or was unleashed in the pages of *The Village Voice*, this whole trend of quality writing, which was negatively known as nonfiction and later got promoted to the more hip category of the New Journalism, came to full bloom around a particular editor and magazine in the late '50s and early '60s: Harold Hayes of *Esquire*."

Hayes himself said, "We make no attempt to impose a style, as *The New York Times* or *Time* does. We want the maximum freedom of style and ideas. And we want the style of each article to reflect the author, to be unique, and personal. It can range from the elegant, to surrealistic, to sardonic, ironic ... . In fact, you might say we like as many sophisticated styles as we can find within the general framework of our point of view."

Brower, a Rhodes scholar who spent time in Paris during the '50s, not in search of Hemingway but American novelist Irwin Shaw, found a place for himself in Hayes's provocative *Esquire*. This profile of Mary McCarthy, on the verge of publishing her greatest selling novel, *The Group*, was typical of the sort of smart and nervy—some would argue flippant and cheap—*Esquire* story of the time. It landed, though not everyone was pleased, particularly McCarthy herself.

In a letter to her ex-husband, the venerated literary critic, Edmund Wilson, McCarthy wrote: "In case you saw a horrible thing about me in *Esquire*, I trust you gathered that I'm not responsible for unpleasant passages about you in it. The author must have dredged them out of the court files. I *am* responsible for being such a fool as to let this young man do the piece—see my friends, etc. The understanding was that it was to be purely literary, and biographic only in that public sense, not a personality piece at all. I do not seem to live and learn."

On the other hand, as McCarthy biographer Frances Kiernan observed, "If one believes that there is no such thing as bad publicity, then the pain caused by the piece was more than offset by the attention it brought her. Not only did it place her in very heady company but it treated her fame as a fait accompli."

DOON ARBUS

Doon Arbus (1945–) did not have a lifelong ambition to be a writer but an aptitude for observation, reporting, and writing crisp, clean sentences was evident in a letter she sent to her mother during freshman year at Reed College, just before she left school for good. Though a personal letter, her mother, the photographer Diane Arbus, a frequent contributor to *Esquire*, shared it with the magazine's editor, Harold Hayes, who included it under an anonymous byline in the magazine's annual college issue. Doon waitressed and took odd jobs, including a stint as Gloria Steinem's gal Friday, but had no designs on a writing career when she proposed to write about autograph hounds for *New York*, the Sunday magazine supplement for the *New York Herald Tribune*, edited by Clay Felker. Doon labored over the short piece as she would over everything she'd ever write—although Doon only wrote a handful of magazine profiles, during her 30-year collaboration with photographer Richard Avedon she wrote the text to several of his books as well as ad copy in their commercial work; it was Doon who came up with Calvin Klein's memorable campaign of nothing coming between Brooke Shields and her jeans. She later penned the exquisite novel, *The Caretaker*, where her lapidary prose and unfailing wit shine. "Dense, visual, and true," observed critic Hilton Als, "this short book speaks volumes about the theater of the mind, and how the ensuing comedic drama we call life unfolds inside and outside our control."

Yet even at twenty years old, Doon's artistic temperament was already formed. She didn't dash anything off, nor was she impressed by status, fame, or celebrity. She was interested in people that inspired her and curious to closely examine anything that captured her imagination, as we discover in her scrupulous 1966 profile of James Brown, also published in *New York*. The occasion: Brown's first concert at Madison Square Garden. Already a legend in Black America, this profile ostensibly introduced Brown to the *Tribune*'s White, middle-class readership (or what was left of it anyway; the newspaper soon folded). Arbus proved the ideal guide—concentrated, alert, receptive. As a writer she is careful with every word. The prose is pristine without calling attention to itself, and we are left with an indelible snapshot of the cloistered show business world of Brown in his prime.—AB

JAMES BROWN IS OUT OF SIGHT

The New York Herald-Tribune, 1966

I've been waiting for ages. After all, he's very big now and getting bigger every minute, so it's not that he's oblivious or inconsiderate. It's a vital part of his social and professional dynamics to keep me waiting outside in the cold, sitting on the wrought iron bench in the front yard, gazing at the mysterious stone cupola with the two tiny, impenetrable cut-glass windows. It's his home, his strangely exotic home in the St. Albans section of Queens; part castle, part hacienda; and somewhere inside he is lying asleep. He works very hard so he likes to sleep as late as possible.

Well, he's a big man. Anyone familiar with the facts admits that. His two latest records, *Pappa's Got a Brand New Bag* and *I Got You* have sold over one million copies each. He tours the country with his own show 335 days a year, performing for an average of five-thousand people a day. Today, March 20, he will be at Madison Square Garden. He and his show will be the sole attraction.

He has never appeared in midtown Manhattan before—only at the Apollo in Harlem and at the Brevoort in Brooklyn, which is why few New Yorkers have seen him or heard him or even know who he is. It's strange, because he has gathered an enormous following throughout the greater part of the nation because of his records and personal appearances. But New York isn't with it when it comes to him.

I only saw him once, in the *T.A.M.I. Show*, JAMES BROWN AND THE FAMOUS FLAMES! It was filmed in Electronovision, which may account for his looking so peculiar; after all, so did everybody else: Lesley Gore and The Beach Boys and The Supremes. But he looked strangest of all—the giant head and broad shoulders, and the rest of him progressively smaller. Short legs. Tiny feet.

Someone finally does let me in the house, after he wakes up and says it's okay. Nobody does anything without orders from the boss, but when he wakes up, and gives the word, someone lets me in through the back door into the den, which looks like a gymnasium all upholstered in black leatherette with a great post in the middle of the room. It's very bare. Photographs of him are crowded onto the wall above the imposing curved bar—photographs of him, beaming proudly as he accepts an award or demonstrating enthusiasm as he signs an autograph for a child or sweating luxuriously on his knees over the microphone. They hang in a cluster amidst the rows of bottles, and there are shelves with rows of plaques and trophies engraved with praise. "To The Hardest Working Performer." Three large white B's are emblazoned on the black upholstered wall at the staircase.

Every few moments someone wanders into the den and pauses in the middle of the room distractedly, standing there muttering about the cold or the time or a lost shoe or what car to take to the airport, then wandering out again. James Brown has to catch a four o'clock plane to Virginia Beach—there is a show that evening. A few people will fly down with him, the few that are still here, like Bobby Byrd and Bobby Bennett and Lloyd Stallworth, the three Famous Flames. All the other members of the show have already left: the musicians in the band and the band leader, Nat Jones; and James Brown's own girl group, The Three Jewels; all the members of the unaccountably popular burlesque comedy acts. They have gone ahead in the private bus. The equipment and the instruments have left in the two-ton truck, and all the costumes have been packed away in the black plastic garment bags, each with a white 11 on the front, and driven down by car. That's the way it always is when the James Brown Show is on tour.

Nobody seems to know exactly how many people travel with the show, or if they do know, they're not sure if it mightn't be some kind of betrayal to reveal the exact number. So some say forty and some say fifty and some just say "a whole lot." That's the way they are: cautious and guarded, afraid to say anything that might he used against James Brown. ("What are you trying to find out? You looking for the good things? Or you just wanna know bad things?") They believe in him. He *is* the whole show; he writes the music and the lyrics, he does the arrangements, and he does the choreography. He designs all the costumes and makes all the decisions. With some mystical, magnetic force, he keeps the whole thing together, all the parts working as a unit. He's got something, but they'll never tell what it is. Maybe they don't even know. All they know is that each has to be *best* in what he does. "The whole show has got to be the *greatest.*"

Bobby Bennett, one of The Famous Flames, has come into the den from upstairs. He wears a shiny brick red suit, black nylon socks, and a big jeweled ring that cost him $10,000, which he has to remember to give to someone to hold for him before he goes on stage. But it doesn't make him nervous, not a bit.

Bobby goes into a small room off the den. It has all sorts of black appliances in it: a black refrigerator, a black sink, a black washing machine. It also has an ironing board, which is what Bobby needs— he has come to iron his clothes. "Yes sir. You gotta learn to do every- thing yourself. No one's gonna do it for you. So you learn. 'Cause there's a twenty dollar fine for having wrinkles in your clothes. Or making a goof on stage. Or gettin' in trouble. It's like the army," he explains cheerfully. "You gotta have discipline. Otherwise, where are you at? Without discipline, nothin' gets done right." The fines go into the treasury to pay for parties and other good things.

Mr. Brown is upstairs in curlers under the dryer. Bobby has just finished putting Mr. Brown's hair up in curlers and Mr. Brown under the dryer. He does it every day, to get the kinks out, and to make Mr. Brown's hair big and round. Bobby says I can't go up yet. Nat Stillwell, the chauffeur, in an elegant blue-gray uniform, comes to collect the suitcases. There are three cars in the garage: the purple

Cadillac limousine, the red Stingray with "Mr. Dynamite" painted on the side, and the white '66 Cadillac. The Cad's the one Mr. Brown has decided to take to the airport, since it's very roomy. Bobby goes upstairs to check on Mr. Brown's hair. Nat Stillwell goes outside with the suitcases to check on the white Cadillac. I sink down onto one of the smooth, black couches to wait some more.

Bobby calls from upstairs, "You wanna come up now? It's okay." I go up the winding staircase into the main hall with the bright glass chandelier and the spongy green carpet protected with long strips of plastic It is as if the whole house were being preserved against the hazards of being lived in, as if it were being prepared for a great future as a museum. It's embarrassingly exhilarating to look through the glass in the front door and see the outside and the wrought iron bench and the three teenagers standing by the white Cadillac, restless, intent on the house. From the outside all that can be seen in the glass is a reflection.

Bobby offers me some house slippers from the giant black suitcase or shoe box or whatever-it-is. It stands almost as tall as he does and has a very strange shape. In a way, it looks like a B, although it doesn't look like one at all. Bobby reaches way into the mouth of it and tosses the house slippers onto the floor, unmatching green and blue scuffs with Japanese-looking flowers or trees embroidered on the toes. I pick the two I like the best and hand him my own shoes, feeling as if I'm about to enter the doctor's office for an examination, or the holy sepulchre, or both. Bobby leads the way up a carpeted ramp through the living room with the Japanese prints and the couches all covered in plastic, into the kitchen.

Yes, he is there. He is enthroned after a fashion on a straight-backed kitchen chair against the wallpaper of orange and yellow flowers, his head of curlers resting lazily against the wall. He looks like the Blackest man on earth. He seems to blot out the light where he sits, which may be what makes him appear so Black.

"Just call me James," he says, smiling grandly, magnanimously. His teeth are set in a neat, gleaming row, a rectangular smile in a dark face. "How about a drink?" He uses my first name right from the start. It puts him in control, implying intimacy while remaining aloof. "Don't you want a drink? Something? Aw, come on. *Sure* now?" He has made himself the host, so *he* directs the conversation. *He* asks the questions.

The short kimono robe hangs open at his chest. A silver thing strung from a chain around his neck rests conspicuously against his chest, but he won't tell what it is. Like a spell, his not telling makes it impossible to guess.

A young woman sits massaging one of his feet, which is stretched across her lap. It absorbs all her attention. He doesn't introduce her, but he treats her with a certain respect, as do Bobby and Nat Stillwell and the maid—as if, in the household, she were second only to James.

Bobby is ceremoniously taking out the curlers, one by one. He is a master. He teases each lock into place, leaning over from behind to get at the front, careful not to obstruct James's view of things. He has learned not to interfere with conversations when he's doing James's hair, creating the great round head. It looks terrific and I tell him so.

"Yeah?" James laughs modestly, as if I were putting him on. "I like *your* hair."

The radio is on and is playing his song: "I Got You" by James Brown. It is number three on WABC *"I feel good. I knew that I would now. I fee-eel good. I knew that I wou-ould. So good. So good. 'Cause I got you!"* It makes him feel real good. He raises his hand and everyone freezes, silent and motionless, listening. But no one listens as well as he. He gazes deep into nowhere. He is part of it and it is part of him. He starts to sing with it. "I like that. *'Sugar and spi-ice.'* " The two voices of James Brown, the two incredible, hoarse voices of James Brown, are straining together. It is a Brown fugue.

We check in at the Admiralty Motel in Virginia Beach, the five of us: James and Bobby Byrd and Bobby Bennett and Lloyd and me. James has armed me with one of his suitcases and a pad and pencil, insisting that I carry the pad and pencil all the time, to prove that I'm a traveling reporter, and to guard against the assumptions of suspicious Southern minds: The pinched-featured white desk clerk with the plastered tan hair straightens up as we enter. He is marvelously meek. "Yes, Mr. Brown. Your room is all ready, Mr. Brown. Suite A20, sir. It's all made up, and we have the three gentlemen in A18, A16, and A14. But as for the young lady," he says, his eyes shifting uneasily from James to me and back again, "well, I'm terribly sorry, but the closest room we have is C15. I do hope that's alright"

James winks. He knew it would be that way; he hadn't wanted me to come at all at first. Back in the house in St. Albans, when I'd asked him if I could, he tried to dissuade me, not just because his Negro fans in the South wouldn't understand if they got the idea he was going around with a White girl, but because he was worried for my *safety*. It's *dangerous* down there. "You remember what happened to President Kennedy." He even sent Nat Stillwell to explain: "Mr. Brown sent me. He wanted me to tell you—about Virginia Beach. He didn't want to tell you himself, didn't want to hurt your feelings. But the fact is you can't do down there like you do up here. Wander around any way you please. That ain't up North no more. That's the *South*, and they don't want you down there. *Anything* could happen. Oh, I ain't telling you what to do. You do like you want. But I'd think twice before going down there. I'd think twice if I were you. Mr. Brown just wanted me to tell you, just so you know what you're doing."

But James seemed to have changed his mind at some point, perhaps sometime while he was dressing, because when he came downstairs again in his shiny purple shirt and purple pants (two inches taller than before thanks to the heels of the pale suede boots) he winked confidentially. "Don't you worry about *nothing*. You'll go wherever I go. I'll look after you. And if you write this the way it really happens, it's gonna be like *I Passed for White*. Only the other way 'round."

So it was no surprise to him that they put me in C 15 a long way from his room; he had figured on it. After we'd all gone to our separate rooms, he sent Gert to fetch me. Dear, round, affectionate Gert is his wardrobe mistress and dresser and she has been with him ten years. She has been through the whole thing with him, looking out for his clothes, looking out for his eating habits, looking out for his worries—everything, like a mother. There isn't anything she doesn't know. She has come to escort me to his room, back through the lobby past the comfortable businessmen, whose knowing eyes turn to watch us as we climb the stairs.

Suite A20 isn't very grand for a suite, just a living room with a couch and two chairs, a dressing alcove, a bedroom and two bathrooms. Both television sets are on, one in the bedroom and one in the living room, and James is sprawled opulently in one of the chairs, talking on the telephone. Bobby is doing his hair again, wielding the expert, inobtrusive comb. Gert is pouring champagne for all. James knows a groovy way to drink it—pour salt in it. It makes more bubbles and stings and also helps you burp. There is some fried chicken. "You dig *hot sauce?*" Eat. Drink. Have a ball. "So long, baby, I'll call ya." He hands Bobby the telephone to hang up. "She's in *love* with me," he laughs negligently. "Well, like I'm *all man*, you know." Lots of them are in love with him; it can sure make life *complicated.* He reaches for some more chicken, a real *hot piece.* It's *out o' sight.* "Hey, Bobby, come put my socks on for me, man, so I can spend these few precious moments talking ... ." He fixes on me with those invincible black eyes, as if there's no one but him and me. He's giving me The James Brown Story.

You wouldn't *believe* how poor he was when he was a kid living in Augusta, Georgia. *Real* poor. He had to pick cotton and shine shoes and dance in the streets for people who would throw nickels and dimes and sometimes even quarters at his feet. "I had a *real* big family. I didn't have no brothers and sisters, but a lot of *close* relatives. Know what I mean? And I had to help support 'em." That can make a guy real determined.

He wants to *do something.* He wants to do something *real* bad, to find a challenge, something in which he doesn't feel completely sure. That's the whole trouble: He's always been confident, and that's no good. "Everything I've done I've always been the number one cat." He's done a lot. He started out as a prizefighter. Former boxing champ Beau Jack spotted his incredibly fast footwork and offered to coach him as a fighter. "Boxing, that's *all work* and none of the *fun.*" Later, he started playing baseball. "I was an extraordinary pitcher," he confesses, shaking his head. He had a chance to play professional baseball, but he injured his leg, putting an end to his career as a ball player. He organized The Famous Flames and started out in show business, singing gospel-derived songs for predominantly adult audiences in the South. But things really began in 1955, in Macon, Georgia. He and The Famous Flames made an unaccompanied recording of "Please, Please, Please" and a local disc jockey played it on his radio show as a personal favor to James Brown. Since then he hasn't needed many favors, because he is a talented singer and dancer and a "very sharp businessman." He works hard and knows how to make friends, and he is a "lucky guy." This is where he's at today: thirty-four years old and "the biggest Negro cat in show business right now." His record sales total well over five million and he has a huge following of adult and teenage fans all around the country and in Europe as well. "All that glamour from sun to sun. It's rough." Some guys might just sit back and take it easy at that point, but not James Brown. He's *ambitious*. He's gotta find the true challenge, expand to the limits of himself. Or further. He can't stop, not with singing; he's got to be moving on. "Maybe into the acting field. I think I'm gonna be an actor next."

"It can be pretty scary up where I am. I mean like everybody's watching. Know what I mean? The whole world. Black and White. I'm carrying the whole thing. Right now, in what I'm doin,' I'm doin' more for the Negro cause than *any* of them *other* cats. I'm talkin' about *Soul*. Forgettin' that other stuff. That's silly. I'm talkin' about bein' *alive*, man. About *feeling*. That's what it's all about." But they're all watching him up there, and he knows if he messes up he's gonna make it rough for every other Negro performer and that's a frightening thing. Any sensitive cat, no matter how tough, would have to be a little scared sometimes, a little mixed up and very much alone.

"I am one of the most alonest guys. You hip to that? Like I'm a very serious person. Know what I mean? I've got *a lot of* problems. I'm real *confused*, you know. But I gotta keep it all to myself. All inside me. 'Cause there ain't no one I can really talk to. Not *really talk*. You dig?"

That's why he's got to do everything himself: he can't trust anyone to do it for him. He's got to know what's going on all the time, firsthand. That doesn't just mean with the songwriting, the arranging, the choreography, and the designs for all the costumes in the show. Sure he does all that. But also, he's got a publishing company, Try Me Music, Inc., and he and his agent, Ben Bart, both own 50 percent of a record production company, Fair Deal Records, Inc. On top of that, James Brown makes a special point of overseeing the whole business end of things: the publicity, the bookings, the contracts, everything. He has to be able to deal with all kinds of people in all kinds of fields. He has to keep his personality changing all the time. "A person who knows me from the way I am when I'm doin' the show would never recognize me as a businessman.

"I gotta be hip to what's goin' on all the time. Know what I mean? When you write songs it's the same with doin' anything creative. You gotta be able to *reach* people. So it ain't enough just to know all there is about any one special thing, like music. You gotta be diggin' *everything that's happening.* You gotta be *at least* eighty-five percent up on everything. And you gotta try *for* 100 percent."

He's trying to tell the real thing; it's not easy, but he's *trying.* "I don't know if you're gonna dig this. I talk *deep.* But when you reach a certain plateau, you can look back and see where you used to be. But when you're below, when you're down below, you can't see up. *Yeah. I* talk *real* deep. Hey, Bobby, I think she digs what I'm sayin', man! You know? She's a Soul Sister."

He knows that the best of James Brown is in his performance. It begins in that tremulous moment before he comes onstage, that *moment* when the whole audience knows he is about to appear. Those rows and rows of clean-cut White college kids packing the arena on a school night are all there to see James Brown. The girls in fuzzy pastel sweaters with their hair in pert flips, the languid-limbed boys in impeccably casual, open-necked shirts, all of them waiting. They are much more than just polite; they are reveling in the suspense, breathless with a tension they cannot explain. All eighteen musicians are standing in a row, rocking back and forth as they *play* something soft and full of promise. The five dancing girls shimmer in the velvety blue-red lights, and small sad-eyed Danny, the quiet stage manager, the master of ceremonies, sits at a desk high up on some box, delivering his introduction. It doesn't much matter what he says; no one really cares. They're all too intent on waiting to be able to listen.

" ... And here he is, ladies and gentlemen. The star of many exciting television shows and movies. The one and only James Brown and The Famous Flames."

The audience screams. First come The Flames, in a row, trotting in time to the music over to the microphone where they dance the ritualistic dance. All three of them are doing the same step, simultaneously—leaning out toward the audience, leaning back, thrusting out their arms. The three of them look so hopelessly different, three different sizes, three different shapes, that even the identical gold jackets can't hide it. But they move as one, and the crowd never stops screaming.

When he appears at the opposite side of the stage in the glamour of a brown-checked, waist-length jacket, matching vest, and sleek brown pants, it all gets wilder. Not just the screaming, but the music, too, and the gyrations of the dancing girls, and the enthusiasm of The Flames. He is coming out to give the audience all he's got, moving with a jaunty stride and a lot of purpose, as though he has come to do something he must do, something he knows how to do, something he loves to do. He is smiling at them, too, a huge, generous smile full of gleaming white teeth. He's magnificent, and he's no time-waster. He grabs at the microphone impatiently and starts to sing.

> "Odansz ed*jerk*
> Pbapasinder*szing.*
> Aindyuooo *hip*
> Tdwotdat nobreed*szayn*
> Ainno *draaaag.*
> Pbap*pas* got*da* brannoooo*bag* ... "

He has all the classic mannerisms: snapping his elbows to his sides to hike up his pants, flinging out his arms for a fresh start at the beginning of each new phrase, pantomiming the lyrics. His style is a phenomenal conglomeration of things: burlesque, gospel, sports, silent films. It is Super-Fine. James cups his ear: "Come on,

John. Play your horn. Play your horn, your baritone." John rocks up to the microphone, feigning a limp, stepping with one foot and sliding the other to meet it, blowing his horn. John takes over at the microphone so James can do his stuff. He smiles at John. "Come on, John." Then his feet are shuffling quadruple time, never leaving the floor, carrying him miraculously all over the stage, so *easily*. His arms are outspread; he is erect. Now his knees are bending; he is sinking toward the floor; he is rising again. And, all the while his feet are working with that phenomenal ease. He claps a hand behind his head, raises one leg, and watches as one foot moves him along with that slippery motion. Then he stops. He bends over his leg, smoothing an expert finger along the crease of his pants and the crowd howls its approval. He sidles back to the microphone to relieve John.

"Hehy*hey*
Come*ohn*
He*hey*
Yuhszetmeup*dtight*.
Yuhrouttas*zight*."

There is no pause between the end of one song and the beginning of another, no pause at all. When James Brown starts giving, he really gives his *all*, gives 'em their money's worth. Once he gets started, nothing can induce him to stop for breath, not even the deafening applause which often drowns out huge portions of his song.

"Mebbed*elass* tdime.
Mebbed*elass*tdimeweshake*hand*.
Mebbed*elass*tdimewemake *roma-ance*.
Oh-o *whah*, Oh-o *whah*, Ah*dunnoh*."

The Flames are cooing, "Hup hup doo-wee-ooo. Hup hup doo-wee-ooo." The dancing girls are holding up their index fingers and saying, silently, "Oh why, Oh why I don't know." The band takes over so James can dance with The Flames. They *face* the audience all in a line, each with his left hand on his left hip, watching each other.

They hop right and bump; they hop left and bump. They each execute a smooth turn and face each other in two rows: James and Bobby Bennett facing Bobby Byrd and Lloyd. Each has his left foot forward, opposite toes almost touching; they are all bouncing their weight on and off the forward leg, smiling, really *looking* at each other and smiling. They love it, being *together*. It's intimate. All at once their heads bow and four arms shoot forward and then four more. "Oh why, Oh why, I don't know."

"Yiaaaaiih. Ahmalla*lohn*.
Ahaintgohtno*body* tocahlma*hohn*.
Causeahdohn*nohf*tmaybedelasst*dime*.
Lookahrounyahovahanhovahagai-*ain*.
Shakehanswidy*ohh*bes*fren*.
Yahmightd*nevahevah*seedemagai-*ain*.
Shakehandswidy*ohh*bes*fren*.
Shake*hands*widyohbes *fren*."

He is back at the microphone, singing for his audience, his people, a modern Moses. He is telling them where it's *really at*. He is holding out his right hand to The Flames, and one by one they move toward it—first Bobby Bennett, then Bobby Byrd, then Lloyd. They each shake his hand and then, inspired, fortified, eager, they stroll cheerfully to the edge of the stage, stretching out their hands to the crowd. They want to shake hands, to shake *everybody's hand*. They move along the edge of the stage with their hands reaching out, inviting.

But it isn't only The Flames who want to shake hands. It can't be because two men in tuxedos are moving out from the wings, forbiddingly. Each grips one of James's arms as he goes to the edge of the stage where the crowd is waiting for him, swarming for his hands. A little shy at first, but frantic if they don't get their turn. They reach up for James's hands, which are scarred by the greedy fingernails of past crowds, as he moves all along the edge of the stage, gleaming and glowing, submitting himself happily to the contest as they try to drag him down to them and the men in the tuxedos tug his arms away. Lots of the time it almost looks as if the men in the tuxedos may lose him, but they never have. One girl faints, just collapses in a heap under all those frenzied feet, and the cops have to come and fight off her hysterical friends and pick her up and carry her out of the theater.

"Ahdlahktuhtellah*somemoh.*
So-*horry.* Ahgottago-*hoh.*"

Then, suddenly, it all stops—everything. For a bare moment the musicians are quiet, the dancing girls frozen with their heads bowed. The Flames have turned their backs. The light is deep purple and James cries into the stillness, "Pleeeeeze. Pleeeeeze, pleeze. Pleee-eeeze." His shoulders heave and he flops to his knees, dragging the microphone with him, pleading over it.

The crowd is hysterical, shattering the stillness. The band music is sighing. The Flames are moaning. The five girls high up on their platforms are jerking in mourning. There are a lot of isolated screams from the audience, erupting out of its momentary silences. Sometimes a particularly long pleeeeeze is what does it, or a shake of his head, or a shiver of his back. When the pace is so insistently slow and the mood so sad, the balance is very delicate.

"Pleeeze. Pleeeze. Pleeeze.
Ohdahlin*plee-eeeze*dohngoh-who-aho-*owhoaaho-o!*
Ahluhvyasooo-o."

He is in an ecstasy of agony, clinging to the neck of the micro-phone, dripping sweat, or tears, or both—screaming out his misery in that coarse voice which rakes relentlessly over the vowels. Bobby can't let him do it, can't let him do this to himself. Nor can Danny. They approach him, Danny with a great purple cape to drape over James's kneeling body. *They raise him to* his feet, swathing him in the robe. Bobby pats his back comfortingly, in time to the music. They guide him toward the wings, still singing, but he stops halfway there. He stops and they can't move him any further. He just won't go, he has to say more, He stamps his feet like a child having a tantrum. No no no no no, in quickening succession, He flings off the cape defiantly and stalks back to the microphone, grabs it and sinks to his knees with it again.

> "Bay*bay!* Yahdone me*wrohng.*
> We-e-e-eh. Yahdone me *wrohng.*
> Yahno*hwyaduhn* duhnwewrohng.
> Yahtuhk*mahluhv* nowyagoh-*hone.*"

Danny comes out with a gold cape this time. He and Bobby pull James up from the floor, drag him to his feet, limp and still crying out his song, telling them about Soul. They understand. Danny and Bobby each put an arm around his shoulders, trying to tell him it's all right, it's all gonna be alright. He stamps his feet again. Again, he flings off the cape. He is back on his knees with the microphone, back where he belongs.

> "Ahjuswannaheahyahsay Aaiii.
> Aaaiii. Aaaiii. Aaaiii. Aaaiii.
> Aaaiii. Aaaiii. Aaaiii. Aaaiii.
> Dahlin*pleee-eeezedohngoh-whoah*-oho-ohyeah-*ohoo.*
> ahluhvyahs*oh-hoh.*"

The audience is still howling "Aaaiii," as they come for him once more. Danny and Bobby wrap him in a flowing black cape. They raise him very gently, very firmly. He is like a victorious fighter, exhausted by the contest, his shoulders are heaving spasmodically. He is weak with the strain of exorcising his misery. He stops again but it isn't possible for him to come back for more. It's just not humanly possible. He raises his arms proudly and the black cape slides off his back into Danny's waiting hands. Expertly, he unfastens his cuff links and before anyone has a chance to guess what he is about to do, he flings them out to the audience in one last glorious gesture and all alone, without any help, he strides away into the wings.

The audience is overwhelmed by the relentless intricacy of it all. The music is still playing. The dancing girls are still swaying. The Flames are still warbling, and the audience is still wondering why they go on. What more could there possibly be? They are wandering until James appears again, triumphant in a clean tan suit, swinging a small suitcase at his side. "Out O' Sight" it says. He stalks across the stage with it, his parting benediction.

It is over, this elaborate personal dream out of the head and body and sweat of James Brown, who really believes in himself so fervently that the whole crowd is ready to follow him, even if he can only lead them to some private narcissistic vision of James Brown. They know it is not for them to ask what it all means. All that really matters is the sheer energy of his belief.

Backstage James sits at a long white dressing table cluttered with hair sprays and make-up kits and soda cans and packages of exotic cigarettes. He is transformed; the magnificence of his presence onstage has vanished, almost as if it had all been a dream. Greasepaint is congealed in the creases of his face, washed there by streams of sweat. It makes his face look cracked and stiff and undefinably cruel. The metamorphosis is shocking. Some open cuff link boxes are arrayed on the dressing table, displaying their goods. He uses one-thousand pairs a month to toss to his audiences. The boxes have been placed there by Gert or Danny for James to choose from—bold, jeweled links, shining in the mirror lights. A gold encrusted pair set with a small black stone in the center seems truly elegant "Ya like 'em? Ah'll give 'em to ya," James says.

He strokes on fresh greasepaint, surveying the room in the lighted mirror like some feudal lord. It's very cozy. Not the room itself, which is stark and white. Still the atmosphere they have brought to it. Bobby works patiently, repairing James's hair. Gert is hanging up the costumes, rearranging them on the rack, the 120 glistening shirts, the slacks, meticulously creased, the jackets, the capes. She attends each article with pride. Good old reliable Kenny is straightening the eighty pairs of shoes and boots, setting them out in neat rows against the far wall. He is harassed, he's always harassed, which is what makes him reliable and James knows that. "When a fellow stops worrying about his job, that's when *I* gotta start worrying. Right?" he says, turning to me, including me as a confederate. Danny is hiding something behind his back, a surprise for James. "Ya got a new ideah fer a costume ya wanna show me. Ain't dat it, Danny? Ah know. Cain't fool me, baby."

"Ah told ya,'" cries Gert triumphantly. "See. Cain't *nevah* fool James. Not dat *James.*"

Danny unfurls the huge sheet and lays it before James on the dressing table. There are eight costume designs. One looks like a costume for Prince Charming, another as if it were made for Napoleon, another like a riding habit, and one like a Sherlock Holmes outfit. "Yeah," purrs James. He stabs a finger at the Sherlock Holmes. He really *digs* that one. Everybody agrees, it's out-of-sight. He flips through the swatches of material Danny has given him. He wants it made up in brown, brown like this, with straight stovepipe pants. "'Cause as long as it's tight from *here* to *here,* that's where the action is. That's where it's happening." Everybody laughs big, knowing and appreciative, doubling over and swatting their thighs. They take turns slapping his outstretched palm with approval.

It's the private world of the show, the James Brown World, warm, intimate, and impenetrable. It even has its own language, spoken in a high grating voice, punctuated by squeals with an accent of elaborately broad vowels, stretching the best words out to the limits of a breath. And slang words and phrases and gestures; not just the classic ones, the ones everyone knows, but *special* ones, made up by James Brown, himself. It's very intoxicating.

He is very willing to teach it—more than willing, he's delighted. "Come on, lemme show ya. Watch this, Gert. Gert's gonna get a kick out o' this. Okay now. Lessee. Well, like when ya see a chick an' she's got a nice shape. Dig? So ya say, 'Man, dat *yo* woman? She's got a *muhthaah* on huh.' Ya hip to that? An' like when ya want somebody to give ya somethin', then ya say, 'Hey, man, dat dollah bill on me.' An' maybe ya want someone to do somethin' *real fast.* You know, no messin' aroun'. So ya do like this." He reaches out for my hand and folds it into a fist, straightening out the index finger. "This fingah ya keep up like dis. An' then ya say to the guy, ya say, 'Git dat on ovah hcah *riaaiight naaahza.*' " As he speaks, he keeps hold of my fist, slowly turning it over, directing it in a leisurely arc down toward the table. As he says "naaahw," he plunges the aggressive index finger against the tabletop. "Now *you* do it!" he crows. "Riaaiight naaahw." Everybody laughs again. "Ya dig dat? She's out o' sight, man. Out o' sight."

But The James Brown Language can't be learned. It's solidly insulated, which is probably why he enjoys teaching it. It's his way of separating the insiders from the outsiders, his way of protecting his secret. The truth is that everyone who is on the outside and makes an effort to get inside appears hopelessly comical, like the White disc jockey who has booked the show. He keeps bobbing in through the stage door to check up on things, to record an interview for his show, to introduce his wife, to report the financial success, to extend his congratulations. He's tall and pale and emaciated with a sharp red nose. Next to James he looks almost translucent. He can't resist affecting his impression of The James Brown Language.

"Well, we really packed 'em in there, James, baby. Like, man, you were out-of-sight. They dug it like wild. Yeah, man. They really flipped. Sure was groovy, alright. Very out-of-sight, James. Cool, man. Boy, James, baby, we'd sure like to have you here during an Easter vacation. When all the schools are out I mean like that would really swing. Of course, I know you're booked up solid. But at Easter, man, we'd really knock 'em dead."

The disc jockey rubs his palms together as he backs toward the door, almost bowing. No one laughs; that would he unprofessional, and the members of The James Brown Show are never unprofessional. Besides, laughter is superfluous: All they have to do is look at each other, just exchange a brief glance. That tells the whole story. He's an outsider. James flashes me a wink.

There's always something to rehearse after a performance, some little thing to go over. Maybe Bobby Byrd has to be straightened out about one of the dance routines. He will come to the dressing room and do it for James, go over it a few times until it's just right. Or maybe the leader of the dancing girls has to be warned to make sure the girls are covered up as much as possible—can't have it looking like a burlesque show, not when there's a fickle audience who could easily go either way, an audience that has to be wooed into the confidence that what they're seeing is something it's okay for them to like. Or maybe there's a phrase of music that's imperfect. Nothing gets left dangling; anything short of perfection has got to be repaired. Nat Jones, the band leader, is summoned to the dressing room for instructions on the introduction to "I Got You," because the way it is now, it's common, the way any old hand would play it. It's not right for The James Brown Show, where everything is *super-fine*. James shows Nat what he means. Hums it and beats it out on the surface of the dressing table. First the way it ought to be, then the way Nat's been letting them play it, then the way it ought to be again, just to show what a big difference it makes.

"You dig it, Nat? The way you're playin' it now, it's too easy. Hear it? It's right on the beat. Try it yourself. Try it both ways. See if I ain't right. It's gotta come *after* the beat. That way it's really got *Soul*." Yes. Nat Jones sees it. He agrees, but something is bothering him. "What is *Soul*, James?" he asks earnestly.

"*You* know!" cries James, almost as if his feelings had been hurt. "It's *feeling*, man."

"Yeah. Yeah, I know. But remember that time we was talkin'? You and me? About Soul? About what it really is?" He glances furtively at me.

James tries to assure him. Tries to tell him it's okay to talk in front of me. But Nat Jones shakes his head.

"No. Some other time," he insists. "Sometime when we're alone, we gotta talk about that some more. Sometime when it's just the two of us."

"Yeah." James has to admit Nat Jones is right. He turns to me shaking his head regretfully. "I dig you. You know. You can see by how I treat you. But I can't let you hear about this. You hip to what I'm sayin'? This is *something else*. I mean like *this*, baby, this is *the whole secret*."

Postscript:

This story was a family affair from the start. Diane Arbus, whose photographs were featured in an array of popular magazines since the early-'60s, was asked by her daughter to take Brown's portrait after Doon proposed the story to Clay Felker. Though she was a young interloper in Brown's world—just twenty years old—Doon was not cowed. She had a native sense of herself from a young age, and a look to go with it too—notice how Brown compliments her hair. Arbus was more than precocious, she was developed and sophisticated and scrupulous from the start. Deliberate, thoughtful, a worker.

"Putting the proverbial pen to paper is a harrowing experience no matter what it is," Doon told me, whether it's articles, books, letters, or an email. "Labor is my middle name. Mostly, I've confronted this nameless, amorphous taskmaster, saying: You'd better do this Right. You're reaching for it and you don't quite get there and the horror of falling short of this thing that you can't define is sort of ever-present. It feels like a tremendous responsibility to something you can't name and that won't give you, out loud at least, instructions on what to do. But it's very demanding, and you just must not betray it. And that sometimes makes you shrink away from doing it at all, which has happened to me by the way."

Doon makes herself a character in the piece—she's the young White reporter in Brown's Black world. It's a logical choice because when she visits Brown at his home in Queens, they discuss the perils of her accompanying them on the road in the South, a White woman traveling with Black men. It's too salient to leave out, and Arbus has a nose for story. But while she is a character, Arbus doesn't get in the way. There are no essayist musings or critical analysis—the only literary effect is the expressive attempt to capture Brown's radical sound on paper. But again, that's expressionism in the service of evoking Brown's talent—his sound—not the author's cleverness or flair. "Being interested in people is a good way to get them to be interested in you," says Doon, whose interest is our reward.

REX REED

The critic Rex Reed (1938-) possessed an abiding passion for old Hollywood glamour. He served as the Age of Aquarius' variation of Addison DeWitt, the sardonic theater critic from *All About Eve*. As a feature writer, he was even better. Tom Wolfe said Reed "raised the celebrity interview to a new level through his frankness and his eye for social detail. He has also been a master at capturing a storyline in the interview situation itself."

Reed's own story was one of ascent, though hardly glamorous—born in Fort Worth, Texas, in 1938 to an itinerant oil rig worker, he lived "anywhere there was an oil boom", he'd note in his reputation-making 1968 collection *Do You Sleep in the Nude?* From Louisiana State University he moved to New York City, briefly worked for 20th Century Fox, and then vaulted into his calling in 1965, nabbing an interview with Buster Keaton at the Venice Film Festival for *The New York Times*. By 1970 he was the trade's go-to magazine writer on film stars, making regular appearances on TV, lecture tours, and bestseller lists. In his cosmos there was room for a rare touch of idolatry—the sheer fun Ava Gardner brought to the interview qualified her but the underlying message was that stars, for all their vanity and allure, were not that godly. And yet, in small doses, they could be a whole lot of fun.—Fred Schruers

Ava: Life in the Afternoon

Esquire, 1967

She stands there, without benefit of a filter lens, against a room melting under the heat of lemony sofas and lavender walls and cream-and-peppermint-striped movie-star chairs, lost in the middle of that gilt-edge birthday-cake hotel of cupids and cupolas called The Regency. There is no script. No Minnelli to adjust the CinemaScope lens. Ice-blue rain beats against the windows and peppers Park Avenue below as Ava Gardner stalks her pink malted-milk cage like an elegant cheetah. She wears a baby-blue cashmere turtleneck sweater pushed up to her Ava elbows and a little plaid miniskirt and enormous black horn-rimmed glasses and she is gloriously, divinely barefoot.

Elbowing his way through the mob of autograph hunters and thrill seekers clustered in the lobby, all the way up in the gilt-encrusted elevator, the press agent 20th Century-Fox has sent along murmurs, "She doesn't see *anybody*, you know" and "You're very lucky, you're the only one she asked for." Remembering, perhaps, the last time she had come to New York from her hideout in Spain to ballyhoo *The Night of the Iguana* and got so mad at the press she chucked the party and ended up at Birdland. And nervously, shifting feet under my Brooks Brothers polo coat, I remember, too, all the photographers at whom she allegedly threw champagne glasses (there is even a rumor that she shoved one Fourth Estater off a balcony!), and—who could forget, Charlie?—the holocaust she caused the time Joe Hyams showed up with a tape recorder hidden in his sleeve.

Now, inside the cheetah cage without a whip and trembling like a nervous bird, the press agent says something in Spanish to the Spanish maid. "Hell, I've been there ten years and I still can't speak the goddamn language," says Ava, dismissing him with a wave of the long porcelain Ava arms. "*Out!* I don't need press agents." The eyebrows angle under the glasses into two dazzling, sequined question marks. "Can I trust him?" she asks, grinning that smashing Ava grin, and pointing at me. The press agent nods, on his way to the door: "Is there anything else we can do for you while you're in town?"

"Just get me *out* of town, baby. Just get me *outta* here."

The press agent leaves softly, walking across the carpet as if treading on rose glass with tap shoes. The Spanish maid (Ava insists she is royalty, "She follows me around because she digs me") closes the door and shuffles off into another room.

"You *do* drink—right, baby? The last bugger who came to see me had the gout and wouldn't touch a drop." She roars a cheetah roar that sounds suspiciously like Geraldine Page playing Alexandra Del Lago and mixes drinks from her portable bar: Scotch and soda for me, and for herself a champagne glass full of cognac with another champagne glass full of Dom Perignon, which she drinks successively, refills and sips slowly like syrup through a straw. The Ava legs dangle limply from the arm of a lavender chair while the Ava neck, pale and tall as a milkwood vase, rises above the room like a Southern landowner inspecting a cotton field. At forty-four, she is still one of the most beautiful women in the world.

"Don't look at me. I was up until 4 a.m. at that goddam premiere of *The Bible*. Premieres! I will personally kill that John Huston if he ever drags me into another mess like that. There must have been ten thousand people clawing at me. I get claustrophobia in crowds and I couldn't breathe. Christ, they started off by shoving a TV camera at me and yelling, 'Talk, Ava!' At intermission I got lost and couldn't find my goddamn seat after the lights went out and I kept telling those little girls with the bubble hairdos and the flashlights,

'I'm with John Huston,' and they kept saying, 'We don't know no Mr. Huston, is he from Fox?' There I was fumbling around the aisles in the dark and when I finally found my seat somebody was sitting in it and there was a big scene getting this guy to give me my seat back. Let me tell you, baby, Metro used to throw much better circuses than that. On top of it all, I lost my goddam mantilla in the limousine. Hell, it was no souvenir, that mantilla. I'll never find another one like it. Then Johnny Huston takes me to this party where we had to stand around and smile at Artie Shaw, who I was married to, baby, for Chrissake, and his wife Evelyn Keyes, who Johnny Huston was once married to, for Chrissake. And after it's all over, what have you got? The biggest headache in town. Nobody cares who the hell was there. Do you think for one minute the fact that Ava Gardner showed up at that circus will sell that picture? Christ, did you *see* it? I went through all that hell just so this morning Bosley Crowther could write I looked like I was posing for a monument. All the way through it I kept punching Johnny on the arm and saying, 'Christ, how could you let me do it?' Anyway, nobody cares what I wore or what I said. All they want to know anyway is was she drunk and did she stand up straight. This is the last circus. I am not a bitch! I am not temperamental! I am scared, baby. *Scared*. Can you possibly understand what it's like to feel scared?"

She rolls her sleeves higher than the elbows and pours two more champagne glasses full. There is nothing about the way she looks, up close, to suggest the life she has led: press conferences accompanied by dim lights and an orchestra; bullfighters writing poems about her in the press; rubbing Vaseline between her bosoms to emphasize the cleavage; roaming restlessly around Europe like a woman without a country, a Pandora with her suitcases full of cognac and Hershey bars ("for quick energy"). None of the ravaged, ruinous grape-colored lines to suggest the affairs or the brawls that bring the police in the middle of the night or the dancing on tabletops in Madrid cellars till dawn.

The doorbell rings and a pimply-faced boy with a Beatles hairdo delivers one dozen Nathan's hot dogs, rushed from Coney Island in a limousine. "Eat," says Ava, sitting cross-legged on the floor, biting into a raw onion.

"You're looking at me again!" she says shyly, pulling short girlish wisps of hair behind the lobes of her Ava ears. I mention the fact that she looks like a Vassar coed in her miniskirt. "Vassar?" she asks suspiciously. "Aren't they the ones who get in all the trouble?"

"That's Radcliffe."

She roars. Alexandra Del Lago again. "I took one look at myself in *The Bible* and went out this morning and got all my hair cut off. This is the way I used to wear it at MGM. It takes years off. What's *that*?" Eyes narrow, axing her guest in half, burning holes in my notebook. "Don't tell me you're one of those people who always go around scribbling everything on little pieces of paper. Get rid of that. Don't take notes. Don't ask questions either because I probably won't answer any of them anyway. Just let Mama do all the talking. Mama knows best. You want to ask something, I can tell. Ask."

I ask if she hates all of her films as much as *The Bible*.

"Christ, what did I ever do worth talking about? Every time I tried to act, they stepped on me. That's why it's such a goddam shame, I've been a movie star for twenty-five years and I've got nothing, *nothing* to show for it. All I've got is three lousy ex-husbands, which reminds me, I've got to call Artie and ask him what his birthday is. I can't remember my own family's birthdays. Only reason I know my own is because I was born the same day as Christ. Well, almost. Christmas Eve, 1922. That's Capricorn, which means a lifetime of *hell*, baby. Anyway, I need Artie's birthday because I'm trying to get a new passport. I tramp around Europe, but I'm not giving up my citizenship, baby, for *anybody*. Did you ever try living in Europe and renewing your passport? They treat you like you're a goddamn Communist or something. Hell, that's why I'm getting the hell out of Spain, because I hate Franco and I hate Communists. So now they want a list of all my divorces so I told them hell, call *The New York Times*—they know more about me than I do!"

But hadn't all those years at MGM been any fun at all? "Christ, after seventeen years of slavery, you can ask that question? I hated it, honey. I mean I'm not exactly stupid or without feeling, and they tried to sell me like a prize hog. They also tried to make me into something I was not then and never could be. They used to write in my studio bios that I was the daughter of a cotton farmer from Chapel Hill. Hell, baby, I was born on a tenant farm in Grabtown. How's that grab ya? Grabtown, North Carolina. And it looks exactly the way it sounds. I should have stayed there. The ones who never left home don't have a pot to pee in but they're happy. Me, look at me. What did it bring me?" She finishes off another round of cognac and pours a fresh one. "The only time I'm happy is when I'm doing absolutely nothing. When I work I vomit all the time. I know nothing about acting so I have one rule—trust the director and give him heart and soul. And nothing else." (Another cheetah roar.) "I get a lot of money so I can afford to loaf a lot. I don't trust many people, so I only work with Huston now. I used to trust Joe Mankiewicz, but one day on the set of *The Barefoot Contessa* he did the unforgivable thing. He insulted me. He said, 'You're the sittin'est goddamn actress,' and I never liked him after that. What I really want to do is get married again. Go ahead and laugh, everybody laughs, but how great it must be to tromp around barefoot and cook for some great goddamn son of a bitch who loves you the rest of your life. I've never had a good man."

What about Mickey Rooney? (A glorious shriek.) "Love comes to Andy Hardy."

Sinatra? "No comment," she says to her glass.

A slow count to ten, while she sips her drink. Then, "And Mia Farrow?" The Ava eyes brighten to a soft clubhouse green. The answer comes like so many cats lapping so many saucers of cream. Unprintable.

Like a phonograph dropping a new LP, she changes the subject. "I only want to do the things that don't make me suffer. My friends are more important to me than anything. I know all kinds of people—bums, hangers-on, intellectuals, a few phonies. I'm going to see a college boy at Princeton tomorrow and we're going to a ball game. Writers. I love writers. Henry Miller sends me books to improve my mind. Hell, did you read *Plexus*? I couldn't get through it. I'm not an intellectual, although when I was married to Artie Shaw I took a lot of courses at UCLA and got A's and B's in psychology and literature. I have a mind, but I never got a chance to use it doing every goddamn lousy part in every goddamn lousy picture Metro turned out. I *feel* a lot, though. God, I'm sorry I wasted those twenty-five years. My sister Dee Dee can't understand why after all these years I can't bear to face a camera. But I never brought anything to this business and I have no respect for acting. Maybe if I had learned something it would be different. But I never did anything to be proud of. Out of all those movies, what can I claim to have done?"

"*Mogambo, The Hucksters*—"

"Hell, baby, after twenty-five years in this business, if all you've got to show for it is *Mogambo* and *The Hucksters* you might as well give up. Name me one actress who survived all that crap at MGM. Maybe Lana Turner. Certainly Liz Taylor. But they all hate acting as much as I do. All except for Elizabeth. She used to come up to me on the set and say, 'If only I could learn to be good,' and by God, she made it. I haven't seen *Virginia Woolf*—hell, I *never* go to movies—but I hear she is good. I never cared much about myself. I didn't have the emotional makeup for acting and I hate exhibitionists anyway. And who the hell was there to help me or teach me acting was anything else? I really tried in *Show Boat* but that was MGM crap. Typical of what they did to me there. I wanted to sing those songs—hell, I've still got a Southern accent—and I really thought Julie should sound a little like a Negro since she's supposed to have Negro blood. Christ, those songs like "Bill" shouldn't sound like an opera. So, what did they say? 'Ava, baby, you can't sing, you'll hit the wrong keys, you're up against real pros in this film, so don't make a fool of yourself.' *Pros!* Howard Keel? And Kathryn Grayson, who had the biggest boobs in Hollywood? I mean I like Graysie, she's a sweet girl, but with her they didn't even need 3D! Lena Horne told me to go to Phil Moore, who was her pianist and had coached Dorothy Dandridge, and he'd teach me. I made a damn good track of the songs and they said, 'Ava, are you outta your head?' Then they got Eileen Wilson, this gal who used to do a lot of my singing on-screen, and *she* recorded a track with the same background arrangement taken off *my* track. They substituted her voice for mine, and now in the movie my Southern twang stops talking and her soprano starts singing—hell what a mess. They wasted God knows how many thousands of dollars and ended up with crap. I still get royalties on the goddamn records I did."

The doorbell rings and in bounces a little man named Larry. Larry has silver hair, silver eyebrows and smiles a lot. He works for a New York camera shop. "Larry used to be married to my sister Bea. If you think I'm something you ought to see Bea. When I was eighteen I came to New York to visit them and Larry took that picture of me that started this whole megillah. He's a sonuvabitch, but I love him."

"Ava, I sure loved you last night in *The Bible*. You were really terrific, darlin'."

"Crap!" Ava pours another cognac. "I don't want to hear another word about that goddamn *Bible*. I didn't believe it and I didn't believe that Sarah bit I played for a minute. How could anybody stay married for a hundred years to *Abraham*, who was one of the biggest bastards who ever lived?"

"Oh, darlin', she was a wonderful woman, that Sarah."

"She was a jerk!"

"Oh, darlin', ya shouldn' talk like that. God will hear ya. Don'tcha believe in God?" Larry joins us on the floor and bites into a hot dog, spilling mustard on his tie.

"Hell, no." The Ava eyes flash.

"I pray to him every night, darlin'. Sometimes he answers too."

"He never answered me, baby. He was never around when I needed him. He did nothing but screw up my whole life since the day I was born. Don't tell *me* about *God*! I know all about that bugger!"

The doorbell again. This time a cloak-and-dagger type comes in; he's wearing an ironed raincoat, has seventeen pounds of hair and looks like he has been living on plastic vegetables. He says he is a student at New York University Law School. He also says he is twenty-six years old. "*What?*" Ava takes off her glasses for a closer look. "Your father told me you were twenty-seven. Somebody's lying!" The Ava eyes narrow and the palms of her hands are wet.

"Let's get some air, fellas." Ava leaps into the bedroom and comes out wearing a Navy pea jacket with a Woolworth scarf around her head. Vassar again.

"I thought you were gonna cook tonight, darlin'," says Larry, throwing his fist into a coat sleeve.

"I want spaghetti. Let's go to the Supreme Macaroni Company. They let me in the back door there and nobody ever recognizes *anybody* there. Spaghetti, baby. I'm starved."

Ava slams the door shut, leaving all the lights on. "Fox is paying, baby." We all link arms and follow the leader. Ava skips ahead of us like Dorothy on her way to Oz. *Lions and tigers and bears, oh my!* Moving like a tiger through Regency halls, melting with hot pink, like the inside of a womb.

"Are those creeps still downstairs?" she asks. "Follow me."

She knows all the exits. We go down on the service elevator. About twenty autograph hunters crowd the lobby. Celia, queen of the autograph bums, who leaves her post on the door at Sardi's only on special occasions, has deserted her station for this. *Ava's in town this week.* She sits behind a potted palm wearing a purple coat and green beret, arms full of self-addressed postcards.

Cool.

Ava gags, pushes the horn-rims flat against her nose, and pulls us through the lobby. Nobody recognizes her. "Drink time, baby!" she whispers, shoving me toward a side stairway that leads down to The Regency Bar.

"Do you know who *that* was?" asks an Iris Adrian type with a mink-dyed fox on her arm as Ava heads for the bar. We check coats and umbrellas and suddenly we hear that soundtrack voice, hitting E-flat.

"You *sonuvabitch!* I could buy and sell you. How dare you insult my friends? Get me the manager!"

Larry is at her side. Two waiters are shushing Ava and leading us all to a corner booth. Hidden. Darker than the Polo Lounge. Hide the star. This is New York, not Beverly Hills.

"It's that turtleneck sweater you're wearing," whispers Larry to me as the waiter seats me with my back to the room.

"They don't like me here, the bastards. I never stay in this hotel, but Fox is paying, so what the hell? I wouldn't come otherwise. They don't even have a jukebox, for Chrissake." Ava flashes a smile in

Metrocolor and orders a large ice tea glass filled with straight tequila. "No salt on the side. Don't need it."

"Sorry about the sweater—" I begin.

"You're beautiful. Gr-r-r!" She laughs her Ava laugh and the head rolls back and the little blue vein bulges on her neck like a delicate pencil mark.

Two tequilas later ("I said no salt!") she is nodding grandly, surveying the bar like the Dowager Empress in the Recognition Scene. Talk buzzes around her like hummingbird wings and she hears nothing. Larry is telling about the time he got arrested in Madrid and Ava had to get him out of jail and the student is telling me about NYU Law School and Ava is telling *him* she doesn't believe he's only twenty-six years old and can he prove it, and suddenly he looks at his watch and says Sandy Koufax is playing in St. Louis.

"You're kidding!" Ava's eyes light up like cherries on a cake. "Let's go! Goddammit we're going to St. Louis!"

"Ava, darlin', I gotta go to work tomorrow." Larry takes a heavy sip of his Grasshopper.

"Shut up, you bugger. If I pay for us all to go to St. Louis we go to St. Louis! Can I get a phone brought to this table? Someone call Kennedy airport and find out what time the next plane leaves. I *love* Sandy Koufax! I *love* Jews! God, sometimes I think I'm Jewish myself. A Spanish Jew from North Carolina. *Waiter!*"

The student convinces her that by the time we got to St. Louis they'd be halfway through the seventh inning. Ava's face falls and she goes back to her straight tequila.

"Look at 'em, Larry," she says. "They're such babies. Please don't go to Vietnam." Her face turns ashen. Julie leaving the showboat with William Warfield singing *Ol' Man River* in the fog on the levee. "We gotta do it … ."

"What are you talkin' about, darlin'?" Larry shoots a look at the law student who assures Ava he has no intention of going to Vietnam.

" … didn't ask for this world, the buggers made us do it … . " A tiny bubble bath of sweat breaks out on her forehead and she leaps up from the table. "My God, I'm suffocating! Gotta get some air!" She turns over the glass of tequila and three waiters are flying at us like bats, dabbing and patting and making great breathing noises.

Action!

The NYU student, playing Chance Wayne to her Alexandra Del Lago, is all over the place like a trained nurse. Coats fly out of the checkroom. Bills and quarters roll across the wet tablecloth. Ava is on the other side of the bar and out the door. On cue, the other customers, who have been making elaborate excuses for passing our table on their way to the bathroom, suddenly give great breathy choruses of "Ava" and we are through the side door and out in the rain.

Then as quickly as it started it's over. Ava is in the middle of Park Avenue, the scarf falling around her neck and her hair blowing wildly around the Ava eyes. Lady Brett in the traffic, with a downtown bus as the bull. Three cars stop on a green light and every taxi driver on Park Avenue begins to honk. The autograph hunters leap through the polished doors of The Regency and begin to scream. Inside, still waiting coolly behind the potted palm, is Celia, oblivious to the noise, facing the elevators, firmly clutching her postcards. No need to risk missing Ava because of a minor commotion on the street. Probably Jack E. Leonard or Edie Adams. Catch them next week at Danny's.

Outside, Ava is inside the taxi flanked by the NYU student and Larry, blowing kisses to the new chum, who will never grow to be an old one. They are already turning the corner into Fifty-Seventh Street, fading into the kind of night, the color of tomato juice in the headlights, that only exists in New York when it rains.

"Who was it?" asks a woman walking a poodle.

"Jackie Kennedy," answers a man from his bus window.

Postscript:

"It doesn't get any easier," Rex Reed said after hosting an event at Lincoln Center for Doris Day's centenary. He meant writing, which he'd done for weeks leading up to the event. He was so wiped after his performance, which included singing three songs, Reed didn't go to the after-party but straight home to his apartment in the Dakota where he's lived for six decades.

Rex's been to enough parties, more than most of us could ever imagine. He's still a tireless ambassador for old Hollywood, something we see in full bloom in his 1967 Ava Gardner profile.

"Ava Gardner was a real movie star," he said. "She was glamourous and beautiful; she was a rebel. She was everything that appealed to me. I idolized her. But she was very difficult because she didn't allow me to have a tape recorder and didn't want me to write anything down. I had to go to the bathroom and scribble notes on a pad quickly. At one point she said to me, 'What's a matter baby, you got a bladder problem?'

"It was wonderful to be with her, I was enthralled, but there was no continuity to what she was saying. She was all over the place. Most writers would have eighty-sixed the whole thing but I decided to structure it like a movie. I was very proud that the piece was chosen by Tom Wolfe to be in his New Journalism anthology. I was the child of Gay Talese. His influence can't be understated. I made a name for myself at *The New York Times*. Seymour Hirsch, who was the editor of the Sunday Arts & Leisure section, gave me my career. But I wanted to be Gay Talese, and I got to do my version of that at *Esquire*. They really cared about writers.

"Well, she went into shock about that piece. I later heard that she told people, 'That son of a bitch knows more about me than I do about myself.' She almost never did interviews again after that. Years and years later, I did a piece for Tina Brown at *Talk* about Ava after she died. I talked to everyone, Artie Shaw, everyone. The person that kept that piece from being a smash was her maid, who knew where all the bodies were buried and everything Sinatra said to her. She knew everything and I couldn't find her, she was from Nicaragua. One day, I'm interviewing Gregory Peck and we were having tea and I told him my dilemma and he said, 'You want to interview her? She just served you tea.' "

Reed got the interview.

BARBARA G. GOLDSMITH

Though Barbara Goldsmith (1931–2016) hailed from a wealthy family, she embarked on a professional career at age twenty-one, interviewing first Clark Gable and then a number of other entertainers of the '50s—John Huston, Danny Kaye, Audrey Hepburn—chiefly for *Woman's Home Companion*. A fixture in the New York art scene, she counted Elaine de Kooning as a pal, along with Larry Rivers, who painted Goldsmith's portrait. Her bestselling books included the memorable 1980 biography, *Little Gloria ... Happy at Last*, about the Gloria Vanderbilt custody trial of the '30s.

"The line between fame and notoriety has been erased," she wrote in 1980. "Today we are faced with a vast confusing jumble of celebrities: the talented and untalented, heroes and villains, people of accomplishment and those who have accomplished nothing at all, the criteria for their celebrity being that their images encapsulate some form of the American Dream ... We no longer demand reality, only that which is real seeming."

It was from this vantage that she wrote about Viva, one of the "superstars" to come out of Andy Warhol's Factory during the '60s, for the fledgling *New York* magazine (it was Goldsmith who lent Clay Felker $6,500 to purchase the name *New York* from Jock Whitney to begin with). The profile, and its accompanying highly controversial photograph by Diane Arbus, helped to established both the magazine and Goldsmith herself as a must-read.—AB

LA DOLCE VIVA

New York, 1968

In Andy Warhol's new loft studio "The Factory," Viva leaned against the whitewashed plaster wall, her cotton-candy hair bright blond under the spotlights. Her fine-boned face and attenuated body were reminiscent of sepia-tinted photographs, found in an attic trunk, of actresses of the early 1930s. She was wearing an Edwardian velvet coat, a white matelassé blouse, and tapered black slacks. "Do I look okay?" she asked Paul Morrissey, Warhol's technical director. "Like a star," he replied grandly.

Underground movies have emerged from Village lofts and moved into uptown movie theaters; consequently underground movie stars have emerged too. Viva, who has appeared in *Bike Boy*, *The Nude Restaurant*, and *Tub Girl*, has been the subject of numerous fashion articles and interviews which present her as gay, hip, and glamorous.

Women's Wear Daily said, "Viva's look is fashion ... she is the kind of person who influences today's fashion ... . She is a presence. Viva's approach to life ... to clothes ... to everything is individual." She has been compared to Garbo and Dietrich *(The Village Voice)*, Lucille Ball *(Vogue)*, an American Rita Tushingham or Lynn Redgrave *(The New York Times)*.

The elevator at The Factory opened, discharging members of the press and friends who had been invited to see a screening of Viva's most recent movie, *The Lonesome Cowboy*. Almost immediately Viva was surrounded by people.

A small dark-haired girl said admiringly, "I saw you on TV today, Viva. You were great." "Thank you, thank you" said Viva, kissing the air in the manner of a Hollywood movie queen. "Now let's settle down and watch the movie."

The movie (which lasted about 200 minutes) demonstrated the Warhol cinematic formula. It proved to be a mélange of homosexual sex, conversation, rape, conversation, transvestism, conversation, homosexual incest, conversation, masturbation, conversation, heterosexual seduction, talk, talk, talk, and an orgy. Viva, the only female in the picture was, quite naturally, responsible for the heterosexual sex and served as a target for the rape.

During the rape scene Viva nudged a friend and remarked, "There were about 40 children watching this scene. All the art students from the neighboring universities came and brought their children. I screamed 'those children will be shocked out of their minds.' You hear me say that in a minute." Viva hunched in a bewildered shrug. "No one complained. They were all artists so they thought it was art."

Andy Warhol is a businessman who is by category an artist. Because of this label, the viewer is either intimidated by what he takes for Art, or, and this is more frequently true, he can indulge the voyeur in his nature in the name of artistic experience. Warhol's studio is accurately named "The Factory" because here he manufactures a blend of peep and ennui for public consumption. His prototype product was *The Chelsea Girls*, the first underground movie to have an uptown run. It cost about $10,000 to produce and the theater gross on this movie is now over half-a-million dollars, causing the taciturn Andy to comment, "The new Art is Business."

"I'm really worn out," said Viva at the end of the movie as she popped a pill in her mouth and washed it down with a glass of red wine. "Andy and Paul are working me to death with all these interviews. How about dropping by to see me tomorrow when I wake up, say about one o'clock."

On the third ring Viva opened the door to her East 83rd Street brownstone floor-through apartment. The young woman who stood at the door wore no makeup and her eyes were a spot of intense green color in a face of light brows and invisible eyelashes. She wore red slacks and an unbuttoned red cotton blouse. Her hair was pulled back in a bun. As soon as I entered words started spilling out. "Oh, God, don't look at this place. I haven't cleaned up or picked up a thing in months. Every night I think I'll die from the smell of dust and that cockroach powder. Just look at those filthy windows. I've got to do something about this, but I don't own a vacuum and I can't buy one. I'm penniless, absolutely penniless. My rent is paid by a man I know."

Viva stepped gracefully over underwear, dresses, bags of laundry, an iron, some dishes, magazines, and papers. She leaned down and from under a laundry bag extracted the velvet coat I had seen her wearing the night before. It was badly burned. "Look at this—ruined. And all the hours I spent on airplanes sewing that lining. Someone dropped a lighted match on it and I didn't notice until it was all burned up. I was so tired and I took two Midols and a muscle relaxer and drank some wine that I made myself last Easter. Then I had two puffs on a pot cigarette and I was so high I didn't notice. It was my favorite. The only other dress I like is a 1920s dress Andy bought but it smells so of perspiration that I can't wear it. Oh, who cares," said Viva, walking through the stuffing that was oozing out of a gold chair and past a wall full of scrawled telephone numbers.

Viva led the way back into the bedroom. It contained a sheetless double bed which occupied almost the entire room. On it lay the remains of pancakes in a tinfoil dish, an orange juice container, some sweaters, a makeup mirror, various types of makeup, a copy of *The Little Prince*, and some photographs. She scooped up the photographs. "I got these for you to see. They are of my family." The first photograph showed a cathedral banked with flowers. "This is my sister Jeannie's wedding picture. She's 24—a year younger than I am.

"There are nine of us. My real name is Susan Hoffmann. Here's my father playing the violin. He has seventy-four violins. He also has four boats, two houses, one in Syracuse and one on Wellesley Island in the Saint Lawrence Seaway, and a farm in Goose Bay. He made it all himself. He's a lawyer in Syracuse.

"My father had an uncontrollable temper and used to take it out on me. Then there was always the difference between how things looked and how they were. He used to raise horses because he said they looked good on the grass of his summer estate but they were never broken so none of his kids could ride them."

Viva flipped another picture. "This is my First Communion picture. The whole atmosphere I was brought up in was absurd. On the one hand my parents were always extremely hospitable, all summer long we had thirty people in the house, but at the same time they were really rigid. My mother was a big Joe McCarthy supporter. She had two looks ... one meant 'Shut up' and the other meant 'Cross your legs.'

"I slept with a cross over my bed—the whole works. My father had a five-foot statue of the Blessed Virgin Mary. At Christmas he put a halo and two spotlights on it. I was with the nuns until I was twenty. I was a virgin until I was twenty-one. Then I spent the next two years making up for it. Now I can't stand the whole clergy, Pope, bishop, priest, nun, anti-sex, authoritarian thing about the Catholic Church. But I think that Christ was probably really groovy.

"After high school I went to Marymount College in Tarrytown where the Sisters said I was the best student in the school in art. I wanted to be a fashion illustrator. Then I went to the Sorbonne and the Academic Julian in Paris and all that time I lived at a convent in Neuilly. The last term at the Sorbonne I became so depressed I didn't attend classes. I just walked around and sat in Deux Magots sipping warm vermouth."

Viva stretched, rubbed her eyes, and yawned. "I'm tired out from that Tucson location trip for the movie. I didn't get any sleep. The first two nights I slept with John Chamberlain who is an old lover of mine. I slept with him for security reasons. Well, then, it was a different one every night. One night Allen Midgette and what's his name, Tom Hompertz, both made it with me. Andy looked in the window and said 'What are you doing in there? I told you not to. You're supposed to save it for the camera.' Then there was Little Joe (Joe D'Alessandro) who was sweet and Eric (Eric Emerson) who was just so rough." Viva looked up and said, "Don't look so skeptical. It's the truth. I always tell the truth. People sometimes say I put them on, but I really don't know what a put-on is. I'm just like everybody else. It's just that I'm too frank.

"The whole point is I really don't care—well, I guess I do. Paul Morrissey thinks I'm a nymphomaniac, but I don't. I just like to sleep with people, because I hate to sleep alone. I have nightmares and I like to have someone in bed to cuddle up. Most men don't know what it's about anyway, they're so insensitive and don't concentrate on it. I guess I expected too much from men. Men just cannot affect me anymore. I haven't been upset by a man in six months.

"In Andy's movies women are always the strong ones, the beautiful ones and the ones who control everything. Men turn out to be these empty animals. Maybe the homosexuals are the only ones who haven't really copped out. They treat me better than any straight men I've known. I was very fond of one girl and we're still friends, but I really like men. Even when I used to make it with that girl, we always wanted a man around, just to watch and everything. You know, if somebody's beautiful, they really turn me on.

"My view of men is that they are pathetic, they are creatures that need help. The only kind of men I like now are men who are fantastically naive and not too bright, like my lover Marco. [For this story Viva was photographed having sexual relations with Marco St. John and his wife, Barbara.] I'd rather have somebody teach me but I never found anybody who could. Anyway, I don't care if I make it much anymore because I feel there is no point. Like the whole dumb *Playboy*-Hugh-Hefner-sex philosophy, that sex without love is better than no sex at all. I think that's a lot of nonsense. You're better off masturbating. When you're with somebody who is not really with you, you feel ridiculous.

"When I was young though, I could really get obsessed with a man. Just after I got out of school I had a fight with my father. I had a fight with him about every two months. So I got a job in Boston and then I moved to New York. I moved in with a photographer. He was my first lover. He was twice my age, a sort of classic situation. I was looking for a father. He was the first person I ever met who I could talk to and tell him all the things I had never told anybody. He was my only friend. He was married but separated. Anyway, he never wanted me to go out anywhere. He was insanely jealous. He even burned all my clothes. We'd have dinner and buy magazines and watch TV and read in bed. He'd make up my face every night. I left him after a year.

"I didn't have a cent and my father didn't give me anything so I got jobs modeling. I worked for three agencies, but I was too disorganized and somehow the word got out that I was unreliable. I guess I was. I kept going back to that photographer and we'd fight because he didn't want me to model for anyone else. It was just a mess. Easily the worst period of my life.

"I had no energy and I just got so depressed. It's not that nobody cares about you; that's only secondary. You're depressed without any reason and that's very scary. I knew I was having a nervous breakdown so I got my sister to drive me to Millbrook, New York, to see Timothy Leary.

"Tim Leary had been the first one to turn me on to drugs. He told me to take Psilocybin, the hallucinogenic mushroom, and I took it out of curiosity. I've tried everything except heroin and opium. I've only taken LSD three times and I don't think I'd take it again because of the health hazard. I don't know about those chromosome changes. The first time I took it, I thought it was a big joke because you think you've got the key to the whole universe only you can't remember exactly what it is. I could see someone taking drugs every day looking for the key. The last time I took LSD I had a bad experience. I was with a guy who wouldn't make love to me so I smashed his TV set and flipped out and he beat me up.

"I prefer mescaline and peyote to synthetic drugs. I can't see anything wrong with taking something that actually grows out of the ground. But peyote is so nauseating to swallow, I don't know if I could do it again. I never take anything regularly. I'm just not organized enough to get a connection. At least half the kids at The Factory are on drugs. We use them in the movies because they are often the most interesting.

"Under drugs I think the answer is love and the constant orgasm. You just keep coming. That puts you in the Kingdom of Heaven. I guess religion is just a whole sexual sublimation. I get into this whole religious thing—I see black-and-white movies of Egypt being played on the walls. I can't figure out whether it's too much of the nuns or too much reading of psychiatry or what."

The phone rang. Viva picked it up and said "OK, OK, I've put the check in the mail. You can't cut off my electricity. I told you. I've been away. It's all taken care of." She hangs up and says "I've got to call Andy to pay my Con Edison bill. Andy gives me $100 here and $100 there whenever I need money. I never ask for much. We're all supposed to go on regular salary soon, but Andy says the company is bankrupt.

"Anyway," she resumed, "I was telling you about Tim Leary. I stayed with him for about a week but he wouldn't let me have anything except a few sniffs of methedrine from my finger so I painted a mural, walked in the woods, and made it with some guys. Then I went home to my family because I knew I wasn't getting any better.

"I told my mother that I wanted to commit myself to an institution so she took me to a place in Auburn, New York, but when we went inside, the attendant locked the door behind us and then clamped a name tag on my wrist. I just got hysterical and begged my mother to take me home, so she did. The next week I lay in bed shivering and I didn't want my mother to leave my side. Then I said to myself 'I'm going back to the womb. I've just got to get out of here.' So I caught a plane back to New York and moved in with my sister Jeannie.

"I took a job at Parsons doing fashion modeling in the morning and nude modeling in the afternoon. It saved all that cab fare I'd have to be paying if I ran around to modeling jobs. After eight months the depression passed. One night I went to see Andy's movie *I, A Man* and I thought it was fabulous. If I had seen one movie like that when I was young, I might not have felt so shy and different. It's just so honest. People hesitate, a girl covers up her breasts because she is embarrassed to show them to you. In Andy's movies people are honest and frank and open. Most people aren't like that at all. Like my parents, everything in their lives is structured by their religion and their politics and their social relationships and anything that doesn't agree with that they think is wrong. Anyway, this whole puritan atmosphere has one advantage ... it makes everything seem more exciting when you break away from it.

"I don't put my parents down, though. They had nine kids and the kids are all against everything my parents stand for so they couldn't have done everything wrong. If they had, the kids would just be carbon copies of them."

Viva stood up, tripped over a cup, kicked at it, and said angrily, "I can't stand this place. You'd think I'd move to the country, right? Right. But I don't. Who am I going to talk to? Almost all my friends are around The Factory. It's just easier to live here and I'm away on college lecture tours with Andy a lot of the time. We pick up a lot of kids on those college tours. That's where we got Tom Hompertz. We show part of our twenty-five-hour movie and we speak to the kids. We tell them we don't believe in goals, no goals, no purpose. We don't believe in art. Everything is art. The only point is to make a movie to entertain.

"I'm nude because Andy says seeing me nude sells tickets. It's hard to believe. I think I look like a parody, a satire on a nude, a plucked chicken. Since I got an IUD [intrauterine device] and stopped taking birth control pills, I don't even have any breasts. But lately I've gotten a lot of attention and publicity. Some dumb reporter said 'Viva has dropped out of the rat race.' A lot she knows. I've just entered the rat race, I want money and I guess a career. Trying to plan ahead puts me in a terrible state. I can tell you what I'm doing at the moment, but if I think about the future I get all neurotic.

"I have Andy now to think ahead and make the decisions. I just do what he tells me to do. Andy has a certain mystique that makes you want to do things for him," Viva looked up, her eyes blank. Then she said slowly. "Sometimes though when I think about Andy, I think he is just like Satan. He just gets you and you can't get away. I used to go everywhere by myself. Now I can't seem to go anywhere or make the simplest decision without Andy. He has such a hold on all of us. But I love it when they talk about Andy and Viva."

The names coupled that way made me think of a time when it was Andy and Edie, so I asked, "What happened to 'Superstar' Edie Sedgwick?"

"Oh," said Viva, circling her lips with the point of her tongue in a nervous mannerism, "Edie looks fabulous. I visited her in the hospital. She's been there for a long time. I brought her a cactus plant because of its shape. They kept a nurse in the room with us the whole time because before I visited somebody gave her an amphetamine."

Viva stood up and took off her slacks. She kneeled before me, naked from the waist down, and began searching through the pile of clothes on the floor. "I've got to go as soon as I find something to wear," she said, "*Eye* magazine is making an official group photograph and they need me."

At Max's Kansas City, after the photography session, Viva, Warhol, and Ingrid Superstar and Brigid Polk, both of whom are featured in Warhol movies, sat at a large round table in the corner. The restaurant accords them celebrity status; Viva sent back her fish, then a steak, meanwhile sniffing methedrine off a spoon. "I take it every three hours," Brigid said. "Don't let anybody tell you speed kills. I've been on it for years."

"I just got out of the hospital," Ingrid Superstar said, "and I'm all set for action." She held up a packet of condoms.

Brigid said, "Excuse me for a minute, it's time to wake myself up," and she headed for the ladies' room.

Viva put her head on the table. "I'm so tired and this place is depressing me." She picked up her bag and left.

Later, Viva returned to The Factory, a loft in a business building. The downstairs door was locked. Viva looked for a telephone to summon someone to open the door. The first five booths had been vandalized and were inoperative. From the sixth she grated, "Listen you bastard, this is Viva. Get down here fast and open that goddamned door." Incredulous, she stared at the phone. "He hung up," she said. Viva then dialed Warhol's home number and got the answering service. The voice asked if she would like to leave a message. "Yes," she said and proceeded to express it. The answering service hung up.

Viva flung the phone across the booth and walked back to the locked door to wait for somebody to come in or go out. "I'll show them," she raged. "They locked me out, and I'm going to lock them in." With a dime and a bobby pin she attempted to remove the doorknob.

During this operation Warhol arrived, "Why don't I have a key to this place? Why don't I have a key to this place?" Viva shouted, "I'm not treated with any respect around here." Warhol regarded her, bland as farina, whereupon she flung her handbag at him catching him across the side of the face. "You're crazy, Viva" he said dispassionately. "What do you think you're doing?"

Postscript:

Tom Wolfe visited the offices of *New York* magazine, then nestled in the fourth floor of a brownstone on Thirty-Second Street, one day in 1968 when editor-in-chief Clay Felker handed him a manuscript of a story. It was going to run in the fourth issue of *New York* and the advertising department was nervous that they could potentially lose a lot of high-end advertisers with this piece. Felker wanted to know what Wolfe thought. Wolfe couldn't sit down. "What I had in my hands was dynamite," he later wrote. "Tout le monde knew about the famous Andy Warhol and his famous Factory full of helpers and hangers-on. But Barbara Goldsmith's was the first story to capture the campy creepy KY/Vaseline-y queasiness of it ... the Warhol style of life."

It wasn't just the nature of Goldsmith's writing, however, that made the piece sensational, it was an accompanying photograph, taking up a page-and-a-half by Diane Arbus. In it, Viva is nude from the waist up, you can see her thin rib cage, hair under her arms, her eyes rolled back as if she were some kind of zombie.

When Wolfe finished reading, he told Felker, "I don't see how you can *not* run it."

Which is exactly what Felker believed and so he ran the piece. The reaction was worse than expected in the short term. According to Wolfe, "*New York* lost every high-end retailer on Madison Avenue and beyond." Felker had to deal with a furious board of investors, but in the end, the magazine survived. This also established the magazine's nerve—a carryover from the scandalous Wolfe-Felker critique of *The New Yorker* back when *New York* was still a Sunday supplement.

Viva, for her part, was furious. "That story is about ninety-eight percent fiction," she later said. "A lot of horrible things have happened to me, but I would consider that the worst. She had me having sex with every single cast member—who were all gay anyway! I ran into that miserable bitch years later. I can't believe I didn't sue those sons of bitches."

While written in an era when writers, even good ones, were known to take certain liberties, big and small, with the truth, Goldsmith was never accused of making things up, at least not that I've been able to find. One thing she understood was the world of fame. "In today's highly technological world," she wrote in a prescient 1983 essay for *The New York Times*, "reality has become a pallid substitute for the image reality we fabricate for ourselves, which in turn intensifies our addiction to the artificial.

"Because it is fabricated, image can be altered at will. Andy Warhol owes the longevity of his celebrity to the fact that his image keeps changing to suit the temper of the times. His 1960s go-go image of black-leather motorcycle jacket, patched dungarees, and drugged companions has given way to the conservative tailored suits and socialite parties of the 1980s."

ALBERT GOLDMAN

It was 1969, "the year of the polymorphous perverse," as Norman Mailer would dub it in *The Prisoner of Sex*, and a *succès de scandale* was about to be loosed upon the land: Philip Roth's ejaculatory escapade *Portnoy's Complaint*. The chapters that had appeared in *Partisan Review* and *New American Review* (one of the excerpts was titled "Whacking Off") had created a wicked sensation. Here was a novel that promised to drag masturbation out from under the sheets in the shame of night and let it run riot, whizzing through the air. Anticipation over the novel was rabid, and not just because of its raunch factor. Its author carried serious literary cred, his beetle-y pair of eyebrows smoldering with Kafka intensity. A wunderkind whose early *New Yorker* stories had notched his reputation, Roth had brought out one popular novella, *Goodbye Columbus*, then being adapted into a movie that would make everyone moony over Ali MacGraw, and two novels, *Letting Go* and *When She Was Good*, which in their slow, plowing, methodical, naturalistic accretion and dissection of experience resulted in writing and reading that seemed labor-intensive, i.e., no fun. He was on a perilous path toward respectability. Now he had made a radical break. With *Portnoy*, the mad parrot of Roth's imagination had broken out of its cage and spoke the language of "Jewish jazz: oral, urgent, and smartassed."

The quote is from Albert Goldman (1927-1994), no minor Jewish jazz-meister himself. A professor at Columbia University, a former classical music columnist at *The New Leader*, author of a study of Thomas de Quincy, Goldman had also assumed the heavy robes of moral seriousness and intellectual responsibility until he finally heeded his own inner call of the wild and went bebop. A student of stand-up comedy, the future biographer of Lenny Bruce, and a man who would answer the phone with a merry "What's up, Green Hornet?," Goldman first met Roth in the mid-1960s, introduced by drama critic and Columbia colleague Robert Brustein. Goldman and Roth became more than friends; they were fellow cutups, coconspirators, cracking each other up in freaky flights of fancy about the mutual plight of being Jewish sons of smothering mothers. These verbal jam sessions helped liberate Roth's rhythm and attack, enabling him to treat his typewriter like a radio mic and follow his id, finding his true voice as an aggrieved monologuist baying on the ragged edge of desperation—and getting laughs with each sonic blast of shock value. The *Life* profile captures Philip Roth on the crest of a career-defining success that he would later treat as a yoke and a curse. Despite *Portnoy*, Roth could never quite relinquish his puritan strain, his sense of higher obligation. Goldman let go of his entirely.—James Wolcott

A COMEDIAN OF GUILT

Life, 1969

The publication of a book is not often a major event in American culture. Most of our classics, when they first appeared, met with disappointing receptions, and even the much-ballyhooed bestsellers of recent years have rarely cut a great swath outside the lanes of publicity and journalism. But this year a real literary-cultural event portends and every shepherd of public opinion, every magus of criticism, is wending his way toward its site. Gathered at an old New York City inn called Random House, at the stroke of midnight on the 21st of February in this 5,729th years since the creation of the world, they will hail the birth of a new American hero, Alexander Portnoy. A savior and scapegoat of the '60s, Portnoy is destined at the Christological age of 33 to take upon himself all the sins of sexually obsessed modern man and expiate them in a tragicomic crucifixion. The gospel that records the passion of this mock messiah is a slender, psychotic novel by Philip Roth called *Portnoy's Complaint* (the title is a triple pun signifying that the hero is a whiner, a lover, and a sick man). So great is the fame of the book even before its publication that it is being hailed as the book of the present decade and as an American masterwork in the tradition of *Huckleberry Finn.*

Heralded last year by several stunning excerpts in the serious literary magazines, *Portnoy* comes to us glowing not merely as a *succes d'estime* but as a *succès de scandale*—the scandal fuming up from the book's pungent language, a veritable attar of American obscenity; and from its preoccupations, foremost among which is the terrible sin of onanism. Presently the object of a cult, which passes selections from the sacred writing from hand to hand at sophisticated dinner parties so that all may have the opportunity to read aloud, *Portnoy* today is still an underground password. But the complete work is being readied for distribution by an international ring of literary agents who are cutting, packaging, and peddling it like a deck of pure heroin. Soon it will be injected into every vein of contemporary culture: as hardcover book, as softcover booklet, as book club offering, as foreign translation, and as American. The TV rights remain as yet unsold, but even without them the book has already earned almost a million dollars prior to the first pressrun.

A million dollars in publicity is what the book will earn next. A chain reaction of cover stories and profiles and critiques and put-ons and put-downs and pictures and cartoons and slogans and quips has already begun to build toward a blast that may set a new record for publicity overkill.

The book that is being blown up by all of this puffing is not so much volatile as it is intense, probing, incisive. A diagnostic novel by a comic Freud, it focuses its lens on a beautifully cut and brightly stained slice of contemporary American life—all sick, black and blue. The hero, an Assistant Commissioner of Human Opportunity for the City of New York, is a man who exemplifies the cherished values of the Kennedy years. Brilliant and precocious as a student, successful as a lawyer, dedicated and sensitive as a public servant to the underprivileged, Alexander Portnoy has devoted his whole life to being good.

Yet when we discover this nicest of Nice Jewish Boys, he is lying on his back on a psychoanalyst's sofa, like an overturned cockroach, spewing out a frenzied stream of angry, resentful, and self-defensive words. Honking through his beaky nose a heavy Jewish blue, he reels off an endless chronicle of suffering, degradation, and terror, interspersed now and then with a little grace and notes of pleasure.

Though Alexander Portnoy's complaint is directed in the first instance against his smothering and seductive mother, and in the second against the succession of maddening females who have poisoned his life, the ultimate truth of his condition is that he has fallen victim to American history in the same way that Oedipus fell victim to fate. For struggle as he will, and analyze as best he can, Portnoy cannot escape the appalling fact that in the '60s, Americans are seeking to live by two completely contradictory moral codes. Maintaining their allegiance to the traditional morality of monogamy, fidelity, self-sacrifice, and the sublimation of sexual energies, Americans are almost equally sanctimonious about those "needs" and "rights" that include the license to experiment with every sort of sexual and sensuous behavior dictated by the most primitive instincts and passions. Walking about in a fallen world, with these two Edens warring in their heads, modern Americans are made borderline schizophrenics.

Something of this sense of the doppelgänger that stalks us has been suggested in a great many works of contemporary literature and comedy. Indeed, the farcical gap between what all Americans are supposed to be and what they are has been the mainstay of our humor ever since this American dilemma found expression in the wit of the so-called "sick" comics of the mid-'50s. Lenny Bruce, Mort Sahl, and Nichols & May were the first to exploit the awkward, spraddling moral stance of the new American; after them the comedy of the Yankee *schlemiel* was developed much further by a whole succession of Jewish novelists, including Saul Bellow, Joseph Heller, Wallace Markfield, and Bruce Jay Friedman. For more than a decade these comic artists cultivated the themes and techniques brought to final fruition in *Portnoy*. For it has always been evident that, though this profound conflict between our better and worse selves might tear us apart, drive us to despair, or make us crazy, it could never be treated with complete seriousness or with the literal-minded simplicity of the sexologists and the public moralists. Comedy alone could provide the lens through which this strangely contorted and grotesquely embarrassing American predicament could be examined.

Philip Roth's achievement in *Portnoy*, therefore, is not the discovery of a theme nor the invention of a mode, but the final perfection of an art, the comic art of this Jewish decade. His book combines in its irresistible funniness all the resources of the tradition: the relentless Marx Brothers energies of *Catch-22*, the self-pitying rhetoric of *Herzog*, the hovering Chagall figures of *Stern* and *A Mother's Kisses*, the pop art sprinkles of *To an Early Grave*, and the self-lacerating ridicule of Lenny Bruce. Purging the Jewish joke and comic novel of their lingering parochialism, Roth has explored the Jewish family myth more profoundly than any of his predecessors, shining his light into all its corners and realizing its ultimate potentiality as an archetype of contemporary life.

Portnoy's Complaint boldly transcends ethnic categories. Focusing its image of man through the purest and craziest of stereotypes, the book achieves a vision that, paradoxically, is sane, whole, and profound. As intimate as the mirror on the bathroom wall, it affords its readers glimpse after glimpse of themselves nakedly living the truths and lies of their innermost lives. Looking into this mirror, the reader—Jew *or* gentile—will be caught between the instinct to cover up and the urge to bare all. Torn, yet relieved by successive shocks of recognition, he will murmur the healing formula of self-acceptance: "It is I."

So intense is the conflict between the two sides of Alexander Portnoy's fractured psyche, so classically clear is his syndrome, that he has been accorded by his psychoanalyst the signal honor of having his illness defined by his symptoms and labeled with his own name: "Portnoy's Complaint—A disorder in which strongly felt ethical and altruistic impulses are perpetually warring with extreme sexual longings, often of a perverse nature ... Acts of exhibitionism, voyeurism, fetishism, autoeroticism, and oral coitus are plentiful; as a consequence of the patient's 'morality,' however, neither fantasy nor act issues in genuine sexual gratification, but rather in overriding feelings of shame and the dread of retribution, particularly in the form of castration."

Portnoy's personality derangement derives, of course, from his childhood relationship with his Jewish mother. Alternately rocked in the soothing seas of maternal solicitude and swamped by the terrifying tides of maternal domination, the boy grows up pathetically seeking some one thing he can call his own. Not until puberty does he discover what he is seeking. Masturbation offers him the thrill of a secret, rebellious, and wholly self-indulgent life. Behind a locked bathroom door, his head thronging with erotic images, his ear alert for the terrifying knock and unanswerable challenge—"Alex, what are you doing inside there?"—Portnoy comes to identify sex with feelings of anxiety and remorse. But the power of his secret pleasure propels him out into the world in search of the beautiful, responsive creatures of his fantasies. Gentile girls with silky hair, button noses, and long slender legs are what he seeks: little beauties redolent of the perfume of America, the alien land that must be plowed to be possessed.

Questing like a nervous knight-errant in search of an erotic grail, he must pass through many encounters, many trying adventures, before he discovers the embodiment of his dreams standing at midnight on the corner of Fifty-Second Street and Lexington Avenue. Springing off the high board of life-as-fantasy with this girl, who is so appetitive and ignorant that he calls her "The Monkey," Portnoy tumbles head over heels in the most extravagant of all erotic, romantic, neurotic relationships. Their dreamlike fall into the depths of sexual debauchery is at first thrilling—in this respect paralleling the stolen pleasures of his boyhood. But gradually they come to demand something more of each other than exchanges of erotic goodies, and the relationship splinters into angry words and exacerbated feelings. Finally, after having inveigled his mistress into a scene of climactic licentiousness, our hero abandons her as a crazy person who menaces his life and happiness.

Leaving the hysterical Monkey standing on the windowsill of their hotel room in Athens, threatening to dash herself to death on the pavement below, Portnoy flees to Israel, where he meets a lady *kibbutznik*, a rugged, self-righteous amazon who reminds him of his mother. Attempting a crude physical seduction, he finds himself impotent. When he offers the lady an alternate form of gratification, she becomes enraged at his degeneracy and kicks him in the heart. Ending his sexual odyssey much where he began it, sprawling prostrate and helpless at the feet of a greatly desired but inaccessible woman, Portnoy concludes his long complaint with a protracted scream of pain. *Portnoy* is not only a funny but an impassioned and angry book. Unlike every other Jewish writer since Heine, Philip Roth knows what's hurting him—and it isn't the *goyim*. He delivers his most soul-gratifying thrusts at those sentimentalized objects of mindless piety, the Jewish mama and papa, the emasculators of generations of Jewish men. Yet his anger is crossed by love for its targets and is distinguished even further by an "Arise Ye Brothers of -----" ardor, a rhapsodic sympathy for his fellow sufferers that bursts forth in passages of ironic eloquence. The crown of the book is his vision of a Jewish *Ship of Fools*, a boatload of Nice Jewish Boys rolling on the seas of guilt:

"I am in the biggest troop ship afloat ... only look in through the portholes and see us there, stacked to the bulkheads in our bunks, moaning and groaning with such pity for ourselves, the sad and watery-eyed sons of Jewish parents, sick to the gills from rolling through these heavy seas of guilt—so I sometimes envision us, me and my fellow wailers, melancholics, and wise guys, still in steerage, like our forebears—and oh sick, sick as dogs, we cry out intermittently, one of us or another, 'Poppa, how could you?' 'Momma, why did you?' ... the retching in the toilets after meals, the hysterical deathbed laughter from the bunks, and the tears—here a puddle wept in contrition, here a puddle from indignation—in the blinking of an eye, the body of a man (with the brain of a boy) rises in impotent rage to flail at the mattress above, only to fall instantly back, lashing himself with reproaches. Oh, my Jewish men friends! My dirty-mouthed guilt-ridden brethren! My sweethearts! My mates! Will this ... ship ever stop pitching? When? *When*, so that we can leave off complaining how sick we are—and go out into the air, and live!" For many readers the strangest feature of *Portnoy* will be the fact that its author is the same man who wrote *Letting Go* and *When She Was Good*, books that reveal Roth's moral preoccupations and literary skills but in no wise prepare one for the high jinks of this latest work (though these high jinks do in fact mirror closely the style and wit I and other friends of Roth have enjoyed for years in private conversations and at parties). Indeed, since 1960, when at the remarkably early age of 27 he won the National Book Award for fiction with his first work, *Goodbye, Columbus*, Philip Roth has given every indication of desiring to be counted among the handful of recent authors more concerned with the values of traditional literature than they are with the currents of contemporary writing.

Educated at Bucknell and the University of Chicago, active for many years as a teacher of English literature and creative writing at Chicago, Princeton, and Iowa, a familiar figure on the college lecture platform and even behind the lectern of the synagogue, a contributor to *Commentary* and *Partisan Review*, Roth has clung through his whole career to the skirts of the university and has counted himself a member of the intellectual and cultural elite. It was to this audience in particular his work appealed.

With *Goodbye, Columbus*, a collection of canny, morally sophisticated stories written in a scrupulously impersonal style—the antithesis of the verbal extravagance of *Portnoy*—Roth focused fiercely on the life of middle-class America in the postwar years, particularly in the American Jewish community where all the traditional values were being submerged in the scuffle to obtain the good things of material prosperity. This volume was followed in 1962 by *Letting Go*, a long and thoughtful novel in which Roth articulated his moral obsession, the theme which underlies all his subsequent writing: the effort of the self to break the bondage of narcissism by renouncing all selfish gratification in favor of a self-sacrificing dedication to the happiness of others. This Christian theme he treated, of course, with a great deal of irony, steadily increasing the dosage, until in *Portnoy* the theme is totally inverted and the hero struggles, with the reader's covert approval, to cast off all traces of moralism and lead a life of guiltless self-gratification.

It was while he was working on his third book, *When She Was Good*, that I first met Philip Roth. Whether it was owing to some congeniality of temperaments or simply to the fact that he knew that I had spent a great many years running with a pack of Jewish comics that included the late Lenny Bruce, our encounters soon assumed the form of spontaneous staging sessions with Roth out in the spotlight working the room like a stand-up comic. Typically we would meet by chance at the Mayhews, a little breakfast shop in Manhattan's East Sixties. I'd be sitting there enjoying the peace of the morning hour and the soothing influence of an egg and butter, when my mood would be shattered by a reproachful voice: "Albert, your father and I have been worried sick about you!" Looking up I would see, not my Jewish mother magically transported from Santa Monica to New York, but Philip Roth, glaring at me maniacally. Looking nothing like the picture of the jackets of his books—that beautiful fem-man face, with its cleft Cary Grant chin, bold intellectual nose, and distantly gazing Mesmer-eyes—this was the comic-crazy Roth, the one lost soul on the pilgrimage, a jarring presence in sending out hysterical waves in every direction.

Slipping into the chair next to mine, fixing me with a hooded maternal gaze, he would continue his exhortation in that guilt-inducing, this-is-not-your-mother-but-your-conscience voice: "Two weeks and not a word. How is it a writer, a person who sits all day behind a typewriter, can't put two words together to send to a mother who lives three thousand miles away?" Then a hyena laugh, fracturing that sorrowful maternal stare into the crazy lights and angles of a Cubist portrait. I'd be gagging, choking, caught between laughter at Philip and anger at my mother, wondering meanwhile (with an instinct as old as the race) what the *goyim* were thinking—particularly that thick-lensed cashier, who has stopped toting up his bills and is staring with astonishment at this strident newcomer.

By this time Philip would be too wound up to notice or to care what reaction he was getting. He'd be doing the Jewish Genet who has written this play called *The Terrace* in which there's a brothel for Nice Jewish Boys where you go every night and they dress you in Dr. Denton's kiddie pajamas and they bathe you and powder you and put mineral oil where it itches. Tucked into your bed, you fall asleep blissfully listening to a little radio with an orange dial. Next morning a voice calls softly, "Wake up, dear, it's time to get up." For that, Philip says, he'd gladly pay $50 a night.

Now the magic word "radio" triggers him into his "Blue Network" bit. "J-E-L-L-O!" He's doing all the voices from the *Jack Benny Show*:

smoothie Jack, fruity Dennis. Yes, yes, I remember them perfectly! But wait, he's reaching even further back for—wow!—*Mr. Kitzel!* Now he's sliding his voice way up in the air in an oral shrug, a vocal curlicue: "Mees-ter Benny!" Oh my pop epiphany, it's Schlepperman! "Awesome, Philip, awesome."

After fifteen or twenty minutes of this comic fuguing, the waiters would be throwing Philip looks, *Wall Street Journals* would be dropping, and some old lady would be giving him the top lens. Everybody would be asking himself, "Who the hell *is* this guy? He must be some famous Jewish nightclub comedian who hasn't gotten to bed yet. Wow! He's really up there. Nine o'clock in the morning and still flying."

After all my years with the funny men, my response to Philip's antics was partly professional. I recognized in him a type not of the stage but of the Jewish living room, the candy store, or luncheonette, where after school the kids take turns driving each other over the edge into hysteria. He agreed that he had learned to be funny when he was a child, probably on those daily walks from Chancellor Ave. grade school in the Weequahic section of Newark to the little Hebrew school fifteen minutes away. In that precious quarter of an hour, those highly regimented Jewish kids could blow off steam and subject the pyramided pieties of their world to a healthy dose of desecratory humor. For a few minutes they could afford to be bad.

Being bad and being funny were much the same thing in Roth's mind, and I often had the feeling that when he wrote his fiction he was intent upon being very good. Having as one of my own obsessions the ideal of a Jewish comic who would be an artist and not just a theatrical or literary entertainer, I often urged Roth to exploit his comic gifts in fiction. I told him that his role was to be the comic messiah, the redeemer of the Jewish joke. When I pressed my arguments and exhorted him to write a novel that would match his hidden talents, a book that would be black, sick, surreal, Kafkaesque, unabashedly vulgar, obscene, and Jewish, he would say with a sigh, "Oh, Al."

In those days, *When She Was Good* was his primary obsession. He had worked on it for years and rewritten it something like eight times.

In his apartment were four big cartons stuffed with manuscripts. After so many years of close-up work, he couldn't tell any longer what he was doing; so one day he packed the latest draft into his briefcase and left his rackety apartment for the calm of the Forty-Second Street Library's reading room. There he read enough of what he had written to realize that, despite the enormous pains he had lavished on the book, it was still so defective that he could not think of publishing it. Walking out into Bryant Park with its pigeons and hobos, he contemplated the future. No longer was he a writer, he decided, nor would he trade off his literary reputation by taking a succession of teaching jobs. At thirty-three he was young enough to go into something else. What would it be? Well, he could always go up to Harlem and be a playground director and die.

Instead, he went off to Yaddo, a foundation-supported estate in Saratoga Springs, which serves as a work retreat for writers, artists, and composers. (Roth's deep attachment to Yaddo owes something to the beauty of the place—it is set among lakes and woods, with a view of the distant Vermont mountains—but it is really its character as a sanctuary from city life, and more especially its comfort as a surrogate home, a home without the annoyance of a family, that explains his frequent and prolonged visits there.) Regulating his life for as much as six months at a time by the soothing routine of the place—they get you up early, feed you breakfast, and pack you off to work in a little cabin with a lunch box full of cold chicken and a shiny apple—he was finally able to bring *When She Was Good* into order and to publish it in 1967.

A stylistic tour de force, *When She Was Good* turns the tone of *One Man's Family* back on itself to produce a highly ambiguous literary texture whose irony is as subtle and deadly as the ripple in a highly polished saw blade. The tension of the book is generated by counterpointing the most gracious of all pop American tones against the moral frenzy and insanity of the heroine, a Midwestern Medea who embodies the horror of the Protestant ethic run amok.

Expecting high praise—at least from the more sophisticated critics—Roth was dismayed to find the reviewers yawning over his novel and offering consoling phrases while they waited for his next book. Perhaps *When She Was Good* was too subtle for those who sat down to write about it. In any case, as soon as Roth had finished it his mind righted itself and all the baffled energies that had blown this way and that during five years of mental doldrums now became a steady breeze which soon shaped itself into a voice—a voice rising and falling with the complaining intonations of an angry and neurotic Jewish boy.

For two years I had seen so little of Philip Roth that when I dialed his number last summer I wasn't even sure whether he was still living in New York. But having read the fourth instalment of *Portnoy's Complaint* in *New American Review*, I had to toss in my penny's worth of praise. Always glad to hear from an old playmate, Philip invited me to his home in one of New York's tallest and baldest buildings. As I walked into his apartment on the twenty-first floor, a flat lined with the brown metal bookcases like the stacks of a library, he greeted me with a routine, singing in the strident voice of a Broadway musical comedy star, "New York, New York, it's a wonderful town!" and gesticulating toward the huge plate-glass windows of the room. Holding a high note, he drew the blind to reveal a stunning panorama of the city skyline.

Stepping offstage, he slumped into an armchair and began to talk. Immediately, I caught a new note in his voice, a lilting note of optimism.

"Wow, what a year I've had!" He reels off an incredible yarn. It starts with his going to a publication party for William Styron's *Nat Turner*. Standing there in his new British tweeds, nibbling on an hors d'oeuvre, Philip begins to feel this pulsing pang in his right side. He'd had the same pain months before and figured he'd licked it, but now it grows worse and worse. The doctors can't tell what it is, so they put him in the hospital and his fever goes up and up, and finally, this crazy scene: A big, handsome surgeon dressed for a black-tie party is pressing down on his abdomen and Philip is going through the ceiling. Appendicitis is the diagnosis and immediate operation the plan, but when they cut him open they find that the cap blew off his gut days before and his belly is flooded with pus. They stick tubes into him from top to bottom and for days he wallows in delirium.

Every time he comes out of it, he finds this exquisite woman, the woman he's been seeing almost every day for three years, standing at the foot of the bed wearing these strange sack-like dresses. "Get out of here!" he screams. "Go home and put a short skirt on. You look like you're dressed for my funeral" (And indeed, as he learned later, by the time they cut into him he was just two hours' walk from the grave—a shocking realization that flooded him with an awed feeling of pride and elation. He had wrestled the *Malekhamoves*—the angel of death—to a fall.)

Then there is his convalescence in Florida, an idyl of sun and water, and the finishing touches of *Portnoy*, and the growing feeling that he has his life back under control at last, when one morning, in this same living room—he's up on his feet now, showing me what happened—the phone rings and he hears his stepdaughter saying, "Mother has been killed." His estranged wife, Maggie, being driven across Central Park at five in the morning, had been instantly killed when the car smashed into a tree. Philip is stunned. He goes through the funeral arrangements in a trance. Then, just as he starts to pull himself together again—wham!—all the hullabaloo begins about *Portnoy*. Fame he's known before, but now, for the first time in his life, he has money—and everybody is shooting zingers into him. He passes the man next door, who says, "Oh, my neighbor, the millionaire!" But what can Philip say? Yesterday a messenger came to his door and gave him a royalty-advance check for a quarter of a million dollars. Philip gave him a tip. What's the tip on a quarter of a million dollars. Philip gave him a tip. What's the tip on a quarter of a million? "I gave him a quarter, Al."

Now he's into this new book. He doesn't know where he's going: he has all these pieces of paper with one sentence on each page. He's just writing this stuff and throwing it away, groping for a new theme—some big semi-comic idea. And he's haunted by this phrase, a simple little phrase: "A terrible mistake has been made." Just that. Now he thinks he may write a book which will stand Kafka on his head. Sort of a marvelous idea: "Instead of having a guy who is more and more pursued and trapped and finally destroyed by his tormentors, I want to start with a guy tormented and then the opposite happens. They come to the jail and they open the door and they say to you, 'A terrible mistake has been made.' And they give you your suit back, with your glass and your wallet and your address book, and they apologize to you. And they say, 'Look, people from big magazines are going to come and write stories on you. And here's some money. And we're very sorry about this.' "

Postscript:

Goldman and Roth would go their separate ways, personally and professionally. It was probably inevitable. Their sensibilities meshed and vibrated in tune with an intensity that would have been tough to sustain even if both hadn't been such tightly wound wizards whose egos needed a lot of elbow room. *Portnoy's Complaint* rocketed Roth into a stratosphere of celebrity that he would spend the rest of his life putting up deflector shields against. Liberated from the rabbit warrens of Quality Lit, as Terry Southern called it, post-*Portnoy* Roth continued to pump the horn of anarcho satire with his follow-up fictions *Our Gang* (a Nixon-Watergate burlesque), *The Great American Novel* (a baseball spoof of which critic Marvin Mudrick wrote, "Poor Roth has lost not only his bearings but his marbles"), and *The Breast* (a Kafkaesque fugue state about a man who turns into a boob), books that read as curiosities today, a carnival of caricatures and god-awful puns. Roth may have needed to get these forays out of his system before facing the reckoning of *My Life as a Man*, a prolonged primal scream about his disastrous first marriage and the most autobiographical of his novels, a self-catharsis; fury spent, he could then tend to the ripening maturity of his talent and his rising status as a literary citizen. His place of honor at the dinner tables of Martha's Vineyard was secure.

"Ripening maturity" was not a phrase that would ever be associated with Albert Goldman, and I say that with fondness and respect. (We became friendly after the publication of his scandalizing Elvis biography and stayed in contact until his death in 1994, victim of a heart attack on a flight bound for London.) He became a pariah in his time and remains so today, his name usually invoked with a sneer, his biographies of Elvis and John Lennon burying him in infamy as an opportunistic ghoul. The *Life* profile of Roth was included in *Freakshow*, a collection of pop culture journalism that provided the springboard for *Ladies and Gentleman, Lenny Bruce!*, where Goldman drew upon his experiences kibitzing with the guys to produce a new species of gonzo biography, where the biographer wasn't a detached observer but a roving eyeball taking in the scene. Goldman always got himself into the full swing of whatever he was investigating, celebrating his fiftieth birthday on a cocaine transport plane. One of the temperamental schisms that developed with Roth was that where Roth wanted to be wanton and daredevil in the fantasy funhouse of his mind, his nostrils would quiver with rectitude and distaste at the sight of actual swingers and their untidy antics; or so Goldman said. (Further evidence is stored in the dossier on Philip Roth that Goldman kept and is now archived with his papers at Columbia University.) The artist as control freak, Roth's appetite for hedonism was strictly regulated and compartmentalized so that it wouldn't interfere with work hours, his conscientious output of typescript. For Goldman, too much was seldom enough, his zeal for Wagnerian spectacle, tribal rites, pagan revels, and sensory overload funneled into ebullient coffee-table books exploring the carnival in Rio and the disco craze. His home office in his apartment overlooking Central Park South was designed like a DJ's booth, as different as could be from the rustic retreat in Connecticut where his former pal Philip Roth consecrated himself to the almighty Novel. Roth's way proved to be the wiser course, if wisdom is what you're after.—JW

Sara Davidson

In order to gain access to the best-selling novelist Jacqueline Susann, who was accustomed to and therefore wary of being mocked by journalists and critics, Sara Davidson (1943-) admits: "I had to play the part of an admiring acolyte." She played the part so well Susann rewarded her with a golden ankh necklace. The novelist and her husband, the press agent Irving Mansfield, allowed the twenty-five year old Davidson—then a reporter for the *Boston Globe*—to fly around the country with them on a publicity tour to promote *The Love Machine*, Susann's second novel, the successor to *Valley of the Dolls* and the sort of fiction that Davidson calls "an escape hatch from the news." They zip from New York to DC, back to New York and then to Beverly Hills, roaming from a bookseller convention to press conferences to bookstores to hotel suite interviews to radio and television programs, including the *Hollywood Squares* game show, where Susann makes a guest appearance, framed onstage within an orange box. The narrative that arose from the romp struck its author as overly caustic. "I hated the story," Davidson says. "Susann was such an easy target. I was having fun with and making fun of her. Hatchet jobs were the tone of the day." Susann, too, ended up disparaging the story. "She told my father-in-law how much she disliked the piece," Davidson says. "I was informed that she based an unfavorable character on me."

And yet for all of Davidson's remorse, "The Writing Machine" remains an extraordinary work of journalism, a vividly detailed, starkly revealing, and comically thrilling account of the manufacture of American celebrity. It has aged much better than many comparable stories from the same period. Davidson began publishing during the rise of New Journalism, when the subject of a profile often became a mere platform for the braggadocio of a writer's voice. The subjects ended up disappearing into the writer's sensibility just as massive amounts of plankton vanish into a whale in a single gulp. Davidson's profile, however, while employing the novelistic techniques of

New Journalism, nonetheless permits readers to feel that they are watching an unmitigated Susann through their own eyes. Around the time "The Writing Machine" appeared in *Harper's*, Davidson says: "I experienced my first spiritual awakening and decided that from then on I would only write about subjects I respected." Within the next decade, she published her own bestseller *Loose Change*, an intimate, generous-hearted nonfiction narrative of three young women, including Davidson herself, moving on from Berkeley in the early '60s into the rest of their lives.—Will Blythe

JACQUELINE SUSANN THE WRITING MACHINE

Harper's, 1969

White lightning slams across the sky as the Eastern Airlines 8:00 a.m. shuttle takes off from New York City to Washington, DC. In a front aisle seat, a tall, slender woman stares straight ahead through a mask of makeup—black penciled brows, heavy false lashes, orange lipstick, and a black shoulder-length fall made of Korean hair. Her body is covered with Pucci designs of yellow, purple, and pink. Her name, Jacqueline Susann, is a household word; her face confronts the American family on the television screen, in magazines, and on the jackets of books seen on beaches, planes, and buses. The best-selling author, who has made the word "doll" a synonym for pill, opens a small gold box and takes out a pink tablet. "I'm going to take a wake-up pill." It is uncustomarily early for the Jacqueline Susann $75,000 road show to be underway. In her baritone voice, Jackie explains she decided to take the early shuttle instead of flying to Washington the night before because of her poodle, Josephine. "She's fifteen, and if I'm away overnight, she has to have a sleepover." Jacqueline washes down the pill with Binaca, a breath freshener she sucks on through the day, and flips through *Harper's Bazaar*.

Beside her is her husband, Irving Mansfield, *né* Mandelbaum in Brooklyn, thin, with a small, round face that carries an anxious expression although it is usually smiling. Irving was once a press agent for Eddie Cantor, then producer of *Arthur Godfrey's Talent Scouts*, and now, manager of the campaign designed to milk the resources of Hollywood, Broadway, and Madison Avenue to convert *The Love Machine* into a commercial fortune.

"Jackie, we wanna be organized," he says as the plane descends through sheets of rain. Irving carries a bag of Jackie's dresses and a hatbox full of makeup and hairpieces. In the limousine, Jackie puts on gray bubble sunglasses. "Where's the schedule, so I can see if I need another wake-up pill?" They check the guest list for a party that evening which will feature a Love Machine Cocktail— crème de cacao, vodka, and Pernod—and a Love Machine Cake decorated with two clasped hands like the jacket of the book. A publicity aide says, "May I suggest that you'll get everyone sick if you serve that drink." Irving says, "How about we put a Spanish fly in it, and have the rolls made up like phallic symbols? Ha ha. That's funny, isn't it?"

They arrive at the Shoreham Hotel, where the American Booksellers Association is holding its annual convention, minutes before a press conference has been scheduled for out-of-town newspapers. Jackie walks in with a demure smile. There are twenty men and women in the suite, and none smile back. After a period of silence, Dan Green, publicity director for Simon and Schuster, asks the first question: "How does it feel to have another book on the best-seller list?" Jackie talks animatedly, perched on her chair. No one in the room takes any notes. A man in the back asks, "Do you read reviews?" Jackie says, "I'd like to have the critics like me, I'd like to have everybody like what I write. But when my book sells, I know people like the book. That's the most important thing, because writing is communication." Jackie describes her writing routine, Irving tells a joke at which no one laughs, even though he adds, "That's funny, isn't it?" At the end, Ivan Sandrof of the Worcester, Massachusetts, *Telegram*, says, "What do you think is the reason for everybody reading your book, apart from the obvious?"

"What's the obvious reason?" Jackie says.

"Sex, pure and simple."

Jackie says it is not sex that sells her books. "I'm a today writer. The novel today has to compete with television and the movies. It has to come alive quickly and be easy to read. When people tell you they couldn't put the book down, that is good writing."

The sex in Susann's books is minimal by contemporary standards. Although a girl is undressed by page three, lovemaking is described only in vague terms. Instead of using naturalistic language, characters employ prudish euphemisms. Men refer to their sexual organs as "Charlie." Women talk about getting "the curse" every month. Jackie says, "I can't stand being clinical. You don't have to say, then he took out his thing and put it in her vagina. For adults, all you have to say is, he took her in his arms."

Susann writes sex not for the liberated woman but for the one with strong inhibitions. Most of the love in *The Love Machine* is joyless, violent, and cruel. Robin Stone, the central character, has to be drunk to make it with the actress Maggie Stewart, beats up a prostitute after taking her, and gets involved unknowingly with a transvestite. Amanda, the high-fashion model, goes to bed in a padded bra because she is flat, and later submits to a sweaty comedian who repulses her. A homely girl does "cold cream jobs" on celebrities who ignore her the next morning. This is the kind of sex which probably discourages going out and trying it.

Michael Korda, Jackie's editor and the editor-in-chief of Simon and Schuster, feels Jackie's promotability is the key to her success. Without promotion, he says, the book would probably sell one-hundred thousand copies, "but it wouldn't have the great impact it does." *Valley of the Dolls* sold three-hundred-and-fifty-six thousand in hard cover and ten million paperback. "Jackie has succeeded where no one has before in tapping all the modern means of communication in one great campaign—movies, television, newspaper interviews, magazines, commercials, all cleverly bound together. Most novelists are not promotable. They don't go on tours because they wouldn't know what to do."

Irving says, "Jackie and I have probably changed the whole book publishing business. For one thing, usually the publisher has a little cocktail party in a dingy restaurant with stale lettuce sandwiches when the book comes out. We had a big swing at El Morocco and we invited everybody—Andy Warhol, Perle Mesta. Also, we sold the paperback rights before we sold the hardcover rights." The film rights were purchased for a record sum of one-and-a-half million dollars.

In the Eastern half of the country, critics and interviewers approach Jackie with condescension. Jackie says, "They walk in with the attitude—how dare you be a bestseller." A television reporter in Washington said, "Are you pleased with what you're leaving behind you in life?" A Detroit newspaperman read Jackie a review which called her writing "trash" and said, "How does that make you feel?" During a Toronto television show, a young woman said, "Don't you ever wake up in the middle of the night and realize you haven't done anything that is really artistic?" Jackie said, "You're sick. Do you wake up and think you're not Huntley-Brinkley?"

Once she has crossed the Continental Divide, and especially in Los Angeles, the feeling toward Jackie changes. Reporters gush at her, and Susann is called America's best writer. One man told her his wife had started referring to his sexual organ as "Charlie." "You're adding words to our language."

Jackie is almost uninsultable. A snide question, a bitchy interview, brings out the best in her. She reads vicious reviews and grins, "I think it'll sell a lot of books." On *The David Frost Show*, critic John Simon asked Jackie in his *echt* Central European accent, "Do you think you are writing art or are you writing trash to make a lot of money?" Jackie lurched forward and threw a torrent of *ad hominems* at Simon: "Is your name Goebbels—you act like a storm trooper." She called him "Simple Simon," a joker, a publicity hound—"How many people have even heard of you?"—all the while Simon kept shouting, "That's not important. Will you just answer the question? What do you think you are writing?" Jackie tried another tangent, saying Simon was "rather nice looking" even though his hair was thin. Simon said, "Cut out all this soft soap. I can smile through my false teeth like you." Jackie bared her teeth and hit them with her finger. "Look, they're caps, not false." Simon kept pressing. Jackie finally said, "Little man, I am telling a story. Now does that make you happy, huh?"

Usually, Jackie succeeds in debilitating her opponents. She watched a young man preparing to have a go at her on *Panorama*, a Washington television show, sitting on his white toadstool chair picking his teeth. "Don't do that," Jackie said, "you'll hurt your teeth." Later, she gloated. "That reduced him to a little boy." (Jackie is one of those women, like the late Judy Garland, Bette Davis, Edith Piaf, and critic Judith Crist, who are beloved by homosexuals. In Jackie's case, it is due not only to her strident personality but to the fact that she treats homosexuals with dignity in her books.)

In her travels from city to city, the one publicity tool Jackie has given up is the autograph party. "When you appear at a bookstore, you are at the mercy of any sex maniac who gets in line. They can say, 'Wanna fuck, baby?' " While promoting *Valley of the Dolls*, Jackie says, "Beastly weirdos would come up and say, 'Wanna go to a pot party?' " Irving says, "They've said the worst things. I've had to acquire the sixth sense of a T-man. In a Detroit bookstore, three guys were standing in a corner. They were daring a friend to go up to Jackie and say; 'Your book stinks.' I spotted it a mile off."

Jackie accepts interviews from all publications, all media, no matter how small or limited their reach, unless she or Irving suspects the writer is out to do a hatchet job. She turned down the *Village Voice*, columnist Dick Schaap, and *Saturday Review*. "I tried to turn you down," Jackie told me. For months, she will give six or more interviews a day, repeating the same stories with unfailing enthusiasm.

At the American Booksellers Association in Washington, Jackie has set aside an hour and a half for William Silverman of the Detroit *News*, who is writing a cover story for his newspaper's Sunday magazine. He asks Jackie to pose for photographs. "I want something that's sexy and glamorous, but I don't want it to be vulgar." Jackie says, "That's marvelous." Irving shakes his head. "The problem is, this is not a glamorous background. There's no satin, there's no damask." Silverman, a grandfather in his sixties who has the shape of a large panda bear, drops to the rug and lies on his stomach, kicking one foot up and, resting his chin on his hand. "Could you be like this, like you were writing?" Jackie obliges, adding, "You know, I write like this every day." Irving dozes for a while, awakens with a smile and sings, "If you can talk to the animals." Silverman is asking Jackie how her success has affected her marriage. "When people work with each other, not in competition but together," she says, "it's like a dance team." She jumps up and strikes an arabesque with her white-stockinged legs. "You could say Irving and I are Nureyev and Fonteyn." She waves her arms in gawky ballet gestures. "We are the Burtons. We are anything that is two people working together."

When she turns aside, Silverman says to me, "Do you believe that?"

Dan Green interrupts the interview to tell Jackie people are crowded around the Simon and Schuster booth in the exhibit hall, where she is scheduled to autograph copies of her book. Because of a feeble air-conditioning system, the hall is steaming hot, with thin red carpets and silver tinsel hanging from the ceiling. A double line radiates out from the alcove where Jackie is seated. The lines completely block access to the displays of Harper & Row, the New York Graphic Society, Fleet Press Corporation, and Bantam Books. Irving says, "Never in the history of the world has there been a writer with this charisma." Jerry Kramer of the Green Bay Packers, Lillian Gish, Kurt Vonnegut Jr., and Tiny Tim also appeared to plug their books but drew scant attention compared to Jackie. The people in line—bookstore owners, salesmen, jobbers, editors, publishing executives, and some reviewers who sat stone-faced during Jackie's morning press conference—wait for more than two hours, clutching yellow pieces of paper on which they have printed their names so Jackie can write personal messages. "For Isabel Smith. All my best."

One of the first in line is Lloyd Severe, a supervisor at Martindale's bookstore in Beverly Hills. "Frankly, this is not exactly my type of book, but my wife wants it." Asked what accounts for Susann's popularity, the tall, bald man stretches his lips into a smile. His eyes twinkle behind rimless glasses. "There's only one word for it. People like thrills."

Irving, in his yellow, green, and pink Pucci tie and Gucci shoes, never moves more than a few feet from Jackie. He sings, "If we could talk to the animals."

When Jackie leaves the floor, the Simon and Schuster group say they have given away six hundred books. When they arrive at the suite, the figure has grown to eight hundred. That evening it is one thousand. A bottle of champagne is brought to the room. Michael Korda, a wiry British blond who wears a bright-blue suit with red stitching, a red handkerchief, a black belt with gold metal studs, a blue wide-striped shirt, and blue motorcycle glasses, walks in and kisses Jackie on both cheeks. "Do you think we'll make number one?" she says softly. "Of course, we will," Korda says. Jackie drinks the champagne in a water glass with ice cubes. Irving makes the toast: "To the first author who's gonna be back-to-back number one on the best-seller list."

In the Chatelaine Room of the Mayflower Hotel, fifty bookstore owners, managers, and buyers from department stores have bypassed the Love Machine Cocktail for whiskey or gin. Since publication of her first book, a biography of her poodle called *Every Night, Josephine!*, Jackie has cultivated friendships with booksellers. She considers some of them among her best friends.

A shout goes up when Jackie appears at the party in a turquoise voile dress. A strawberry blonde book buyer from Oregon grabs her arm and pumps it. "I want to shake the hand of the lady that's been makin' me so much money the past two years." The book buyer, an angular, freckled woman, in a black chiffon dress with ruffles around the scooped neck, says she doesn't think *Love Machine* will sell as well as *Valley of the Dolls* because "it's an over-again, the same jenner. (Genre?) It's Jackie's husband that puts her across with all that Madison Avenue hoopla, and I love it! The pa-toy they speak! (Patois?) It's just marvelous. I don't care what's in the book as long as it sells."

Irving and Jackie move to a different table for each course—crab cocktail, vichyssoise, beef en brochette, wine, and cake. When the *Love Machine* cake is wheeled out with seven candles, Jackie carries it around the room. "For a finale, I fall into it." She and Irving leave just before 10:00 p.m. to catch the last shuttle back to New York. As they settle in the limousine, Irving swivels around. "Jackie, will you stop already with these goddamn books! Ha ha. That's funny, isn't it?"

The Mansfields live in a three-room apartment in the Navarro Hotel overlooking Central Park South. The decor is theatrical, with black lamp bases in the shape of human torsos, red shades, ivory linoleum floors, and a large bar. The walls are lined with photographs of Jackie with celebrities, Irving with celebrities, and celebrities who have appeared on television shows Irving has produced. On a late Friday afternoon, just before leaving for California, Jackie is having caviar and imported Russian vodka, straight, with her press agent for *The Love Machine*, Abby Hirsch, a fashion-conscious young woman who radiates self-assurance and efficiency. Abby's salary is paid by Simon and Schuster, which guaranteed to spend $75,000 promoting the book, and has spent considerably more.

The Love Machine dominates Simon and Schuster this year. In the reception hall, red-and-white buttons with the book's title are pinned to the rubber tree plants. Michael Korda has written on the walls of his office in blue ink: "Three bottles of Dom Perignon, '59 or '61, *The Love Machine*—fifty-thousand advance. Sixteen ounces of caviar when we reach number one." There are bets recorded as to when the book would hit the top spot. Korda says the advertising budget for *Love Machine* is larger than for any book they have published. In addition to Abby, they use a press agent in California, Jay Allen, and a full-time press agent in New York, paid for by Irving.

Both Abby and Michael Korda, like Jackie, wear around their necks a gold chain with the ankh, an Egyptian symbol of life, which Jackie made the motif of *The Love Machine.* She first saw it on Janet Leigh, wearing it in the form of a ring at a party. Janet Leigh gave the ring to Jackie, who had her jeweler make it up into necklaces. She has presented these large gold crosses with a loop on top to John Lennon, the Beatle; to Muriel Slatkin, daughter of the owner of the Beverly Hills Hotel; and, among others, to me. On television, Jackie likes to describe how Cleopatra carried the ankh as a symbol of eternal sex. But it is not Cleopatra of the Nile she conjures up; it is Cleopatra of 20th Century Fox. Two New York designers have started production of ankh necklaces, pins, wrist and ankle bracelets, and there is talk of a *Love Machine* perfume. The Mansfields have avoided these projects. "It's a little too much," Irving says. "Jackie's a writer, an artist. Inside this little breast beats a heart that is not as commercial as people think."

The Mansfields's lifestyle has not changed since they struck gold in publishing, because they have always lived conspicuously well. They commute between Central Park South and the Beverly Hills Hotel, where they have had the same suite—at seventy-eight dollars a day—since 1959. Jackie does not cook. In Los Angeles they dine at Chasen's, in New York at Sardi's, Danny's Hide-a-way, "21," and, if they are feeling informal, P. J. Clarke's. They are city animals and have no desire for a yacht or a country estate. On Sundays in New York, they like to walk to the out-of-town newspaper stand in Times Square, have breakfast at Nathan's—two dozen cherrystones for Jackie, two hot dogs for Irving—and go to a movie like *The Green Slime.*

Like the characters Jackie has created in her books, she and Irving seem to be rootless, tieless. Jackie writes in *The Love Machine*: "Nothing is as dull as a woman without a past. And once you know all the details there is no past. Just a long, dreary confessional." Jackie and Irving have sealed off their own past with vague and contradictory references. Jackie often says she was born in 1963, the year her first book was published. When a reporter asked her age, Jackie said, "You could say I'm a young woman in her thirties." The reporter looked up. Jackie smiled. "*Newsweek* printed my age—it's forty-two." Jackie looks younger than forty-two; her figure is slim and her hairpieces are set in youthful, shoulder-length flips.

I accepted the age of forty-two until I met an actress at a party who said she remembered Jackie from the theater in the late 1930s. When I called other theatrical figures, I found they were reluctant if not terrified to talk of Jackie's past. One woman said, "Jackie will be furious if this gets out. She doesn't want the country to know she's been around all that while. She doesn't want to shock the country. If

I looked as well as she does, I'd be proud. I'd want everyone to know how old I was."

Programs on file in the Lincoln Center Performing Arts Library show that Jackie appeared in Max Cordon's production of Clare Boothe's *The Women* in 1937; in *She Gave Him All She Had* and *When We Are Married* in 1939; in *My Fair Ladies* and *Banjo Eyes* with Eddie Cantor in 1941; and in *Jackpot* in 1944. She was not playing child roles. As the reluctant actress put it, "You can't put two and two together and get forty-two."

A subject Jackie and Irving never bring up is their son. When questioned, they say the boy is sixteen and in school in Arizona. In Jackie's novels there are no children (except for an occasional infant), no families living and growing up together. She creates a dream world of stardom, money, and power where personal ambition and lust are the only forces. The hero of *The Love Machine*, Robin Stone, blazes his way from delivering news on a local television station to controlling the national network. In the process, he is loved by, without loving, a breathtaking, breastless model, a voluptuous actress, and the blue-blooded wife of the chairman of the network. Although the story is set in the 1960s, there is no mention of Vietnam, the generation gap, racial tensions, urban riots, inflation. The book, like *Valley of the Dolls*, is an escape hatch from the news. It shoots the reader to a fantasyland where there are no babysitters, no commuter trains, no supermarkets, but at the end of the trip, the reader is psychologically prepared to get off, reassured that there is no place like his double-mortgaged home.

Susann's characters experience no guilt about sex or anything that might be considered "sin" in the Judeo-Christian tradition. When a girl loses her virginity, or a baby through abortion, she gives it no more thought than if she had lost a tooth. The relationships traced are not marriages but love affairs. Because all the characters have miserable, bathetic fates, the mainline American family can feel its own values have been upheld.

A young man with green eyes and an easy smile is sitting on the cream-colored couch in Jackie's suite at the Beverly Hills Hotel. "I saw a lot of myself in Robin Stone," he says. Irving says, "So did Peter Lawford." The young man, in a voice that has no distinguishing inflection, says, "I've learned to hide my feelings and not show emotions ever since I was little." He turns on a tape recorder. "This is Dick Spangler. My guest on *The Forum* is Jacqueline Susann. Miss Susann, you've been criticized as not being the best writer, although you are the best-selling writer." Jackie says, "Way back they didn't think Shakespeare was a good writer. He was the soap-opera king of his day. They called Zola a bad writer, a journalistic writer. Everything changes in writing. I think James Joyce is a bore. *Ulysses* is a bore. In fiction today there is no time to do great exposition on a landscape. Writers like Harold Robbins, Leon Uris, and Irving Wallace have given the novel new life, new excitement. They're storytellers. That's the place for the novel today."

Breakfast is brought in on a gold tray. Jackie drinks iced tea and cuts off pieces of a kosher salami she was given by a television sponsor. She removes the butter from the tray and puts it in her icebox. Irving says, "Would you believe it? A woman as rich as Jackie stealing butter?"

The Beverly Hills Hotel is an island of New York theatrical people transplanted to the glades of Southern California. The building with its pink cupolas rises from a slope of palm trees. From the sliding glass doors of their suite, Jackie and Irving look out on a red-tiled patio with rows of geraniums, a green picket fence, and green garden furniture. In the distance, the yellow and white cabanas of the pool stand out from the hibiscus and coconut palms. Through most of June, the landscape is muted by gray haze.

Jackie and Irving have been in Beverly Hills for two weeks, visiting bookstores in Monrovia, Pasadena, and Westwood. Jackie has appeared on more than thirty-nine radio and television shows, including a week on the midmorning game show, *Hollywood Squares*. She has been on television more hours in the past two years than most actors. The only show that has turned her down is Art Linkletter. For *Hollywood Squares*, she is driven to the NBC studios in Burbank with five costume changes, since a week's worth of programs are to be taped in one night. In the back of the studio, the stars—Wally

Cox, Shirley Jones, Jack Cassidy, Vincent Price—pop in and out of their dressing rooms as if they were playing a slapstick comedy.

"Hey, Vince."

"I just bought a house on the beach."

"Look at my new dog."

On the set, the warm-up man, burly, red-faced, with dandruff on his shoulders, bellows at the audience, "Hello, my name is Ken Williams. I'm from Baltimore. Where are you all from?"

"Eddyville, Iowa." "Mayville, Tennessee." "Mt. Eric, North Carolina." This is Jacqueline Susann country.

Peter Marshall, the emcee, introduces Jackie. "You ladies know all about this guest. She wrote *Valley of the Dolls*, which sold a couple books, and *The Love Machine*, which just knocked *Portnoy's Complaint* off number one on the best-seller list. Which shows, if you write family, beautiful, sweet things, you're gonna make a buck." The audience is cued to laugh. The game is played like tic-tac-toe. Each star sits in a separate box of a large orange steel contraption. Two contestants try to earn boxes by picking a star, listening to the star answer a question posed by the emcee, and then deciding whether the star is right. If the contestant is right, he gets the box. The first to win three in a row gets $200 in cash, and possibly luggage, a car, a vacation, or a mink coat. The contestants, chosen from the audience, are all young, bubbly, not overly bright, with no long hair, even on the girls. There is one black girl, but she is the antithesis of the Afro look. She could be a model for Breck shampoo. A large portion of the questions are based on articles in *Ladies' Home Journal* and *Woman's Day*. Jackie is asked what Benjamin Franklin used as his pen name for *Poor Richard's Almanac*: Richard Benjamin, Richard Small, or Richard Saunders. Jackie says, "I'm going to guess—Richard Saunders." The contestant says Jackie is wrong. Jackie squeals when told Richard Saunders is right. "You should have trusted me," she says to the contestant. "One writer with another." On the last show, when Jackie is introduced in her blinking orange box, she mouths the words, "Hello mother." Mrs. Susann watches the program every morning in Philadelphia.

They finish just after 11:00 p.m., and the producers, directors, and several of the stars drive to the home of Mary Markham, an independent producer and talent coordinator, on Beverly Drive. It is a lavish house of excessive symmetry. There is a fake fire blazing in the den, where Jack Cassidy is playing pool. Mary's dog, a white animal she says is a "cockapoo—a cross between a cocker spaniel and a poodle," is lurching through the house bumping into furniture. Three men begin playing a dice game called canoga over the long, sunken bar. Jackie is the first of the women to join, throwing dollar bills into the pile. She wins the first two games and claims the cash pot with a cold smile. Irving sits on the couch saying, "No, no!" as the cockapoo laps at his face. Cassidy confides in Jackie that he wants to write a book. Jackie says, "You should. I think any good actor is a good writer, because he is able to mimic life."

Jacqueline sets many scenes of *The Love Machine* in the pink and green Polo Lounge of the Beverly Hills Hotel. During the day, the theatrical crowd, who greet each other with cries of "Marvelous," pronounced "mah-velous," is filled out with wealthy women whose daughters are always married in the hotel's grand ballroom. In the ladies' lounge, a blonde girl who looks to be nineteen is curled on a couch, sucking her thumb. Her mother is stroking the girl. "I've ordered those nice chicken pancakes. We don't want them to get cold."

In the Polo Lounge, Jackie is seated on a green banquette in front of a trellis with plastic ivy. She has been giving interviews for several hours and is eating a hamburger and a glass of water as part of her meat and water diet, which she describes in detail to each reporter. She devotes an hour to *People Today* magazine, another to the Long Beach *Independent Press-Telegram*, and then sees a young reporter from the Los Angeles *Herald Examiner*. When asked if she expected her books to be so successful, Jackie says, "I came up the hard way in acting, so with writing, I was going to start right at the top. I had always written for myself—stories, poems, I had a play produced on Broadway (*Lovely Me* in 1945). When I saw people reading my first book, *Josephine*, I would think, there's someone reading the baby. When I saw people reading *Valley*, I would think, they have very good taste."

In the evening, Jackie is a guest on *The Steve Allen Show*, taped in the Hollywood Video Center on Vine Street. The sidewalk of Vine, like that of Hollywood Boulevard, is pink inlaid with gold stars bearing the names of actors. Jackie is shown to a spartan dressing room with a couch and a director's chair. A young man with a beard walks in and asks her to sign a release. Looking at herself in the mirror, combing the Korean hair, she says, "Is this an AFTRA contract?" The young man frowns. "I'm an AFTRA actress. I don't go on a show without getting paid."

Jackie and Irving watch the beginning of the program on a monitor. "It's *The Steve Allen Show*, with Jacqueline Susann … ." A stagehand comes for Jackie. She stands, pulls up her white stockings, straightens her Pucci dress, and waves, "See ya." When she appears on the monitor, Irving says, "She's just radiant, isn't she? Even when the show is terrible." Steve Allen invites members of the audience to ask Jackie questions. As on all her West Coast radio and television appearances, the audience asks how she learned to write, what is her technique. What they mean is: If you can do it, why can't I? Jackie says her father, a portrait painter, taught her to study people's faces and voices. She does some sloppy imitations of Zsa Zsa Gabor and Tallulah Bankhead. Jackie is asked to play a running-jumping game with a girl swimming champion and a black comedian. After she hears the rules, she says, "I'll watch."

As the show ends, Bob Shayne, the twenty-eight-year-old talent coordinator, says to me, "I hope you're not going to be as kind to her as we were. We had no intention of giving her such a plug. We had review sheets all ready for Steve. We were dying to plant someone in the audience to ask a leading question. I read the other book she wrote. She can NOT write."

The inescapable fact about Jacqueline Susann is that even those who denounce her have probably read *Valley of the Dolls*. According to statistics kept by *Publishers' Weekly*, more people have bought that novel than any other published in America in the twentieth century. She is a national phenomenon, and we are stuck with her. There is a built-in audience of ten million for every book she turns out. She is as compulsive about writing as the legendary British popular novelist who kept a rigid schedule of writing five hours every day.

If during that time he finished a novel, he would type, "end," insert a new page and type the title of the next book. Jackie has already written a first draft of a new novel to be called *The Big Man*, about a girl with a dominating, magnetic father.

She writes the first draft in the period between the time she finishes a novel and the day it is published and she embarks on the promotion tour. "Then I don't return to an empty typewriter."

Even after the film rights of *The Love Machine* were sold for a million and a half dollars, even after the book had hit number one, Jackie continued to plug it as if she were an unknown author. "Maybe it's my bag, but I feel I have to keep going around and doing it," She was autographing books for Higbee's in Cleveland when she learned *Love Machine* had made number one. Her immediate response was, "We've gotta keep it up there." Irving says that with Jackie, staying number one is a matter of pride. "Simon and Schuster wanted us to hold off publication for a month because *Portnoy's Complaint* was so hot. But Jackie said no. She wanted the title shot. She's a natural born competitor."

Irving has taped on the wall of their creamy bathroom in the Beverly Hills Hotel a cardboard facsimile of the *New York Times* Best Seller List of June 22, the first week *Love Machine* was number one. "It's great to watch when you're on the head," Jackie says. "It makes you relax. It's good for the soul."

Irving looks up from his copy of *Variety*. "That's funny, isn't it?"

Postscript:

The photographer Diane Arbus plays an unseen roll in this collection. Not only did her daughter, Doon, write the James Brown piece, but Diane contributed a photograph to the article as well. She took Viva's picture, of course, and also took a portrait of Susann and her husband, Irving Mansfield for *Harper's*. "They had no idea who she was," Sara Davidson told me, "or they never would have let her take the picture."

Only 25, Davidson arrived at the assignment with plenty of seasoning. "My first job after I graduated from the Columbia school of Journalism was at the *Boston Globe*. I went to work there in the late summer, early fall of '65. I worked as a general assignment reporter at the *Globe*—and they assigned whatever came up. But they were receptive to ideas, and I was very ambitious and proposed most of the stories I wrote. Really, I wanted to write about movies and their film critic was an older woman who got to write about all the A movies. I would write humorously scathing reviews about B movies. I also got to interview directors like Alfred Hitchcock and Roman Polanski and others.

"I became more interested in the work I was doing in regular reporting. At 23, I wanted to interview the mayor about something. The city editor said, 'Do you think you can handle the mayor?' 'I think I can, sir.' But I wanted to get back to New York. 'You don't go right to the *Times*' is what we'd heard in school, and I was very lucky to get a job at the *Globe*, not the hinterlands. So, I moved back to New York and for a few years was the New York correspondent for the *Globe* which was a lot of fun. Then I quit to go freelance.

"I read all the magazines. As it happened my husband at the time, Jonathan Schwartz, knew the managing editor of *Harper's*. I proposed a story about a rock band named Rhinoceros and they agreed but said I'd have to write it on spec. I did and they liked it enough to give me an assignment—Jacqueline Susann. It wasn't my idea. I certainly hadn't read her books.

"She tried to turn me down, but I told her, 'My editor says you're really important in the literary scene and would appreciate an interview.' She was very flattered that *Harper's* wanted to do a story on her. I don't think she had any idea who I was. She read my first story for *Harper's*, and she and her husband, Irving, figured I would write a positive piece.

"*Harper's* loved the piece but she hated it and bad-mouthed me. I was proud of almost everything I did. That one left me feeling kind of squeamish. I didn't feel it was my finest hour. I was glad to work for *Harper's* but I made a conscious decision that I was no longer going to write about someone or something I didn't have a genuine interest or respect for. It felt cheap. She was an easy target. But I didn't feel good about it. After that I didn't take those assignments— and I wasn't offered them, either."

NORA EPHRON

Before Nora Ephron became Nora Ephron (1941–2012), before she introduced Harry to Sally and three Oscar nominations for screenwriting decorated her CV, she stepped into a world she had only glimpsed in *The Front Page* and *His Girl Friday*. She was a reporter for the *New York Post*, this nice girl from Beverly Hills with a Wellesley education, surrounded by ink-stained curmudgeons who drank breakfast after working the overnight shift and remembered every great lede—civilians call it an opening paragraph—they ever read word for word. There were rock stars, jewel thieves, and seals that refused to mate out there, and she wrote about them all with the flair, wit, and intelligence that told anyone who cared she wouldn't be doing this for long. Helen Gurley Brown, who was revolutionizing women's magazines at *Cosmopolitan*, spotted Ephron first and hired her to write about how the chorus line was chosen at the Copacabana. Ephron held her nose and delivered, thinking nothing good would come of it. But something did: an assignment to profile Brown for *Esquire*. When she delivered an empathetic piece about this doyenne of false eyelashes, formal dinners, and orgasms, the magazine knew it had found the perfect columnist to explain the modern woman to its largely male readership. Who else could watch a porn film consumed by the fear that the female star's glass dildo just might break? —JS

HELEN GURLEY BROWN ONLY WANTS TO HELP

Esquire, 1970

A girl can do anything she wants to, don't you think? She can start out hillbilly-poor in the Ozarks and end up having Chinese food with Darryl Zanuck every Sunday. She can be married to a top executive and still bring in scads of MONEY as a magazine editor. She can change her nose, her wigs, her image, and manage to remain as sincere and pippypoo as ever. I've done all these things, and thank goodness there's one magazine that seems to understand me. I guess you could say I'm That COSMOPOLITAN Girl.

They are still screaming at her after all these years. They are still saying that Helen Gurley Brown is some kind of scarlet woman, leading the young women of America into reckless affairs, possibly with married men. And every time they say it, she sits there, little puckers beginning in her chin, and waits for the moment when the talk show will be over and she can run offstage and burst into tears. You might think that by now they would stop screaming—after all, this small, thin, dreadfully sincere woman is not to blame for the moral turpitude in America; you might think that by now Helen Gurley Brown would stop crying—after all, her attackers simply do not, cannot understand. But no. Just the other night, it happened again. On *The Merv Griffin Show* or *The Joey Bishop Show*. One or the other. She was just sitting there, talking in her underslung voice about how a single girl must go to lunch with married men, that a single girl with no other men in her life must somehow make the men who are there serve a purpose. She finished her little spiel and the screaming began. A singer on the panel started it. "Is this the kind of thing we want the young women of our country to listen to?" he said. "I wouldn't want any daughter of mine to go and date a married man." Then he turned to the audience and said, "Everyone out there who agrees with me, raise your hand or clap." And it began. Thunderous applause. Hundreds of hands flapping on the monitors. And as soon as the show was over, Helen Gurley Brown began to cry.

As it happens, Helen Gurley Brown cries quite a lot. She cried for three hours at Trader Vic's the night Jerry Lewis attacked her on *The Tonight Show*. She cried one day in the beauty parlor just after returning from a trip to see her mother. She cried the day a Hearst executive refused to let her run a cover of *Cosmopolitan* magazine because there was too much boosom showing. (That's the way she pronounces it. *Boosom*.) She cried the day Richard E. Berlin, president of The Hearst Corporation, put his foot down over a cover line that said, "The Pill that Makes Women More Responsive to Men." She cries all the time because people don't understand her. Jerry Lewis does not understand her, her mother does not understand her, and, from time to time, The Hearst Corporation does not understand her. They don't understand what she is trying to do. They don't understand that she knows something they don't know. She knows about the secretaries, the nurses, the telephone company clerks who live out there somewhere, miles from psychiatrists, plastic surgeons, and birth control clinics. Only eight percent of *Cosmopolitan*'s readers are in New York City—the rest are stuck in the wilds, coping with their first pair of false eyelashes and their first fling with vaginal foam and their first sit-down dinners and their first orgasms. These are the girls who read Helen Gurley Brown's *Single Girl's Cookbook* and learn—yes, *learn*—that before guests arrive for dinner, it is smart to put out the garbage. These are the girls who buy *Cosmopolitan* and swallow whole such tidbits of advice as: "Rub your thighs together when you walk. The squish-squish sound of nylon ... has a frenzying effect." These are the girls who have to be told "How to Tell If He's a Married Man." You don't believe there are girls who cannot tell if a man is married? Listen, then, to this letter to Helen Gurley Brown from a young lady in Savannah, Georgia:

"My problem is a common one. I am an expectant unwed mother. The father of my child turned his back on me after he found out. Besides, he is married. However, I was not aware of this until after our affair had begun, and too weak to break it off until I realized he had never been serious about me. By this time it was too late."

Helen Gurley Brown knows about these girls. She understands them. And don't you see? *She is only trying to help.*

We are sitting in her yellow and orange office across the street from Hearst headquarters at Fifty-Seventh Street and Eighth Avenue. On the floor is a large stuffed tiger. On the bulletin board is a picture of her husband, David. She calls him Lambchop. On the wall is a long magazine rack, containing, along with a number of popular periodicals, the last twelve months of *Cosmopolitan* magazine. Read all about it. "Why I Wear My False Eyelashes to Bed." "I Was a Nude Model." "I Was Raped." "I Had a Hysterectomy." On her desk—along with some dental floss she uses before all editorial meetings—is a tear sheet of the next in a series of advertisements she writes for *Cosmopolitan*; this one, of a luscious girl, her hand poised deftly over her cleavage, has the following to say:

"What does a girl do if she's wearing a hairpiece and she and her date are getting quite romantic? Well, we all know that a hairpiece can't live *through* very much in the way of stress and strain so I just take out the pins and take mine off. So far, no boy I've known has ever fainted dead away because everything that basically counts is *me* ... adding extra hair is just an *accessory*. When I think of all the subterfuge and pretending girls once had to go through I'm thankful I live now when you can be truthful ... and there's a wonderful magazine to help me be the honest female-female I really am. I love that maga-zine. I guess you could say I'm That COSMOPOLITAN Girl."

Helen Gurley Brown is now in her fifth year as editor-in-chief of *Cosmopolitan*. She took it over when she was forty-three and it was in trouble, turned it around, breathed new life and new image into it, became the only editor in America to resurrect a dying maga-zine. She is now forty-eight and tiny, with tiny wrists, tiny face, tiny voice. "I once heard her lose her temper," a former *Cosmo* editor recalls, "and it sounded like a little sparrow—she was chirping as loud as she could but you still couldn't hear her." She wears Rudi Gernreich dresses, David Webb jewelry, a Piaget watch, expensive hairpieces, custom-cut false eyelashes—but it never quite seems to come together properly. An earring keeps falling off. A wig is askew. A perfectly matched stocking has a run. All of which not-quite-right effect is intensified because Helen Gurley Brown relentlessly talks about her flat chest, her nose job, her split ends, her adolescent acne, her forty-minute regimen of isometrics and exercises to stay in shape. She does not bring up these faults to convince you she is unattractive but rather to show you what can be done, what any girl can do if she really tries. "Self-help," she says. "I wish there were better words, but that is my whole credo. You cannot sit around like a cupcake asking other people to come and eat you up and discover your great sweet-ness and charm. You've got to make yourself more cupcakable all the time so that you're a better cupcake to be gobbled up." That's the way she talks when she gets carried away—exhortation, but in the style of girlish advertising copy. She talks about "hot-fudge-sundae-kind-of-pleasure" and "good-old-fashioned-popcorn-eating-being-transported-to-another-world-going-to-the-movies." Ten years as an advertising copywriter pays off for this girl. Yes sir. She can package anything. Titles for articles fall out of her mouth involuntarily. A staff member will suggest an article idea, and if she likes it, she has the title in an instant. "The Oh-So-Private World of the Nurse," she will squeal. Or "The Bittersweet World of the Hillbilly Girl." Or "The Harried, Happy World of a Girl Buyer." One day someone suggested an article about how most girls worry about having orgasms. "Yes!" cried Mrs. Brown. "We'll call it, 'It Never Really Happens to Me.'"

I am in Helen Gurley Brown's office because I am interviewing her, a euphemism for what in fact involves sitting on her couch and listening while she volunteers answers to a number of questions I would never ask. What she is like in bed, for example. Very good. Whether she enjoys sex. Very much. Always has. Why she did not marry until she was thirty-seven. Very neurotic. Wasn't ready. It all seems to pour out of her, her past, her secrets, her fears, her innermost hopes and dreams. Says her husband, David: "Whether it was group therapy or what, there's nothing left inside Helen. It all comes out."

It all comes out—in interviews, on television, in editorial conferences, in memoranda, in the pages of her magazine. Helen Gurley Brown spends twelve hours a day worrying, poring over, agonizing about her magazine; if her insomnia is acting up, she may spend most of the night. She writes endless memos, in lowercase letters, to her writers, full of suggestions for articles she is particularly concerned about, "would like to go into a little detail about what goes through a girl's *head* as she is unable to have an orgasm," went one recent memo, "maybe a soliloquy, this subject has been treated so *clinically* … as though she couldn't do push-ups." She writes memos to her editors praising them, nudging them, telling them how to fix stories that need fixing. "She has a very clear picture of what will and will not fit her magazine," says Hearst special-projects editor Jeannette Wagner. "If she sends you back an article with a note that says, I want a lede that says thus-and-such, you go back and do exactly what she says."

She works over every piece that goes into the magazine, doing the kind of line-by-line editing most editors leave to their juniors, rewriting, inserting exclamation points and italics and capitalized words and *Cosmopolitan* style into everything. "I want every article to be baby simple," she often says. Not surprisingly, most of the magazine sounds as if it were written by the same person. And in a way, it is. *Cosmopolitan* is Helen Gurley Brown. Cute. Girlish. Exhortative. Almost but not quite tasteless. And in its own insidious, peculiar way, irresistible. Says *Cosmo* articles editor Roberta Ashley: "Helen manages to walk that line between vulgarity and taste, which isn't easy. The magazine is like a very sexy girl—you don't mind that her dress is cut down to her navel because her hair is clean. If her hair were dirty, you'd be revolted."

And if, at times, Helen Gurley Brown and her magazine are offensive, it is only because almost every popular success is offensive. Mrs. Brown—like Hugh Hefner and Dorothy Schiff, to name two other irritating publishing successes—offends because she is proving, at sizable financial profit, the old Mencken dictum that no one ever went broke underestimating the intelligence of the American public. She is demonstrating, rather forcefully, that there are over one million American women who are willing to spend sixty cents to read not about politics, not about the female-liberation movement, not about the war in Vietnam, but merely about how to get a man.

I have not been single for years, but I read *Cosmopolitan* every month. I see it lying on the newsstands and I'm suckered in. "How to Make a Small Bosom Amount to Something," the cover line says, or "Thirteen New Ways to Feminine Satisfaction." I buy it, greedily, hide it deep within my afternoon newspaper, and hop on the bus, looking forward to—at the very least—a bigger bra size and a completely new kind of orgasm. Yes, I should know better. After all, I used to write for *Cosmopolitan* and make this stuff up myself. But she gets me every time. I get home—or sometimes, if I simply can't wait, I open it on the bus, being careful to remove my glove so that onlookers will see my wedding band and will know I'm not reading *Cosmopolitan* because I'm That COSMOPOLITAN Girl. And there it is. Buy a padded bra, the article on bust lines tells me. Fake it, the article on orgasm says. And I should be furious. But I'm not. Not at all. How can you be angry at someone who's got your number?

In a recent article in *The Antioch Review* linking *Cosmopolitan* and *Playboy*, Peter Michelson wrote, "*Cosmopolitan*, or more likely the Hearst hierarchy, had recognized how *Playboy* was making the world safe for pornography, and it very neatly cut itself in on the sex-profit nexus." That explanation, while interesting, gives The Hearst Corporation more credit than it is due. In 1964, about all the Hearst people realized was that *Cosmopolitan* was in bad shape. Circulation had dropped to under eight-hundred-thousand copies a month. Advertising was down to twenty-one pages an issue. Early in 1965, Helen Gurley Brown came to see Richard Deems, President of the Hearst Magazines Division, with a dummy for a new magazine. He had vaguely heard of her, had no idea she was at all controversial, and had never read her 1962 best seller, *Sex and the Single Girl*. But he liked her, he liked her idea for a magazine aimed at single women, and, most of all, he liked her long list of companies that might be willing to advertise in such a magazine. It is safe to say that if Deems had thought that Helen Gurley Brown was going to turn *Cosmopolitan* into something that would repeatedly be called the female counterpart to *Playboy*, he would not have employed her. "We happen to be a company with a conscience about what it publishes," he said recently. "Our paperback division is the only book company that doesn't have a married-sex book. We're very studious about this kind of thing."

There are, of course, many similarities between *Cosmopolitan* and *Playboy*. Both magazines contain nudity. Both are concerned with sexual freedom of a sort. Both are headed by people who are the prod-ucts of repressed, WASP backgrounds. Both publish the worst work of good writers. Both exalt material possessions. Both are somewhat deprecating to the opposite sex: *Playboy* turns its women into sexual objects; *Cosmopolitan* makes its men mindless creatures who can be toppled into matrimony by perfect soufflés, perfect martinis, and other perfectible manipulative techniques.

This year, Helen Gurley Brown even commissioned a *Playboy*-type foldout picture—of actor James Coburn, nude, his vital parts some-what obscured by a potted palm. "It was a very pretty picture," said Mrs. Brown. "But ... I don't like to be in the position of turning James Coburn down ... but the particular picture I needed didn't come out of this shooting. The pictures were very hippie and mystical, strange and ethereal and a little sad, and Jesus, that isn't what I had in mind at all. I wanted a cute, funny, wonderful foxy picture, with that great mouth and marvelous teeth. I am going to do a foldout—I'll take another whack at it—but I haven't got the picture I want yet."

There is one major difference between *Playboy* and *Cosmopolitan*. The Playboy man has no problems. The *Cosmopolitan* girl has thousands.

She has menstrual cramps, pimples, budget squeeze, hateful room-mates. She cannot meet men. She cannot think of what to say when she meets them. She doesn't know how to take off her clothes to get into bed with them. She doesn't know how to find a psychiatrist. She even gets raped, though only by rapists with somewhat unlikely dialogue. (In "I Was Raped," *Cosmopolitan* introduced the only rapist in history who lay down on his victim and murmured, "Let's make love.")

"It drives my management wild to be compared with *Playboy*," said Mrs. Brown. "We are not like *Playboy*. We are all the things we've been talking about—onward, upward, be it, do it, get out of your morass, meet some new men, don't accept, don't be a slob, be everything you're capable of. If you're a little mouseburger, come with me. I was a mouseburger and I will help you. You're so much more wonderful than you think. *Cosmopolitan* is shot full of this stuff although outsiders don't realize it. It is, in its way, an inspirational magazine."

There is very little that has happened to Helen Gurley Brown that she has not managed to extricate a rule from. Or learn a lesson from. Or make a maxim of. Or see, in hindsight, that it was all part of a plan. If it weren't for her unhappy childhood, she says, she wouldn't be enjoying herself so much now. If it weren't for her years of diffi-culty, she would never have had such a drive to improve her lot. She has led a hard life, a perfect life out of which to build inspirational books and an inspirational magazine.

She was born in Green Forest, Arkansas, in the Ozarks, the second daughter of Cleo and Ira Gurley. Both her parents were schoolteachers, but her father turned to politics and was elected to the state legislature. In 1925, he moved his family to Little Rock. He was killed in a freak elevator accident in the State Capitol Building seven years later. His daughter Helen was ten and his daughter Mary was fourteen.

"That really changed our lives considerably," Helen Gurley Brown remembered one day recently. "That sort of finished things, finished a phase of my life which I never will get back. The security ... . They say a great deal of your life is formed by the time you're about seven, so these drives and rages and ambitions and yearnings and needings and cravings of mine must have been formed before that time, some of them. I never have gotten to the bottom of all that. Why am I so driven? It seems logically to have derived from things that happened to me after my father died, but some of it must be residual from very early. I don't know.

"But anyway, here we are in Little Rock, little fatherless children. I don't think my mother and father were particularly happy together, but my father's death was a horrendous thing in her life. She and my father had been very poor. She gets disgusted with me because I keep carrying on about how poor I was. I always ate. I always looked okay. I really never was eating pork and beans out of a can and putting cardboard in the soles of my shoes. But it's what you get in your head, it's how it seemed to you that motivates you. Whereas my parents were really poor, and just about the time things were beginning to go rather well, she and my father resolved whatever differences they had, poosh, he's taken away, snapped off.

"We stayed in Little Rock for about three years after my father's death," she continued. "But he left a limited amount of insurance and apparently our house was mortgaged to the hilt. So because mother felt we couldn't keep up the nice little standard of living in Little Rock on this particular stipend she had been left, she decided we'd all go move to Los Angeles. It was very brave and gutsy of her. But my sister didn't want to go to California. I didn't either. And my mother didn't level with us, because you didn't in those days. She said, 'Oh, I think it would be nice to go to California, we have relatives there.' So we move to California and Mary gets polio." She paused. "She was nineteen. There was no March of Dimes and there was nobody to help. Schlurp, in one big thing, in one year, it took all the money we had. I really got good and scared out of my wits about that time."

Another pause. "I just didn't know what was going to become of us. It was still the end of the Depression, jobs were very hard to get and my sister—she's never walked again. I don't know, we were sort of a pitiful little tribe." Her voice cracked and she began to cry. "My word," she said. "I never talk about this anymore." She daubed at her eyes with a handkerchief. "Well, this is the way I was for years. It was the three of us sort of huddled together. My sister was in a wheelchair and needed constant care. My mother couldn't go back to work or do anything for a number of years." Tears continued to roll down her face. "I was terrified," she said.

The Gurleys moved to the East Side of Los Angeles near the Los Angeles Orthopaedic Hospital, and Helen enrolled at John H. Francis Polytechnic High School. Her memories of that period—aside from her sister's illness—have mainly to do with having acne. "I was kind of a cute little girl, but who could see past those pus pustules?" Like that. She became a student leader, graduated as valedictorian, and was taken to the prom by the student-body president. "It was the coup of the year," she recalled with some amusement. "He had a real case on me, because he got close enough to find out what I was like. I always have to get men close enough to me to be interested in me. I have to do what I call Sinking In before they pay attention. I'm never anybody that some man sees at a party and says, 'Get me her.' Never. But once they get near me and I turn on what I call Plain Girl Power—well, it worked with the student-body president."

Following high school and a year at Woodbury Business College, Helen went to work answering fan mail at radio station KHJ to pay for her second year of college. Her mother worked in the marking room at Sears, Roebuck. Her sister did telephone work for the Hooper rating service. Then Mrs. Gurley and Mary moved back to Arkansas and Helen was left as a single girl in Los Angeles. Friends who knew her in the 1940s, when she held eighteen consecutive secretarial jobs, remember her as a shy, self-effacing, attractive girl who always did the sorts of clever things that seemed astonishing twenty years ago, like putting egg in spinach salad. She was, they recall, completely neurotic about money. She sent one week's salary each month to her family and she was convinced no one would ever marry her because of her financial obligations.

To make ends meet, she took the bus to work, drove her car only on weekends with gas she pumped at the serve-yourself station on Beverly Boulevard, brought her lunch to the office in a paper sack, read other people's newspapers, made her own clothes, traveled by

Greyhound bus. She tried every angle. Because she washed her hair in Woolite, she wrote the president of the company to tell him—and he sent her a free box of the stuff. She wrote an unsolicited memo to the proprietor of the beauty salon in her office lobby telling him how to hype up business—and he did her hair for nothing. She entered the *Glamour* magazine Ten Girls with Taste contest three years in a row, and finally won. "I used to enter all the contests," she said. "I bought so many bars of Lux soap to enter the 'I like Lux soap because … ' contest. I couldn't enter under my own name, because I worked in an advertising agency, so I would send them to Mary and say, 'Please, Mary, have a picture made of yourself in a wheelchair and send these off.' Well, that didn't work. That's one that failed. But I did it. I tried."

She tried everything. Vitamin therapy. Group therapy. Psychoanalysis. Hair therapy. Skin therapy. Her persistent self-improvement dazzled her friends. "She decided the kind of person she wanted to be, the milieu in which she wanted to live, how she wanted to look," said one longtime California associate. "In a very real sense, she invented herself." There were a number of men in Helen Gurley's life—two agents, a married advertising executive, and a Don Juan whom she spent nine years off and on with—but to hear her tell it, her job always came first. She became secretary to Don Belding, a partner in Foote, Cone & Belding, and after five years she was made a copywriter. "It was so heady," she recalled in a near-whisper. "I adored it. Instead of making $100 a week I'm making $10,000 a year, and this is in 1955 and that was considerable money for a girl then, very heady. You know, everything adds up. It's what I keep saying in my books and in *Cosmo*. If you do every little thing you can do in your own modest position, one thing leads to another. So *do* it and *be* it and *write* the letters and *make* the phone calls and get *on* with it. And this is what I was doing every hour of the day, every day of the year.

"But I'm still living in my frugal way. I'm still bringing my lunch to the office. And I was conservative enough to have saved a little money. I had managed to save $8,000." One day, Helen Gurley walked into a Beverly Hills used-car lot and paid $5,000 for a Mercedes-Benz. Cash. "The next weekend I went to the Beldings's ranch in total shock because of this money I spent. It just was not like me. I was in pain, physical pain. Everyone told me all the reasons I should have that car—that I was a successful writer and a gifted girl—they pumped me up and held my hand. But every time they looked at me I was sitting over in the corner in a catatonic heap thinking of this money I'd spent.

"A week or so later a friend of mine set up this famous date with David Brown, whom she'd been saving for me. I thought it was going to be a big thing. I felt it in my bones before I met him. She'd been talking about him for three years, and it felt right. It was an interesting, lovely evening. And he took me to my car after dinner. I could see him looking at this car, this nice car. And I said, Yes, I just bought it and I paid all cash for it. And that was a nice thing, he liked the fact that I'd been able to save all that money, because he had been married to very extravagant women, particularly his last wife."

Helen Gurley and David Brown were married one year later, in September 1959 at the Beverly Hills City Hall. He is now executive vice-president of creative operations and a director of 20th Century-Fox, and his wife continually says she could never have become what she has become without him. He gave her the idea to write *Sex and the Single Girl*. He gave her the idea to aim a magazine at single women. He was once an editor of *Cosmopolitan*; and in her early days there, he helped her run the magazine, rushing over in taxicabs for street-corner conferences about copy. He still writes all the cover blurbs for the magazine. Both Browns live work-oriented lives—long office hours, dinners out with business friends. They spend at least one night a week at Trader Vic's with Darryl Zanuck; they travel to Palm Springs and the Riviera with Richard Zanuck. Several nights a week they eat at home, in their Park Avenue apartment, and spend the evening working.

At one point in 1968, Mrs. Brown was also emceeing a television show and overseeing the editing of Hearst's *Eye* magazine. Both operations are now defunct, and she is left with just *Cosmopolitan*. Now selling 1,100,680 copies a month. Now pulling in 857 advertising pages a year—compared with 1964's 259. There are still the little setbacks, of course: old friends who are jealous; reader complaints over increasing nudity in the magazine; The Hearst Corporation's censorship. But though Helen Gurley Brown cries frequently, she cries much less now than she used to.

Why just the other day she managed to get through a major flap without crying once. It all had to do with the breast memorandum. Perhaps you remember it—one of her staff members leaked it to *Women's Wear Daily*, and many newspapers picked it up. The memo began, "We are doing an article on how men should treat women's breasts in lovemaking. It will either help us sell another 100,000 copies or stop publication of *Cosmopolitan* altogether." Its purpose? "To help a lot of men make a lot of girls more happy." It went on to say … . But stop. Let her tell the story.

"It started with my idea of how boosoms should be handled," she said. "Ninety-nine percent of the articles here are assigned by the other editors, but this particular thing was a secret of mine that I felt only I understood. I called my own writer in California and told her about it. She tried it and turned it in and it was beautiful, but God, it didn't have *anything* to do with how men should treat women's boosoms. It had to do with *love* and it had to do with *companion-ship* and the wonderful relationship between men and women, but it just didn't have *anything* to do technically with the subject. I wanted techniques. What does she like and how does she tell him and what does he do and how does he shape up. So I called my writer and said, 'This is your personal reminiscence of all your love affairs, and fascinating as it is, it doesn't have *anything* to do with boobs.' And she said, 'I know. Can you supply me with any material?'

"That's when I sat down and wrote my memo to the girls in the office. Just give me your thoughts about boosoms, I said. Has anybody ever been a real idiot in making love to you? How could men improve their techniques? What would you like done that's not being done? I just got a wonderful response. All the girls responded except two. I'd like to know who the two were because I don't think they'd be happy at *Cosmopolitan*, but I had no way of knowing because a lot of girls didn't sign their memos. I've sent many memos before— give me your definition of a bitch, have you ever dated a very wealthy man—and this was just another one of those memos. Then I saw it in *Women's Wear Daily* and I really did hit the roof. A lot of people said, ho, ho, ho, how lucky can you be? You probably mailed it yourself in an unmarked envelope. But that's not true, because I tread a very careful path with Hearst management and I don't want to get them exercised about anything. If I just very quietly developed these articles and show them the finished product, it's much better. But this big brouhaha started because this little bitch, whoever she was, sent the memo to *Women's Wear*, and I would still fire her if I knew who she was. Because then the turmoil started. My management said to me, We want to see a copy of the boosom article the minute it's finished. I didn't want this attention to be called to what I was doing. Furthermore, we have trouble with supermarkets in the South and I didn't want them stirred up ahead of time.

"Well, the girls wrote their wonderful memos, I put two other writers on the story—because the girl in California suddenly got very haughty and said she didn't want to deal with the material. She just went absolutely crackers about the whole thing. So these two writers took it on and between them they turned in wonderful stuff, their own ideas plus all my material. I got this fantastic article. But my management won't let me run it. The actual use of anatomical words bugs them. Well, you cannot talk about love and relationships when you're talking about how to handle a breast. You must be anatomical. You've got to say a few things about what to do. I'm not mad at them—they do it because they're afraid we'll have too much flak. But I plan to lie low for a while and come back with my boosom article later. I read it tenderly, like a little love letter, every so often. I'll try it again after a while."

One day a couple of years ago, a *Cosmopolitan* editor named Harriet La Barre called me and asked if I wanted to write an article on how to start a conversation. They would pay $600 for one-thousand words. Yes, I would. Fine, she said, she would send a memo Helen had written on the subject. The memo arrived, a breezy little thing filled with suggestions like "remember what the great Cleveland Amory says—shyness is really selfishness" and "be sure to debunk the idea that it is dangerous to approach strangers." I read it and realized with some embarrassment that I had already written the article the memo wanted, in slightly different form—for *Cosmopolitan*, no less. I called Harriet La Barre.

"Omigod," she said. "And I even edited it."

We talked it over and decided that I might as well take the assignment anyway.

"After all," said Miss La Barre, "if it doesn't bother us to *run* the same article twice, it shouldn't bother you to *write* it twice."

"I have just one question though," I said. "What is this about the great Cleveland Amory and his theory that shyness is just selfishness?"

"Did she say that?" said Miss La Barre. "She must be kidding—I don't even think she likes Cleveland Amory."

A few weeks later, I turned the article in, and Harriet La Barre called. "We're going to run it," she said, "but there are two things we want to change."

"All right," I said.

"First of all, I was wrong about Cleveland Amory," she said. "I'm afraid we do have to say that shyness is really selfishness."

"But shyness *isn't* really selfishness," I said.

"Well, I know, but that's the way we have to put it."

"What's the second thing?" I said.

"Well, it's just one little change Helen made, but I wanted to read it to you. You have a sentence that reads, 'It's absurd to think that any girl who asks a nice-looking man how to get to Rockefeller Center will be bundled up in a burlap bag and sold into a Middle Eastern harem.'"

"Yes," I said, realizing it wasn't much of a sentence.

"Well, Helen changed it to read, 'The notion that any girl who asks a nice-looking man how to get to Rockefeller Center is immediately bundled up in a burlap bag and sold into a Middle Eastern harem is as antique and outmoded a myth as the notion that you can't take a bath while you're menstruating.' "

"What?"

"Is that all right?" she said.

"Is that all *right*? Of course it's not all right. How did that particular image get into my article?"

"I don't really know," said Harriet La Barre. "We're thinking of doing a piece on menstruation and maybe it was on her mind."

I hung up, convinced I had seen straight to the soul of Helen Gurley Brown. Straight to the foolishness, the tastelessness her critics so often accused her of. But I was wrong. She really isn't that way at all. She's just worried that somewhere out there is a girl who hasn't taken a bath during her period since puberty. She's just worried that somewhere out there is a girl whose breasts aren't being treated properly. She's just worried that somewhere out there is a mouseburger who doesn't realize she has the capability of becoming anything, anything at all, anything she wants to, of becoming Helen Gurley Brown, for God's sake. And don't you see? *She is only trying to help.*

Postscript:

This marked Ephron's debut in *Esquire* where she enjoyed a memorable run in the '70s as an essayist, chiefly in a column about women during the height of the women's liberation movement, and another about media. She wrote hilariously about breasts, her mother's mink coat, and Eric Segal's massively successfully but unbearably corny 1970 novel, *Love Story*, yet only a handful of what we'd call traditional profiles which gives this piece on Gurley Brown an added appeal. After all, Ephron would go on to know something about fame and celebrity herself.

According to Helen Gurley Brown biographer, Gerri Hirshey, in *Not Pretty Enough*:

Helen gave Ephron the name and phone number of a married ad executive she had an affair with during her single years. Ephron interviewed the man, who was still married and was perplexed that Helen would identify him. She judged it too awkward to use in the article.

"I can't believe you gave me his name," Ephron told Helen later. "Oh. Well. Yes."

Gurley Brown's success at *Cosmo* can't be understated. Within a short time of taking over the venerated but atrophying title, Brown's *Cosmo* practically printed money for Hearst and would continue as the flagship magazine at the company for decades to come.

Ephron didn't do too badly herself. Her 1979 novel, *Heartburn*, a not-so-thinly-veiled fictional account of her marriage to *Washington Post* reporter Carl Bernstein—of Woodward and Bernstein fame—was a bestseller, and soon Ephron left magazine writing behind for Hollywood, first as a screenwriter—*Silkwood, When Harry Met Sally*—and then as a writer-director of chatty romantic comedies such as *Sleepless in Seattle* and *You've Got Mail*. She eventually married Nick Pileggi, a veteran *New York* magazine reporter and all around beloved guy—also Gay Talese's first cousin—whose 1988 book, *Wise Guy*, is the basis for Martin Scorsese's genre-busting 1990 epic, *Good Fellas*, and lived happily ever after.

HELEN LAWRENSON

By the time Helen Lawrenson (1907–1983) interviewed Warren Beatty for *Cosmopolitan* in 1970, she understood the fickle nature of celebrity better than most. She'd worked at *Vanity Fair* during the early '30s, first as movie critic, then managing editor. She enjoyed love affairs with magazine mogul Conde Nast, political advisor Bernard Baruch, and numbers-runner Bumpy Johnson—making her a kind of Eve Babitz of her time. After *Vanity Fair* folded, she spent six months in Havana; when she returned, she dashed off a quick humor essay debunking Latin machismo. She titled it "Latins Are Lousy Lovers" and sent it to *Esquire*, then just a few years old. Published under an anonymous byline it became, according to founding editor Arnold Gingrich, the most famous piece the magazine ran in its first forty years of existence. The title phrase became part of the pop culture lexicon and made Lawrenson notorious for reasons that perplexed and annoyed her, but also gave her a beat—sex.

Even in the '60s, Lawrenson was still relevant in the ever-young magazine world, specializing in celebrity interviews, with her pieces notable for their frankness. She was never flippant or vicious, remembering how much grief the "Latins" piece caused her. "With one shot of my typewriter," she later recalled, "I made myself unpopular with the male population of an entire continent, three countries in Europe, and more than half a dozen islands. At this late date I have no desire to widen the horizon of hostilities." It was with this sensitivity in mind, that she approached Warren Beatty, whose caginess with the press was already well-established. He agreed to make an exception for Lawrenson, which tells you a little something about one of the finest profile writers of her time.—AB

WARREN BEATTY HAS BEEN WRONGED!

Cosmopolitan, 1970

Ever since his first film (*Splendor in the Grass*) ten years ago, Warren Beatty has been one of the most talked about figures in Hollywood—and the least understood. It is an open secret that the reason *Bonnie and Clyde* didn't stand a chance of winning the Best Picture Oscar in 1968, or Warren the Best Actor award (despite both nominations), was because of his controversial status in the movie colony.

He should worry. Today, at thirty-two, he is world-famous, successful, respected, rich (estimates of his total take from *Bonnie and Clyde* vary from $6 million to $12 million), and one of the most eligible bachelors alive. His reputation as a lothario would make a healthy mink look impotent. But what is he really like? What kind of man is this Warren Beatty?

I first met him in late 1961, when I went to interview one of his famous friends in her suite at the Plaza Hotel in New York. Their romance was still in full flower, so I was not surprised when a door opened and into the living room came Warren, wearing jeans and a rumpled shirt and looking as if he had just gotten out of bed, which he probably had (it was around noon and the table was laid for breakfast). His famous beautiful young friend introduced us, but Warren only grunted and shuffled out again. I thought him utterly resistible.

It was about five years and a lot of girls later before I saw Warren again. During the interval I had heard plenty about him, none of it flattering. Whenever his name was mentioned, people reacted with an automatic spasm of resentment. They said, among other things, that he was conceited, arrogant, rude, selfish, pretentious, obnoxious. (I should have figured that anyone universally disliked by so many executives, directors, actors, press agents, and reporters would be interesting, at the very least.) The mildest comment was from a female publicist: "He's not well-liked. He's not like Cary Grant."

He sure isn't. Nor is he easy to interview. Having discovered how easy it is to sound asinine in print if you are misquoted or misinterpreted, Warren has grown increasingly wary of the press. "I don't mind if they make me out a bastard," he told me recently, "I just don't want them to make me out an idiot." Intense, moody, sensitive, he is basically serious, with no talent for glibness. He doesn't give prepacked answers. Instead, he thinks out what he wants to say—and there are long, awkward pauses while he searches carefully, doggedly, for the word he feels will best express his meaning. But the average reporter couldn't be less impressed with the Beatty precision of language, because what Warren wants to talk about is his theory of acting and what the reporter wants to talk about is the actor's sex life.

Warren has consistently refused to discuss his love affairs, a reticence unappreciated in a community whose denizens are wont to telephone columnists to report their romances, their wives' pregnancies and miscarriages, their marital quarrels, and how much they paid for presents to their loves ones. Warren won't play the kiss-and-tell game. "One of my few virtues is discretion," he says. He carries the practice of this virtue to such extremes that he riles people who don't understand his motives. A male writer who interviewed Leslie Caron at the time of *her* romance with Warren had the same experience I had at the Plaza. "He never even spoke to me," the writer said indignantly. "He just walked out of the room." I realize now that in each case Warren's behavior did not stem from an insolent lack of courtesy, but from dismay at having walked into a press interview with an actress with whom he was having an affair and his determination not to contribute in any way to publicity about the romance.

Warren's desire for privacy in this personal area has been frustrated, in part, by the fact that his prowess as a lover has, until recently, overshadowed his skill as an actor. Without intending any disparagement of the women involved, it should be pointed out that one doesn't have to be Superman to be successful with girls in Hollywood. Warren may not be the *only* unquestionably heterosexual male in town, but the field has not been exactly overcrowded. So, not surprisingly, he has gained a reputation as the year-round champion stud of the film colony, a sobriquet that hasn't necessarily endeared him to men of more mediocre—or ambivalent—sexual ratings.

Nevertheless, whatever the competition—or lack of it—the Beatty myth has grown. In her book *Scratch an Actor*, Sheilah Graham, the famous Hollywood columnist, wrote, "The girls he has loved, famous or unknown, are legion"; and last year an article in *Life* contained the flat statement: "With Warren Beatty there is no worry over whether seduction is possible, only when and where and who's next." Certainly, the list of women with whom his name has been linked is a glittering one, and includes Joan Collins, Natalie Wood, Vivien Leigh, Leslie Caron, Vanessa Redgrave, Barbara Harris, Candice Bergen, Inger Stevens, the Russian ballerina Maya Plisetskaya, Madame Dewi Sukarno, and, of course, Julie Christie.

Not *everyone* succumbs to Warren's charm, but his record is such that if he is seen talking at length to any girl, people assume a subsequent bedroom scene is inevitable. Last year gossip columnists reported that he had left Julie Christie for Brigitte Bardot. I asked him about the alleged affair and he said, "I've met Brigitte exactly twice, both times in public. I've never seen her alone."

As for Mme Sukarno, the beautiful, estranged wife of the former Indonesian President, she met Warren at a party in Paris given by Mia and Louis Feraud, the designers. According to a guest at the party, Mme Sukarno did indeed appear smitten with Warren: "She did everything to attract him and she certainly looked gorgeous ...

practically exploding out of a low dress—no man could have ignored her. She made a spectacular exit, wearing a floor-length brocaded cape and carrying a long bamboo pole with a lighted candle on the end—don't ask me why. But Warren didn't leave with her. I don't know if he ever saw her again, but if he did, he isn't going to say so."

Warren in bed is said to be living proof of the old adage that practice makes perfect. In fact, it's been reputed that he's practiced his way to absolute perfection. But how does he get the girls there in the first place? Faye Dunaway, one of those who did *not* becomes involved with him, possibly because she was too much in love with someone else at the time she and Warren played *Bonnie and Clyde*, has been quoted as saying that the secret of Warren's appeal is his "totally unconventional approach to women. It's a direct approach. He plays it for shock. He doesn't waste time on amenities."

Faye's assessment tallies with a report of a photographer who told me, "I've seen him go up to strange girls and say, 'I'm Warren Beatty. How would you like to sleep with me?'" I repeated the anecdote to Warren and he laughed. "For Christ's sake, it's the old joke," he said. "You know the one: a guy goes up to girls and says, 'How would you like to go to bed with me?' and a friend asks him, 'Don't you get your face slapped a lot?' and the guy says, 'Yes, but you'd be surprised how often I make out.' "

"You mean you *don't* operate that way?" I asked.

"Don't be silly," he said.

Although personally I don't dig the Beatty kind of looks—too boyish, the type of adolescent male face you see everywhere—I can understand why most women would think him devastatingly handsome. He's tall—six one—has a good build, and quizzical, deep-set, blue-green eyes under shaggy eyebrows, a dimpled chin, and a sensual mouth with full lower lip. The habit of narrowing his eyes and baring his bottom teeth I guess is sexy, and he has a really warm, dazzling smile, although he doesn't use it often. Bob Benton, who along with Dave Newman, wrote the screenplay of *Bonnie and Clyde*, told me that girls fall apart when they see Warren on the street: "He has this fantastic thing with women. If he looks at them and smiles, they collapse, sometimes in tears. They're overcome."

Once or twice I caught an inkling of how Warren's appeal works. We had an argument that grew out of a previous interview, and one day I stormed into his suite at New York's Delmonico's Hotel, huffily saying what I thought of him. He was striding up and down the room and suddenly he *yelled* at me: "Will you sit down and shut up and listen to what I have to say?" I sat down and shut up and listened. "Hmmm," I thought. "This kid has more to him than I'd given him credit for." I hadn't expected his reaction to be so honest and direct and *human*. He wasn't a movie star intent on his image, spraying push-button charm at the interviewer. He didn't try to fob me off with evasive tact. Instead, he met the issue—the source of our disagreement—head-on. Among the many plastic narcissists of the film world, Warren's real-life masculinity must provide an often riveting contrast.

The first interview I ever had with him took place in his penthouse suite atop Los Angeles's Beverly Wilshire. He likes living in hotels: "I have no cook, no maid, no butler, no valet, no secretary, no chauffer. Nobody else up here … just me. And I like it this way." The room was in disorder, with stacked books on the coffee table and piles of records spilling off the couch and chairs onto the floor. He keeps books stashed in all the hotels where he stays in different cities, and when he's in New York for more than two weeks, he gets Delmonico's to move their dining-room piano into his suite so he can play when he feels like it. He's certainly not acquisitive. He has only one car, a black Lincoln convertible. "My entire adjustment to cars is very square. I just like them to have soft seats and good engines and radios. I don't care for spritzing around." Nor does he have a big wardrobe, and he's not a collector of luxury gadgets or cultural status totems: "I have practically no possessions, but I have difficulty throwing anything away. I clip things from newspapers and magazines and save them, and then they pile up and I hate to throw them out."

Warren has been up until five in the morning and I'd woken him at eleven, but he was cheerful and friendly. He wore a clean white shirt with the top buttons undone, charcoal-gray slacks, a black cardigan, black loafers. Going to the phone, he ordered breakfast: grapefruit, yogurt, eggs, and toast. (No gourmet, Warren likes meals consisting of sandwiches and a bottle of ginger ale. He stays away from alcohol, and on those rare occasions when he lights a cigarette, he doesn't inhale and takes only a few puffs before he puts it out.)

Before breakfast arrived, Warren started asking me questions about *my* life, and I had a hard time getting him to talk about himself. This reversal of roles is a studied technique on his part by which would-be interviewers wind up telling him their own life histories, go away thinking what a great guy Beatty is, and then get home and look at their notes and realize they don't have anything. Warren distrusts all journalists and says he is fed up with being asked questions he considers silly or superficial or too personal. He once yawned in the face of a *Saturday Evening Post* writer and said, "I've given you too much of my time, much too much. You haven't asked me a single question about my ideas on acting ... or anything I consider important ... . All you're interested in is trivia."

I expected to dislike Warren Beatty this time because of my first impression during the interview with his friend at the Plaza, and also because his Hollywood press agent had said to me on the telephone, "This is the brightest guy you'll ever meet in *your* life!"— a remark which instantly fired my hostility. (Warren's associates have an unfortunate reluctance to let you discover his intelligence for yourself. A production man on *Bonnie and Clyde* told me, "What separates him from other actors is his *brain!*" and a friend Warren suggested I call in London kept repeating like a stuck record, "He's so bright ... Christ, this guy is bright.") Warren *is* bright, but he isn't *that* bright, and it doesn't help him any when others try to oversell him. On his own he can be immensely likable and appealing.

To his credit, he is disarmingly modest when you meet him. He doesn't boast or volunteer self-congratulatory items. In fact, he doesn't volunteer *any* information; you have to extract it. I experienced an example of this Beatty reticence when I saw him again a couple of weeks later in New York, knowing he had been invited to the White House by President and Mrs. Johnson—to a dinner in honor of Princess Irene of Greece. (I would never have learned about the invitation from *him*; his press agent had told me.) "I heard you're going to the dinner at the White House," I began.

"Who the hell told you that?" Warren was visibly annoyed.

"John did."

"Oh." Then silence.

"Well"—I asked—"how did it happen?"

"I'm invited to dinner, that's all. Is there anything wrong with going to dinner at the White House?"

"No, of course not. But it is one of those semiofficial cultural gatherings or it is just a social affair?"

"It's just a social affair."

"Do you know the Johnsons?"

"I can't say I *know* them. I've met them." That was all I could get out of him. (I didn't even learn the dinner was for Princess Irene until I read it in the papers.) But the point I want to make is that a few hours later, during lunch, he took several telephone calls from friends and not once did he mention the White House dinner. He just said he had to go to Washington and would be back the next day. I don't know anyone else who would have shown such restraint.

At the time of the Beverly Wilshire interview Warren had just finished shooting *Bonnie and Clyde* and no one had any idea of the smashing triumph it would be. In the seven years he had been in films he had made only seven pictures (*B&C* was the eighth) and turned down more roles than possibly any other actor in history. "I have a certain truculence about not doing things I don't think are right for me," he said. It is easy to understand how Warren's choosiness has annoyed the Hollywood Establishment—because, as Arthur Penn, who directed *B&C*, pointed out to me, "If people keep offering you fat parts and you keep turning them down, the implication is you think their taste is lousy."

Penn had also directed Warren some years before in *Mickey One*, a curious, fascinating, frustrating film (Warren calls it "a complicated, brave picture that failed") and Penn is characteristic of the people who do like Warren. (Lillian Hellman, who suffers gladly neither fools nor phonies, is another who admires him.) "I saw Warren in *The Roman Spring of Mrs. Stone*," Penn told me, "and took the script of *Mickey One* to him at Delmonico's. I thought him a very attractive young man—deeply confused, but attractive. He had a reputation for being uncooperative and difficult, but overall, it was a pleasant experience to work with him. I never found him lacking in a willingness to engage, and I think that an admirable trait. He has a strong native intelligence and a richly inventive mind. Oddly, his literary taste is exquisite—not from any broadly educated base, but from a visceral appreciation of good writing ... . He's not a frivolous person; he's profoundly responsible. I don't think anyone can question his integrity, and I would take his word on anything."

Warren was born March 30, 1937, in Richmond, Virginia, but he grew up in Arlington. His father, Ira O. Beaty (Warren added the extra "t" so the name would be pronounced "Batey" instead of "Beety"), used to be a teacher of educational psychology and philosophy (he's now in the real-estate business) and his mother taught acting and directed local amateur theater groups. In high school Warren played basketball and baseball and was star center on the football team. He was offered ten scholarships to as many colleges but turned them all down to go to Northwestern University's School of Speech. Quitting before the year was out, he went to New York in 1956, determined to be an actor. A cheap furnished room was his Manhattan home, and his job as sandhog on the construction of the Lincoln Tunnel paid the bills while Warren studied acting with Stella Adler. He auditioned for a *Kraft Theatre* television play and got the lead, the role of a young vagabond rebel. After that he did other TV plays and winter stock in New Jersey, picking up extra money and playing the piano in a New York bar and in what he calls "gin mills and dumps on Long Island."

Director Josh Logan and playwright William Inge saw Warren perform on television and gave him a screen test (on viewing the results Logan said, "this boy is the sexiest thing around"), which led to MGM's signing him for a film that was never made. Then, in November 1960, Warren opened on Broadway in Inge's play, *A Loss of Roses*—a short-lived flop, but Warren received unanimous critical praise and through Inge met Elia Kazan, who signed him to play the lead opposite Natalie Wood in *Splendor in the Grass*. The movie opened in 1961, and Warren's reviews were again spectacular; he was acclaimed as the successor to James Dean and Marlon Brando, and *Life* called him "the most exciting American male in movies."

He was then twenty-three-years old, had been a star in his first play, and was a star in his first movie—literally an overnight success in both. Further, Warren had risen to the top entirely on his own, as he had determined to do without any assistance from his older sister, Shirley MacLaine, who by then was an established actress. He has a stubborn inner probity, I feel, which makes him reject the easy way, the quick money, the professional shortcut—and this reliance on self has often been misinterpreted as arrogance by those less close to him.

That initial year in Hollywood Warren made two other films, and then turned down the first of many roles, which, as I mentioned before, alienated the moneymen around town and earned the actor a reputation as a bumptious young smarty-pants. Among the movies he rejected were *The Victors*, *West Side Story*, *Act One*, *The Carpetbaggers*, *Youngblood Hawke*, and *PT 109* (he was John F. Kennedy's choice to play in the film version of the President's written wartime experiences). When I asked him about turning down the JFK part, he told me, "Frankly, I get embarrassed when people say, 'Why didn't you do it?' I'd been saying no to so many pictures because I thought they were crap, and I hadn't worked for two years. It was getting almost ludicrous … I'd turned down two million dollars and hadn't made a cent. Then Jack Warner asked me if I would fly to Washington and meet with President Kennedy. I didn't think *109* would make a good picture and I felt if I read the script later and didn't like it, I couldn't say no to the part *after* I'd already met the President and discussed it with him. So I said I wouldn't fly to Washington. Someone in the office said, 'Why not fly the President to Hollywood?' He meant it as a joke, but a newspaper columnist printed the line and claimed *I* had said it. I was terribly upset. Later, when I did meet President Kennedy on another occasion, he was very funny about that." (Cliff Robertson was in the film, finally.)

While his career languished, Warren's private life flourished, and though he never talked about his love affairs, everyone else did. The general tone of commentary was an equal mixture of malice and envy, but Warren's girls were devoted and loyal, and remained so even after he left them. To this day, none of them will talk about him, not out of any feelings of hostility, but apparently because they respected and admired (as well as loved) him.

Warren is not your typical philanderer. Indeed, I would think his earnest, innate decency would lend any affair an aura of dignity which would be reassuring to the female ego. Women have left their husbands and lovers for him and, according to their friends, have never regretted it, although "transitory" is the qualifying Beatty adjective for romance. When Joan Collins was making a film in Europe, she flew back to America three times to see Warren, but during that period he switched to Natalie Wood, who was still married to Robert Wagner. Natalie followed Warren to Miami, where he was making *All Fall Down*, and everyone expected her to marry him after her divorce—but once again the lover moved on. When Warren was filming *Mickey One* in Chicago, Leslie Caron flew there every weekend to be with him, and when Leslie made a picture in Jamaica, Warren was on hand to keep her company off the set. Her husband, Peter Hall, then director of the Royal Shakespeare Company in England, divorced Leslie, naming Warren as correspondent, but again an expected marriage did not take place. When I asked Warren about his reluctance to take a wife, he said, "I don't know why it's anyone's business or why people should get so indignant. They say, 'He never marries the girls.' Well, it so happens none of the girls wanted to get married. As for myself, I have an ambivalent attitude toward marriage. I'm not against it, but I'm not especially for it."

A man who knows Warren fairly well said, "I've felt at times he's been somewhat envious of people like myself who are reasonably happily married. His inclinations are toward a home and roots, but his pattern of living out of a suitcase is heavily ingrained. Besides, Warren sees these god-awful examples of broken marriages everywhere among actors. He's extremely aware of what this business does to a man and wife. Then, too, he has a big ego—and he's aware of that also. I think he'll keep on his own style until he gets halfway satisfied with his professional achievements. Ever since *Bonnie and*

Clyde, his problem has been, 'How do I follow it?' I think if he hadn't made that picture, he would have married Julie [Christie]. They complement each other. They really admire each other, and the ego thing gets dispelled when they're together."

Warren started going with Julie in 1967, while she was making *Petulia* in San Francisco. ("When I met her," he told me, "I thought she had the most wonderful face!") According to reports, he was in town at the time visiting a Russian ballerina who was staying in California, while Julie was still in love with Don Bessant, the English painter with whom she had been living for several years and who had flown over from London (peripatetic people!) to see her. (I met Julie and Don four years ago in Spain, when they were on vacation in a small Costa Brava fishing village. "I cannot imagine not being in love with Don," she told me then. "I also can't imagine a time when I wouldn't be with him. But—forever? I don't honestly know. Forever is a long, long time." Indeed it is.) At first Julie did not appear interested in Warren, but the ballerina went on tour and Don returned to London—and Warren stayed in town. The next anyone knew, actor and actress were with each other in Mexico, and they've been together ever since—although no one is taking bets on permanence.

I saw Warren several times last year in Paris, where he was filming *The Only Game in Town* with Elizabeth Taylor, his first picture since *B&C*. I asked why he decided to accept that film after having turned down so many other good offers, and he said, "The people are extremely pleasant and I get weekends off." (An unusually flimsy answer for Warren!) *Only Game* is about a love affair between a compulsive gambler and a nightclub dancer in Las Vegas. Frank Sinatra was originally signed for the movie, but when Elizabeth had to postpone filming because of her hysterectomy, Sinatra had to keep other commitments and Warren agreed to replace him. His reason for taking the job may have been the realization that he couldn't wait forever for something spectacular with which to follow *B&C*, and that the longer he waited, the more difficult it might became to make a choice.

Warren still wants to produce, direct, and star in a film he has written and on which he has been working, off and on, for the last few years. "I was set to start filming in Prague," he told me, "and then came the Russian invasion. I'm now thinking of trying it in Russia and Yugoslavia. In the meantime, this is an agreeable job in Paris. Elizabeth is sympathetic, straightforward, and ethical. Working with her is one of the most pleasant associations I've had."

Julie was in Paris with Warren when I saw him, but he wouldn't let me talk to her. I heard that she made only a couple of visits to the film set—and had lunch in Warren's dressing room. The rest of the time that he was working, she amused herself by visiting antique shops and the Flea Market. "We seldom go to parties," Warren said. "No discotheques or nightclubs. We like good restaurants where we can sit and talk. Most of our time is spent alone. I'm studying Russian and French, and we're being very quiet."

The last time I saw Warren in Paris we met in the bar of the Hotel George V, where he and Julie were staying. He suggested we get something to eat and we tried four restaurants in the neighborhood, but they were either closed (it was Sunday) or not serving dinner because it was too early. We finally went back to the hotel bar, where Warren tried to order sandwiches. No luck—they wouldn't serve food in the bar—so again we got up and moved out to the lounge. The only reason to mention this little episode is to illustrate how good-natured and pleasant Warren was throughout. Contrary to what journalists have written, he *doesn't* throw his weight around or demand special attention. There is no movie star grandezza about him.

We spent a couple of hours together and Warren was willing to talk about anything except his personal life. He is seriously interested in politics and national affairs, civil rights, the student revolution, and the war against poverty. On all these issues his views are liberal and humane, reflecting an intelligent effort to keep informed. (When asked to do television appeals for VISTA—the domestic peace corps— he first visited Los Angeles's Black neighborhood of Watts, telling the VISTA people, "I'd be happy to help you, but I must learn about your program and see if I really believe what I'm saying about it. I'll be sort of a pain to you, because I have to make sure I really believe in what you're doing.") He knew and liked Bobby Kennedy, for whom he campaigned in California and Oregon, and after the assassination he traveled around the country making speeches in favor of gun-control legislation. Warren also attended the Democratic Convention in Chicago in 1968 and has firm opinions on various politicians (Carl Stokes, the Black mayor of Cleveland: "A terrific man ... charming, intelligent ... a serious, good man." Teddy Kennedy: "Here we're dealing with someone whose potential appeal is unlimited.")

Conversation with Warren is interesting and uninhibited—so long as you can stay off the subject of his personal life. Before I left him I asked him again why I couldn't see him with Julie. "Because it's a private relationship," he said. "Anyway, I've decided not to give any more interviews. I'm seeing you because I promised I would, but I'm not going to bring Julie into it. If she and I were making a movie together and I thought our being interviewed together would help the film, it might be different." (Since then, Warren has visited Russia in connection with filming his own script, and recently it was announced that he and Julie would star in the picture together, although when I saw him last, he thought she wouldn't be in it.)

One notable thing about Warren is that his triumph with *Bonnie and Clyde*—which enhanced his professional reputation and filled his coffers—doesn't seem to have changed him. He has *always* insisted on doing what he felt was right for him; the only difference is that now he can well afford such independence. He remains basically the same person—honorable, talented, and intransigent, but with a knack for arousing antagonism, chiefly in members of his own sex.

Postscript:

In her tasty 1978 memoir, *Whistling Girl*, Lawrenson writes:

"Contrary to the opinion of some, I do not do hatchet jobs. There are a lot of things I will not do for money. One of them is to betray my political principles and another is deliberately to write an inaccurate profile. I never got to an interview with a preconceived 'angle.' I let the story evolve from the interviews. I try to be fair. Some women journalists seem obsessed with their own importance and demand to be treated like queens. I've occasionally been treated like a doorstep salesman, but I would never dream of writing an unkind piece just for the sake of retaliation. Furthermore, if anyone asks me not to mention something, I don't mention it. Once an interview is over, I avoid even those persons I really liked and with whom I got along well. If I should see one of them on the street I would duck into a doorway.

"Another thing is that I get bored with an interview long before they do. If I force myself, I can come on strong but I can't sustain the effort. There comes a moment when I think, 'Oh, fuck it. How can I get away?' I never stay as long as I'm expected to. I was supposed to spend a week in Berlin for a profile of Michael Caine, but I left after three days, although I think that I probably liked him the best of anyone I've ever interviewed. He's exceptionally intelligent, well informed, perceptive, witty, kind, thoughtful, with no side, not a smidgen, of anything phony. He's also a fine actor. But I just can't stand hanging around movie sets. It's boring and exhausting."

And from her first, and equally appealing memoir, *Stranger at the Party*, Lawrenson writes:

"Many people probably think I've been a fool. I suppose it is true that I haven't 'made the most' of what talent and opportunities I've had. I certainly haven't contributed anything to the world, or made my mark, or lusted after fame and fortune. I could look back on mistakes, humiliations, failures, and writhe with embarrassment, but I don't. I consider that I have been a fortunate woman and have had a happy life, by and large. I can survive tragedy, not through self-delusion but through acceptance. I accept. I don't mean that I accept cruelty or hypocrisy or injustice. I accept whatever happens to *me*. What you lose on the swings you win on the roundabouts."

BRAD DARRACH

Brad Darrach (1921–1997) spent fifty years at Time Inc. when coffee tables across America sagged beneath the combined weight of its magazines along with the millions of words he wrote that defined not just his subjects but the art of capturing celebrities on slick paper. His march to legendary status began when he succeeded James Agee as *Time*'s film critic. Darrach spent years on the job establishing his mastery of beguiling first sentences, compressed anecdotes, word-play, and puns. Loosed on the world of show business, he charmed his way past Marilyn Monroe's defenses and convinced her to discuss her Dickensian childhood for a *Time* cover story. The only writer Elizabeth Taylor wanted at her side when she discussed her brain surgery for *Life* was Darrach. He crafted each piece with a jeweler's precision and rapier wit. Talk show host Dick Cavett "looked a little like a marshmallow lightly haired over" while miscast leading man Jack Webb "lips onto a horn, or a woman, with about as much feeling as other men show for a K ration." If there was ever a perfect subject for Darrach, it should have been Robert Mitchum, the forever cool Hollywood rebel, but *Life* turned the piece down—too racy, perhaps. So Darrach reworked it for the exuberantly gynecological *Penthouse*, then just three years old and starved for quality writing. Turned out, the piece was too racy for Mitchum. Want to bet which piece you turn to first in this book?—JS

THE LAST OF THE IRON-ASSED LONERS

Penthouse, 1972

Robert Mitchum slipped into his slate-gray shades and glared warily at Yale University. "A cat like me in a place like this," he muttered, "could get busted for mopery with intent to gawk." As he scowled back at the scowling gargoyles on the gothic turrets I took in the busted beak, the cuts around the eyes, and the ragged ditches underneath, the little fatty pockets forming in the jowls. It was a face out of an Eighth Avenue gym, but I liked it. There was power and humor in the blade-thin lips and skewering stare. And the star quality was still there. Through every movement oozed the heavy sensuality that for more than thirty years had made Mitchum a glamor-charged image of the elemental male.

Turning to gape, a passing coed spilled her books on the sidewalk. Mitchum brightened. At fifty-three, he dug the compliment. He also savored the invitation to give a seminar on the subject of himself at a major university. In mock-professorial manner he announced to the welcoming committee of the Yale Law School Film Society: "Gentlemen, shall we get it on?" And swelling his formidable chest he went rolling across campus in the languid powerful glide that is known to the trade as the Mitchum ramble.

In the lecture hall he rambled down to the dais and then turned to face an audience of students and professors that filled every chair and most of the aisle space in a 300-seat auditorium. "I have been asked," he presently announced in a vigorous bass voice, "what it's like to be a personage of the cinema." He gave his audience a slow ironic glare. "It's like being trampled to death by geese."

Five years ago Robert Mitchum was an aging screen lover with a slumped career and an unbankable reputation for what he calls "the simple virtues"—boozing, wenching, and sampling the hemp. Today his assets are worth $5 million and his career is a pleasantly expanding exception in an era when Hollywood's giants have collapsed like overinflated latex dinosaurs at the end of a parade. With a boost from *Ryan's Daughter*, Mitchum remains one of the few superstars who can command the super-salary of the '60s and a crack at the best roles in his age bracket. "After twenty years of playing a comic strip character called Superstud," says director David Lean, "Mitchum at last is being recognized as the gifted actor he has always been. He is a master of stillness. Other actors act. Mitchum is. He has true delicacy and expressiveness but his forte is his indelible identity. Simply by being there, Mitchum can make almost any other actor look like a hole in the screen."

Most of Mitchum's fans are over thirty, but in no small part he owes his new career to a younger generation of moviegoers. To the kids he is a "brother" who grew up poor on the fringes of Harlem and got leaned on by The Man; a "heavy dude" who got busted for cannabis way back in 1950; a rugged individual who time and again has risked his career by refusing to trim in the presence of power. To the campus crowd, from Yale to Fresno State he is the scruffy icon of the Mitchum cult.

No man more merrily relishes the side dishes of stardom—the money, the girls, the roar of the crowd, the company of the great. No man more keenly longs to give the best that is in him and have it appreciated. Yet Mitchum has responded to the people who are calling him the Bogie of the '70s as he has always responded to adulation: with skeptical aloofness and a snake-quick ironic wit that unerringly fangs a flatterer. Alert and elusive, he shies from close contact and guards carefully against revealing any need or tenderness that the geese could trample.

"Zilch," he says with his trademark sneer, "is what this latest frammis means to me. I got half the bread in North America and I need success like I need an extra keester. Why don't the kids just do their thing and stop tryin' to recharge my wig. Somebody always wants to own ya, y'know? No way. I'm the last of the iron-assed loners."

I was in a Philadelphia TV studio when I had my first glimpse of Mitchum in action. He knew I was there and couldn't resist doing his own Mitchum imitation—in this instance a takeoff on Superstud. I was watching through the glass window of the studio and all around me forty cute little things stood giggling and wriggling. "Ooooo!" a girl in her early twenties gasped in tones of adoration, "doesn't he look *funky!*" In the center of the studio Mitchum lounged alone, and I had to agree that funky was the word. He was wearing clay-gray slacks crisscrossed with wrinkles behind the knees, and a London-tailored dark-blue sports jacket that gaped at the collar and shirt like a bargain off the rack at Robert Hall's. The hair was stringy, the skin as gray as an aging undershirt, yet the figure was commanding. Mitchum is only moderately tall, just a cowlick over six feet, but his waist is narrow, his shoulders wide, his legs lean and elegantly bowed in the calf, like Flash Gordon's. And when he turned to look at the girls on the other side of the glass he moved his head with slow majesty and flashed his eyes like an old lion sighting a flock of tempting impala. Then he swelled up his chest and bore down upon the ladies in the inevitable feline glide. Enveloped in squeals, he signed a dozen autographs while carefully inspecting the game. Then without a word he reached out to the young woman who had said "ooooo" and, grasping her firmly by the back of the neck, steered her through the crowd and out to his limousine. As he passed me, looking like a small boy who had just stolen a piece of candy, he let one eyelid droop about a third of the way toward a wink.

"You gotta have three legs and two heads to keep up with that cat," a publicity man warned me on the way back to the hotel. Mitchum was making the East Coast loop of a promotion tour and at times he was blue with exhaustion but the show never stopped. That night in his room he loosed the opening gust of the roughest three-day word-storm I ever weathered, beginning on a note of graceful self-deprecation.

"Me? I'm just a movie actress," he said with a carefully erased smile. "They want a freak, they got a freak ... If Lassie can be a star, it can't be very difficult, can it?" I knew he was a man of surprising talents, but when I tried to discuss them I got nowhere. I asked about his eloquent romantic poetry. "Mother liked it." About his children's stories. "Kids are easy to fool, aren't they?" About his hit songs (friends say he did the first drafts of *Can't Get Started with You* and *Praise the Lord and Pass the Ammunition)* and the oratorio Orson Welles produced "Puerile aberrations." He is also a secret chef with the gift of sauces, and a self-taught "street intellectual" who can give you back from memory pages of Dryden and whole acts of Shakespeare, but these subjects were also off-limits. Some of the damnedest subjects were substituted.

Gathering afflatus, Mitchum held oral concert for the next six hours. Of all the great gabbers I have heard—W. H. Auden, Buckminster Fuller, James Agee, Brendan Behan, Dylan Thomas. Alwyn Lee—Mitchum has the most richly conglomerate idiom. English on his tongue becomes a Joycean bedlam of broken Yiddish ("*eppis*," "*stumer*"), Swinburnian alexandrines ("sculptured in awareness with immediate clarity"), pusher Spanish ("mojo," "ganja"), Tin Pan Alley talk ("begorra music"), cockney ("minge"), Harlemese ("that mother had muscles in his hair"), a species of Sydney slang called Strine ("'e pulled a furphy"), and pert tags from Pope and Dr. Johnson along with some snatches of Norse. I lost him at the first turn of phrase, and conversation collapsed into harangue. I remember he did three or four Irish accents, eight or ten English, a dozen or so from the US South. After that came peculiar lore (the Sasquatch of the Sierra Nevada, he said, are a race of abominable snowmen eight feet tall and covered with long brown hair) and some saucy anecdotes. By 2 a.m., well beyond amazement, I was ready to tie my smile to my sideburns.

Next morning Mitchum paused for a press conference. Asked how he got his exercise, he snapped: "I run around and witness the intolerable follies of my times." Then he was off to the horse races at Laurel, Maryland, where he chatted wittily with the British Ambassador, made stable talk with Willie Shoemaker and some passing Mellons and signed several hundred autographs with exemplary patience. ("I think you're wonderful, Mr. Lancaster," a little old lady told him; "Thank you very much," Mitchum gently replied.)

The strain of being a good boy told on him, though, and Mitchum took advantage of a break in his tour to "blow the seat out of these balbriggans." After hoisting quite a few in an elegant restaurant, he confronted a Montrachet '59 and announced: "I'm happy to say I have no dry vices." With that he was off on a string of salty stories related with skill and mordant relish—among them a droll tale about how Trevor Howard once substituted the urine sample of a famous actress for his own and was duly informed that he was pregnant. As the evening wore on and the bars closed down. Mitchum became indignant. "Well, if you won't give me a drink," he declared gravely to a young waiter at a posh hotel, "you might at least give me a kiss!" Grinning uneasily, the waiter backed off, but Mitchum caught up to buss him resoundingly on the lips.

It was part of an act we both knew was wearing a bit thin. I wondered when he would stop being Mitchum and start being himself. There was a big man in there somewhere and I wanted to meet him. But I couldn't get under his jab-jab-jabber.

Once, when we were alone, I ventured to suggest that he was developing a slight paunch. He strolled toward me sleepily. "Tap that gut," he said. I tapped his diaphragm. It was as hard as a tree. Another time, about 2 a.m. in a hotel room, I wondered out loud if he was really as fierce as he sometimes sounded. His eyes slitted and his teeth gleamed in a sinister smile. "If I ain't a bear," he said softly, "I'm a rough pole on a tall hill on the way to it." Then all at once his eyes blazed, his voice rattled. *Double wild! Hang or die! Born that way!*" His tone fell to a purr. "Like to play rough? Right on, Jack! Take yer best shot. But when you fuck with the ape, be ready to go the route. *Because he might just come unglued.*" He was roaring again, his face bulging with fury less than two feet from mine. "*He might just tear yer eye out and hand it to ya! Rip a finger off and bring ya to attention!*"

If I'd had the nerve I'd have hollered: "Print it!" But I was afraid he might get carried away by his performance and actually hit me. Also, curiously, I didn't want to hurt his feelings. There was something almost flirtatious about Mitchum's aggressive displays. I sensed they were meant to make me admire him, even to like him. Ferocity concealed an offer of affection.

It wasn't until I'd been with him day and night for almost a week that Mitchum dropped his guard a little. "On the whole," he mused. "I'm hopeful about today's kids, though God knows they're a Breughel of freakers. I don't mean the drug thing. That's just the latest Hula-Hoop and it'll go away. I like their adventurousness and up to a point I like their politics. I resent any system that tabulates men. A terrorist is always preferable to a bureaucrat. And I tend to agree that the world has too long been ruled by a conspiracy of constipated grandfathers and a tax structure that ties us all to the trellis of competitive materialism ... But I wish the young'uns'd pay more attention to the reality and less to the ritual of resistance. I mean they come on with cardboard sunglasses, a knapsack full of raisins and walnuts and a Molotov cocktail degree in sociology and really think they can solve the world's problems. It's a head ramble ... I'm a revolutionary conservative, a Republican radical, and these days I feel like a lone maggot in a collapsing cheese."

The cheese collapsed around Mitchum quite early in his life. His father, half Scottish-Irish and half Blackfoot Indian, died in a railroad accident before Robert was two years old. His mother moved the family from Bridgeport, Connecticut, to her father's farm on the eastern shore of Maryland. Her father, Gustavus Adolphus Gundersen, was a 295 lb. Norwegian-born sea captain who, according to Mitchum, could back-lift a wagon loaded with 4,000 pounds of hay. Gus was a sadist. He hated cats, and once when he came home from a voyage to find six kittens in the kitchen he made all the children (Robert among them) watch while one by one he brained their little pets with a ballpeen hammer. The women, by contrast, were overprotective. Mitchum still has nightmares about being smothered in powdered bosoms.

All this trauma produced a child prodigy. At five, put up to it by his gifted mother, he wrote some precocious verse that was published in newspapers and children's magazines (*A rod, a reel, a quiet mood;/a boy, a book and solitude*). But by this time Mitchum and his family had moved to a part of Manhattan just south of Harlem where five-year-old poets were not notably appreciated. One day a boy somewhat larger than Mitchum washed his face with horse apples. The grandson of Gundersen went berserk and knocked his attacker cold.

The victory established the Mitchum style. He built up his skills as a street kid—cracking vending machines for cigarette money, selling candy apples in the local bordello. At fourteen, he quit school forever and rode the rods to California and back. On the way he was introduced to marijuana, peyote, and the roughhouse tactics of the railroad police. On a later junket, nabbed for vagrancy in Georgia, he was handed six months on the chain gang but soon escaped.

At twenty-one, after a two-year career as a boxer that concluded when his left eye was temporarily knocked out of his head, Mitchum married his childhood sweetheart and they arrived in California with a cardboard suitcase and one dollar and fourteen cents. During the next eighteen months, while he and his bride inhabited a slightly remodeled chicken coop in West Hollywood, Mitchum scrounged along as a comedy writer, musical arranger, and lyricist. With a baby due, he got a war job at Lockheed Aircraft but hated it so much he went stone blind. The day he quit his sight came back.

Remembering his success in amateur theatricals a couple of years earlier, Mitchum went to see an agent and wound up on the posse in a Hopalong Cassidy movie. Eight pictures later a director named Bill Wellman (*The Oxbow Incident*) cast him as Lieutenant Walker in *The Story of G.I. Joe*. With that movie Mitchum was established among the best of a new breed of Hollywood stars, the hardjaws who came up during World War II to replace the pretty pusses (Robert Taylor, Tyrone Power) of the late Depression years.

Mitchum at first was a docile celebrity. He was so pleased to be famous he didn't at all mind being typecast as a handsome brute. But when he mildly requested a role in which he could show his acting talent, the studio head laughed in his face. It was the wrong way to handle Mitchum. All his life he had heard that he was "common." Now he was being told that he was stupid. Hurt and angry, he turned the insult back in his own ironic way. Tough they wanted him? Tough he would be. For a love scene with Greer Garson, who seemed to him too sniffety, Mitchum primed his breath with Bermuda onions. To express his displeasure with David Selznick, a producer who happened to own half his contract, Mitchum slouched into his office and, standing on an expensive white rug that was Selznick's pride and joy, urinated.

With directors, Mitchum could be really brutal. "I have a terrible temper," one director told him at the start of a picture. "When I lose it I shout at actors. But don't let it worry you. Next day I've forgotten all about it." Mitchum said he understood. "I have a temper too. When a director shouts at me, I flatten him. But don't let it worry you. Next day I've forgotten all about it." The director did not lose his temper. Another, who did, had a remarkable experience. Mitchum tied his shoelaces together and hung him upside down from a lamppost.

And that was mild. "Mitchum is one of the great dirty fighters of our time," says a friend who once boxed professionally. "In a free-for-all, no one stands a chance against him. Breaks your fingers, thumbs your eyes out. And he can get heavy wood on you with either hand. He's got the reflexes of a leopard—and the blood lust." He has whipped four men at a time, and once in a Colorado bar he took out with one punch a professional fighter who later went three rounds with Marciano. Mitchum fights less frequently nowadays. He considers it a miracle he has never killed a man, and he hopes to keep the miracle intact. "The thing I'm most afraid of in this world," he told me one night, "is me."

What is it that makes Mitchum so angry? Usually the same thing. "I tell 'em but they won't listen. Gotta be their way—keep crowdin' in. But can't two people be in the same place. Can't nobody be me but me. Stand back, Jack. No? *Whap!*" I wondered who had first tried to crowd Mitchum out of his existence and I remembered Gus Gundersen. Would Mitchum ever finally prove he was tougher than that wild Skowegian?

In the early days Mitchum was sometimes rough with women too—"had to be, man." Dozens, often 100 girls, waited at the studio gate when he was on the lot, and on location he had to enlist two bodyguards to fight them off. Men were known to offer him their wives, and on one occasion a woman tried to force him into bed at gunpoint. Mitchum escaped through a bathroom window.

It was a woman problem, according to his close friends, that almost wrecked Mitchum's career. They say that a studio executive, enraged because his girl had been with Mitchum, tipped the narcotics squad that the actor was smoking marijuana at a house in Laurel Canyon. Mitchum did sixty days on the work farm and so admirably kept his cool ("It was just like Palm Springs," he explained, "without the riffraff") that he came out of the mess the darling of the downtrodden and a bigger star than ever. But the episode cemented his disgust with Hollywood ("I've met nicer people on freight trains") and considerably shortened his fuse.

Of all the women in Mitchum's life, only three are now important. To know Mitchum you have to know his wife of thirty years, his nineteen-year-old daughter and his secretary-manager. I saw his wife, Dorothy, briefly in Philadelphia. She arrived in Mitchum's suite about 9 p.m., a bit flustered by planes and taxis, a tall, slender woman, fiftyish, expensively dressed, pretty in a clear Nordic way. Mitchum greeted her with a smile that seemed to me somewhat strained and even hostile; she hurried into the next room. I was embarrassed for her, and later sympathetic when she talked about her loneliness. Then at the end of the tour, I saw her at home, a comfortable but unassuming four-bedroom California colonial in suburban Bel Air, and realized I had been too quick to commiserate. When Mitchum growls, more often than not she hisses. "When he goes too far," says a friend, "she packs his bags and puts them outside the front door. After one day in a hotel, he is destroyed. Mitchum is a man who needs his home, his tribe." He also needs Dorothy, though he hates to admit it. He needs her strength, her continuity. "He needs a full-time woman who always puts him first," says Dorothy. "I do." Mitchum is grateful for what she does, but it seems hard for him to say so.

It is almost as difficult for Mitchum to show his daughter, Trina, how he feels about her. He obviously feels deeply—what father wouldn't? She is a heart-stopper with long glossy hair, a subtle tone of red, and enormous liquid eyes that change color with the light like watered silk. Whenever Mitchum comes into the house, he asks the same casual question: "Treen around?" When she is in the room his face brightens. But they seldom exchange two sentences at a time.

"When I was little," says Trina, "I was I so scared of him I couldn't speak when he was there. Now I understand him and I love him, but it's still hard to talk about serious things." Yet Trina's reentry after three years in a psychedelic orbit is mostly Mitchum's doing. When she came to tell him about a flipped-out marriage she was going to make, he calmly let her talk herself into tears and then said: "If anything hurt me that bad, I'd walk away from it." Trina is now living at home and taking film classes at UCLA. "I've been on some weird trips," she says, "but no way would I blow it. I have too much respect for them both."

Mitchum in some ways is closest to the third important woman in his life, Reva Fredrick, the wife of a high-ranking film executive named Max Youngstein. Reva is Mitchum's secretary, business manager, agent, artistic adviser, psychiatrist, bartender, chauffeur, shopping service, friend. Mitchum calls her "Spider Lady" and never makes a business deal she hasn't vetted or a movie she hasn't approved. She knows all his faults and couldn't care less. "Don't let the noise fool you," she once told me. "He's double kind."

Mitchum's kindness often takes the form of generosity. On impulse he gives sports coats, record players, cameras, money to his friends. I'm told he once gave a new car to a stranger he met in a bar. And, year in, year out, he supports six relatives outright and contributes to the support of six others. But Chris, the second of his three children, a twenty-seven-year-old actor who has appeared in the last three John Wayne movies, refuses to accept his father's bounty. "It's because his offers aren't just offers," Chris told me. "They're tests. If you accept, he figures you don't care about him—just his money. I care about him and I care about myself so I'll never take his money." Reva provides a larger view. "Giving money is sometimes a substitute for giving himself, which is too painful. Rawb feels love, sometimes feels it very strongly, but doesn't dare to risk expressing it."

Several people told me that in Gus Gundersen's family, people who expressed love were considered weak, and it wasn't safe to be weak with Gus around.

The Mitchum clan gathered one day when I was there. Trina came down the spiral stairs at the center of the house. She wore clinging leather slacks and in her hands she was twirling a tiny boa constrictor. "Hey!" she said to no one in particular.

Mitchum was sprawled in a big low bed-like easy chair in the family room, expounding to Chris's wife, Cindy. Chris was in Mexico with John Wayne but Cindy had brought the two children down from their split-level shack in Topanga Canyon. She was a small, slender, quietly pretty young woman with intelligent eyes, but she looked guarded now. Her children—Carrie, six, and Robin, four—were screaming a lot, and Mitchum occasionally shot them a look loaded with shrapnel.

The noise got worse after Jim and Wende came in with their contribution—Tiffany, seven, and Josh, three. Jim is even bigger than his father but looks so much like him that people stare when he walks down the street. He's thirty, has also appeared in movies, and seems determined to make it as big as his father did—but on his own terms, which are radical and unbarbered. Meanwhile, father is footing many of the bills. Wende is small, dark, vivid: an actress and, I'm told, a good one. Mitchum said hello but didn't get up. Josh toddled over and grabbed his grandfather's thumb. Mitchum smiled benignly—Josh is his favorite. "Only kid his age I ever saw," he says wonderingly, "that's got developed triceps."

Once the clan had gathered, two bottles of champagne were drained in five minutes. Somebody put a Crosby, Stills, Nash, and Young album on the record player and the men began talking horses. Cindy and Trina went on about Trina's film class. Over at the bar, Wende was telling Dorothy that she and Jim and the kids were all going up to Taos soon to visit Dennis Hopper.

"You're wrong, Jim!" Mitchum suddenly was bellowing. "You put a bottom like her under that cold-jawed mother, you'll get a short stroker couldn't run to the mailbox and back!" He was off on a tirade about horse breeding that soon had Jim glassy-eyed and then fighting back with a tirade of his own. At the height of it little Robin arrived in the center of the room and began to screech uncontrollably. Mitchum crossed the room, put his mouth an inch from the child's ear and shouted: "SHUT UP!"

Robin shut up. So did everybody else. Cindy went white but said nothing. Six more bottles of champagne arrived. Corks popped rapidly. Talk got very loud. Mitchum sat sullen, realizing he had gone too far. Jim, getting stoned, cornered his mother behind the bar and all but asked her directly to buy him a $50,000 house he'd just seen. "Jim," said Dorothy, getting smashed, "stop suckling!" Jim flared up and reminded his mother of the time his father had promised to star him in a movie and at the last minute had let him down. "Now hold on, Jim!" Mitchum bellowed across the room. "No, *you* hold on!" Jim bellowed back. Wende made frantic little signals. Cindy gathered up her kids and left. I headed for the kitchen. For the next ten minutes it sounded like a barroom brawl in a Mitchum movie—the men roaring, the women screaming. I heard Wende shriek: *"No, Jim. no!"*

And then suddenly they were all in the kitchen, cheeks flushed and eyes bright, smiling broadly. "Now make up!" said Dorothy. The men grabbed each other and hugged heartily. The women hugged. Jim and family left. "Jesus!" said Mitchum, his eyes flashing with pride, "that Jim's a *wild* mother! I mean, when he picked up that bottle he was ready to go the route!"

Next day Dorothy told me that five minutes after I had left she and Mitchum had started fighting again. At 1 a.m., Mitchum had packed a bag, jumped in the Chrysler, and driven away.

I never had a chance to watch Mitchum make a picture, but while he was "scarin' up the backblocks," as he later put it, I had two days to talk with actors and directors who had worked with him. In recent years, they agreed, his professional manners have been impeccable. He never hogs the camera, never plays the star. He admits to facility—he regularly commits a page of dialogue to memory in one reading, and in two readings actually learned a fifty-word speech in Swahili—but to nothing more. "I don't act. I just stand there and let 'em talk to me." But that's just it, says Deborah Kerr. "He's the best reactor in the business. He listens to every line, as if hearing it for the first time, and alters his response according to your reading. It throws your lines right out of your head, it's so real."

Another quality of Mitchum's work that many professionals mention and few critics have noticed is his humor. "He is a master of the put-on," one director told me, "but it's such a subtle put-on that the public doesn't get it. All these years he's been laughing at the masculine ideal of middle America. It's been a very lonely joke."

About thirty-six hours after he had left his Bel Air home, Mitchum turned up at his ranch in the country. When I met him there, I didn't ask where he had been. Usually when he wants to get lost, he just takes his front teeth out and puts up at a motel. Nobody recognizes him. "It gives me the temporary illusion that I'm real," he says.

The Mitchum ranch is a small spread, about seventy-five acres, all good bottomland crosshatched with seven-foot fences and well grassed-over. There is a five-room bungalow for the trainer, a four-stall stable and a carousel for training the colts. Mitchum keeps thirty or thirty-five of the best quarter horses on this continent there.

When I arrived, Mitchum and his trainer, Pete Woods, were watching the exercise boy breeze a yearling mare around the oval. Mitchum was at ease. His eyes were bright and his skin, freshened by the morning chill, had a healthy flush for the first time since I'd known him.

With squirely pride he showed me his fiery little horses. Gold, orange, black, they were loping poems. Mitchum races them, but his passion is improving the breed. As we strolled among the warm animals, he recited the breeding of every horse for three, four, five generations back, and most of the bloodline's trace to Man O'War, Equipoise, Nasrullah, or a sire almost equally illustrious.

Back at Mitchum's motel room he took out a pipe no bigger than his thumb and as he smoked it, spoke his mind.

"I've dirtied my ticket some over the years, but I do respect those who battle for their innocence. Men of character and destination. If it's a matter of belief and you sell out for forty dollars or fourteen million you're a fink. A man who doesn't have something to die for doesn't have anything to live for. The Masai understand this. Before he can be a warrior, every Masai boy must kill his lion." He paused and puffed. "In our world, the moral equivalent of the lion is a man's work," he said, and was silent awhile. I sensed that for the first time he was trying to tell me something essential about himself.

"Bogart once laid it on me," he went on, "that a man who really wanted to be a man would always feel ashamed to be just an actor, and I guess he was right. Literature was my lick, but instead of writing novels. I've lived them. And there are times," he added with an ironic tilt of the head, "when I suspect I have run out of ink."

We both knew what he was saying—that he had never killed his lion and now he was getting old.

"Is it really so," he asked, "that the supreme value in a man is his continued existence?" Through the smoke he smiled a gently sardonic smile. "I don't know what God is, but then I don't know what else there is. We seem to have some sense of divinity, an impulse to refine life to a crystalline substance. Smoke it, shoot it, stick it in yer eye. Some way or other, make a connection. I don't sleep so good, and the nights are pretty long. You wonder about these things, y'know?" He drew deep on his pipe. Our eyes met. For an instant his look was clear and childlike; then all at once it was ironical again. "What I need," he said, "is a black void. Black voids aren't too easy to come by these days. But someday I'll find one."

In the bar and grill where we went for dinner there was a short, fat, loud woman who looked like Betty Boop. Earlier in the day she had come cantering onto the Mitchum place on a hairy little quarter horse with an Arab head, and for the next half hour she had jabbered movie-magazines and flirted like rural sin. Mitchum looked bored then and he looked bored now. But all that pink flab covered with black net was no common eyesore, and I suspect it was Mitchum's fine sense of the absurd that made him invite her to eat with us. After five minutes he was sorry. She took over the conversation and pawed him as though she owned him—two things you just don't do with Mitchum. He kidded her along for a while but when she started to analyze him astrologically he gave out and, excusing himself, went to sit with some strangers at a nearby table. There was another fat woman there and for the next three hours she exclaimed over and over in a high silly voice: "Oh, I just can't believe it! I'm *really* having a drink with Robert Mitchum!"

It just wasn't his night. He got mildly smashed and about 1 a.m. we went back to the motel. "Oh, no!" Mitchum groaned. Betty Boop was there. When he opened the door to his room she ran in. He rolled his eyes but I knew he wouldn't kick her out. For one thing, he couldn't bring himself to hurt her feelings—he could knock her teeth out but he couldn't embarrass her. For another, anything was better than being alone.

"Hi diddle-de-dee. An actor's life for me," he said. And went in.

Postscript:

"Watching Brad Darrach write a story was exhausting," remembered his friend, and editor at *Life* magazine, Jay Lovinger. "First he would take voluminous notes on yellow lined notepads, writing in an elegant, precise hand that was so compact it looked as if he were compiling an endless EKG. Next he would study the notes, committing to memory everything of meaning in them before putting them aside to think about what he wanted the story to say. Sometimes he would do this for three or four days. Finally, when all around him were losing hope, Brad would begin to write, never going on to the next sentence until the previous one was, to his mind, perfected.

"This lapidary approach to writing, which has largely disappeared from the world, had three effects. The first, which never concerned Brad in the slightest, was to drive editors—including this one—temporarily insane. The second was to delight readers. A third, almost incidental effect, was to inspire several generations of magazine writers at Time Inc. During his fifty years of writing for *Time*, *People*, and *Life*, Brad helped create and refine the Time Inc. writing style—heavy on knockout opening lines, compressed anecdotes, wordplay, puns. In the process, he probably committed more words to slick paper than any Time Inc. writer who ever lived. In Brad's hands, words could do almost anything—from thrill to kill to break your heart.

"But as sharp as his brain was, he more often followed his heart, which went out to almost anyone in need … . Generous is the right word for Brad. He never seemed to lose any part of his ego by offering brilliant help to others, and he never wanted recognition for it. He didn't have to be credited. It was always a free gift."

A year after the *Penthouse* article appeared, Grover Lewis profiled Mitchum in *Rolling Stone*. Here's Mitchum's daughter Trina, then 20-years-old:

"Dad has kind of an aversion to reporters these days," she reflects, expelling a long blue spume of mingled smoke and cold-breath. "Mainly, that's because of a single guy, a writer named Brad Darrach. Darrach trailed Dad around for months in order to do a piece about him for *Life*. And Dad treated him like a friend—the whole family did. Well, for one reason or another, *Life* wouldn't take the piece, and Darrach rewrote it for *Penthouse*, and it turned into something else, if you understand what I'm saying. *Penthouse* wanted stuff that *Life* wouldn't have ever printed. You know—about Mom and Dad squabbling, and Dad's various women, and Dad fighting with my brothers, Christopher and Jimmy, and me being some kind of acid crawlback or something like that. Well, sure, I went through that routine a little bit, I guess. Just as much as anybody my age growing up in California and being exposed to those things. But not very heavily, you know.

"The thing is, it was all so *private*. It hurt Dad, and made him mad too. It did all of us. Oh, it was a fairly accurate story, sure, but I don't think it was a fair story. I just don't believe in invading people's privacy to the point where you expose their family fights and stuff like that. I think, personally, if you can't say something good about somebody, there's no point in writing at all."

O'CONNELL DRISCOLL

"O'Connell Driscoll," (1951-) said Stevie Wonder, decades after Driscoll profiled him in *Rolling Stone*, "that's a name that's hard to forget. That boy still drinking ginger ale?" Between 1974 and 1985, Driscoll wrote seven exquisite celebrity profiles—five for *Playboy*, two for *Rolling Stone*—that feature a kind of penetration we rarely see anymore, in this era of limited access. Driscoll's refined, fly on-the-wall style, reminiscent of Lillian Ross and Gay Talese at their best, was already evident in his first profile, "Jerry Lewis, Birthday Boy," which appeared in the twentieth anniversary issue of *Playboy* alongside such literary heavyweights as John Updike and Vladimir Nabokov. That he was in fact a mere twenty-one-year-old senior at the University of Southern California at the time makes it a rare, almost freakish debut, the *Citizen Kane* of celebrity profiles, capturing Lewis in the act of editing his famously misbegotten—and never released—tragicomedy about the Holocaust, *The Day the Clown Cried*.

"I was living my dream," Driscoll says. "Working for *Playboy*. I was on the airplane with Jerry. Everything just fell into place for me because there was material galore there. Nothing ever worked out like that ever again." Driscoll got an agent and wrote six more stellar magazine profiles; signed a contract to a write a novel that he never finished; and messed around Hollywood for a while, polishing scripts and working on screenplays that went unproduced. Then, abruptly, he moved to Santa Barbara, took a job in management with Nordstrom, and said goodbye to the writer's life. He left behind a string of gems, none more arresting than the first, which captures, with unsentimental clarity and a master's eye for detail, the midlife crisis of a fading superstar. —AB

JERRY LEWIS, BIRTHDAY BOY

Playboy, 1974

"**A**nd then they say, 'Now, ladies and gentlemen, here's the star of our show,' and we both come out and go for the microphone, and you grab it and start right in, 'Good evening, folks, it's so great to be here in Miami,' and I say, 'Wait a minute, what are you doing out here? I'm supposed to be on first, I'm supposed to open the show,' and you say, 'No, they told me *I* was supposed to open the show,' and we go back and forth like that until you say—no, *I* say—'Look, didn't you see the sign when you came up to the hotel? Didn't you see that name up there with all the neon lights? Well, that's *me*.' And then you look and take a beat and say, 'Oh, you must be Air Conditioning.' "

Milton Berle stopped to light his cigar. "You have to be sure to take that beat, Jerry," he said. "Then you say, 'Oh, you must be Air Conditioning.' "

Jerry Lewis looked at Berle but said nothing. He stood in his narrow dressing room backstage at the Deauville Hotel, dressed in a tuxedo, holding a plastic cup of white wine in one hand and a cigarette in the other. He took a sip of the wine.

"So then I'll say, 'Look, Jerry, why should you be on first?' And you say, 'Well, you heard me last night,' and I say, 'Yeah, you were very funny,' and you say, 'Funny? Are you kidding—you could hear them laughing across the street.' I say, 'Oh, really? What was playing over there?' "

Berle puffed on his cigar, then reached out and grabbed Lewis by the arm. "Listen, Jerry, I have to tell you about the ending." Lewis dropped his eyes quickly to where Berle held him, then raised them again.

"When I finally introduce you," Berle said, "you start in telling some story, right? And I back up a couple of steps and say, 'Listen to this, this is a terrific story, you'll love it,' and you turn around and say, 'Would you mind? Could you just back off?' I say, 'Sure, Jerry,' and I go a couple of more steps, and as soon as you start again, I turn to the band and say, 'This kills me, this story; wait'll you hear it.' And you say, 'Look, would you just back away, I'm trying to do a show here. Back off.' Then I walk up and say, 'How far do you want me to go?' And you say, 'Have you got a *car?* "

Berle tightened his grip on Lewis's arm and pulled himself toward him. "Now, you can't jump on that line, Jerry. You got to give it some time. When I say, 'How far do you want me to go?' you have to look at me and take a beat before you answer. Then you deliver the line. It's funnier that way. Last time," he said, "you rushed that line."

Lewis still said nothing, but he gave his arm a slight twist and pulled loose from Berle's hand.

"I think we got it all set, Jerry," Berle said, heading toward the door. "Just remember the pause. These people need time to think down here."

Berle started out of the room, then turned and looked at Lewis. "How far do you want me to go?" he said. Then he paused dramatically and counted three beats in the air with his cigar. "And then you say, 'Have you got a car?' " He put the cigar back in his mouth and walked out the door.

Lewis stood and watched him leave. Then he walked over to his dressing table and dumped the rest of his wine into the sink. He filled the plastic cup with water and used it to put out his cigarette. The cigarette hissed and then floated on the water like a dead fish.

Lewis shook his head and looked over at his wife, Patti, who was sitting in a corner of the dressing room, doing some needlepoint.

"He didn't let you say a word, Daddy," Mrs. Lewis said, looking up at her husband. "I don't believe it. Milton came in here and did the whole opening routine and he didn't even let you speak."

"I don't have to speak," Lewis said. He sat down in a high-backed chair and shut his eyes. "Milton does all the parts. He even does audience reaction."

Lewis opened his eyes and leaned forward to look at himself in the lighted mirror. He turned his head slightly to one side and then to the other. Under a layer of makeup, his skin was deeply tanned; and although his face had become fuller and more mature-looking with time, it had also retained a good deal of youthfulness. Jerry Lewis did not look his age, today, on his forty-seventh birthday.

"Rehearsing," Lewis said, patting back his hair. "That's all Milton has on his mind. We've gone over that routine a million times since yesterday. And it's just an opening bit, for Chrissake."

"I don't see why Milton behaves that way," Mrs. Lewis said.

"Well, Milton is the master of his craft," said Lewis. "Everybody learned from him. He's a perfectionist and a consummate showman. And for that I love him." Lewis closed his eyes again and rubbed them. "But he's driving me fucking bananas with all his rehearsing."

"I think he goes a little too far, Daddy."

"You could walk up to him and say, 'Good morning, Milton,' and he'd give you three other ways to read the line. On the way to his funeral, he's going to be telling the guy how to drive the fucking hearse."

Lewis stood up and began to look through a pile of mail that was sitting on his dressing table. He picked up a telegram from Bill Harrah, the nightclub owner, wishing him a happy birthday, and held it as if he were weighing it.

"We were wrong to come here," Lewis said. "The place is wrong. I don't belong in Miami."

"I know," said Mrs. Lewis.

"Jesus *Christ*," said Lewis suddenly, throwing the telegram back on the table. "Milton's coming in here and telling me how to deliver my fucking lines. I *wrote* the whole fucking routine, I should know how to deliver the lines."

"Milton shouldn't act like that," Mrs. Lewis said.

"And he's explaining to *me* about timing. He's telling me about timing." Lewis looked in the mirror. "I'm forty-seven years old today. I don't need lessons in timing."

"Of course you don't," Mrs. Lewis said.

A tall man with a mustache, who was the announcer for the show, stopped in the doorway and stuck his head into the room. "Are you just about ready, Mr. Lewis?" he asked.

Lewis nodded without turning around. He straightened his jacket and his tie. Then he leaned over and kissed his wife. "Good luck, Daddy," she said to him.

"You know that Milton has always been my idol," Lewis said as he stepped out of the room. "But I think he's turning into a prick."

Mrs. Lewis watched her husband as he left to go onstage; then she went back to her needlepoint.

The day before his forty-seventh birthday, Jerry Lewis stood in the lobby of the Deauville Hotel, looking out through an enormous picture window at the swimming pool area. "Momma!" he said. "Come here and look at this! Look at this Ping-Pong table!"

Mrs. Lewis, wearing a summery pantsuit and sunglasses, went over and stood next to her husband. "Look at what those people are playing on," he said.

Lewis pointed through the window. Beyond it lay a huge swimming pool that nobody was using. The pool was flanked on two sides by narrow cabanas, most of which were open, occupied by post-middle-aged people sipping drinks and avoiding the hot afternoon sun. A number of other people were sitting out in the open, on deck chairs, some with silver reflectors strapped around their necks, and their heads thrown back like astronauts' on takeoff.

In an area directly beneath the picture window, a man and his wife were playing an energetic, if somewhat unpolished, game of Ping-Pong. Both wore broad-brimmed straw hats, and most of their efforts were directed at retrieving the ball after a missed return. The table they were playing on, the only Ping-Pong table in sight, was a warped piece of plywood painted green, nailed onto two sawhorses. The adhesive tape that had been applied to mark off the playing surfaces was fluttering lightly at the edges.

"Can you believe that?" Lewis asked, his eyes fixed on the table. "People here are paying a hundred, a hundred and fifty dollars a day for a room, and look at that piece of shit they provide in the way of recreational facilities. That is absolutely unexcusable." He turned away from the window. "Welcome to Miami," he said.

It was about noon and Lewis had just arrived at the Deauville to rehearse for the opening of his show that night. He had come from The Jockey Club, where he was staying, a twenty-five-minute ride by chauffeur-driven limousine across the bay from Miami Beach.

"Let's find out where we're supposed to go and go there," Lewis said. He started off across the lobby, followed by his wife and by his assistant, a man named Bob Harvey.

"Look at the carpeting!" Lewis called out as he walked along. "Holes in the carpeting!" He stopped above one of the holes and examined it. Two silver-haired ladies sitting nearby looked on with interest.

"Now, it would be one thing," Lewis said, "if they said that the carpeting had been torn in the last fifteen minutes and they just hadn't gotten around to fixing it yet. But those holes have been there since Lindbergh landed in Paris."

"This used to be such a groovy hotel," Harvey said, catching up to Lewis.

"This was the best," said Lewis. "This was class. Now take a look."

"The '50s was the best time for Miami," Harvey said. "The late '50s."

"The town was alive then," Lewis said. "The people were alive. Now everyone in sight is on his way to fucking death. He looked around at the silver-haired ladies and lowered his voice. "It makes you sad to see a town deteriorate like this."

Mrs. Lewis came up and joined them. "Did you see the carpet, Momma?" Lewis asked. Mrs. Lewis looked at the carpet and shook her head.

Lewis led them toward the stage door entrance. Harvey asked him if he'd seen the room in which he was performing. Lewis shook his head. "It's big, Jerry," he said.

They went through the door and into the room. "Holy Christ!" said Lewis, looking around. "Is this where the Dolphins play their home games?"

"Why, it's like a convention hall," said Mrs. Lewis, laughing. "They could hold a convention in here, Daddy."

"They must be out of their minds," Lewis said. "They're never going to fill this place every night. There aren't that many people in Florida."

A number of people were moving unhurriedly around the room, setting up the lighting and sound equipment. Onstage, the band was being led through the numbers in Lewis's act by his accompanist and conductor, Lou Brown, a full-faced and pleasant man who has been with Lewis for twenty-three years.

"Some room they got here, huh?" Brown said as Lewis walked over to the edge of the stage.

"Nice," said Lewis. "Especially if you want to fly an airplane."

"Maybe that's what the show needs," Brown said.

Lewis smiled and took some notes out of a briefcase. He glanced through them, then stood listening to the band. "When do you need me, Louie?" he said.

"Not right away," Brown said. "We'll go through it all first. Then you can come in and tell us how we did it all wrong."

Lewis and his wife came out of the Deauville together and alone and walked over to the car that was waiting for them. The night air was misty and muggy. The neon time-and-temperature board on the delicatessen across the street said that it was 72 degrees, a few minutes before midnight.

Lewis was wearing the tuxedo that he had performed in, except for the jacket. He had left the jacket backstage. He had on a dark-blue nylon windbreaker zipped up to the throat and a white bath towel wrapped around his neck. His make-up was smeared and running from the perspiration that dripped from his hair and his forehead, and both the collar of his shirt and the bath towel were stained with the tan-colored grease.

He slumped into the seat and put his head back, his eyes shut. The driver turned around and gave him a questioning look. Mrs. Lewis made a small motion with her hand and the car pulled away from the hotel.

"There won't be any sleeping tonight," Lewis said in a tired voice. "I have to look for some answers. There have to be some answers."

"What did Milton have to say?" Mrs. Lewis said.

"Milton was very understanding," Lewis said. "He said to me, 'What can we do?' He told me that he knows he went way too long. I said, 'Milton, that's only a small part of it.' The thing about chemistry is that there are particles, and pieces, and small factions that build into the totality of the end result. Time is just one thing."

Lewis took the corner of the bath towel and wiped some of the sweat off the side of his face.

"You can't plan a concept," he said, "and then change it, and expect it to work after you've made the change. When we originally planned to do this, it was going to be Milton and myself and the Louis Prima outfit—and we were going to work in concert and build a kind of revue. Then Prima became unavailable. And then Lee Guber, who put the show together, said that it would just be Milton and myself, and that it would work just as well that way, with each of us doing about an hour. And I really had some reservations about that. But I knew how important it was to Milton, I knew how much he was looking forward to us working together, and so I really didn't put up any resistance to the show's changing from the original concept. Because I didn't want to make waves.

"But you know I talked to Milton, *months* ago, and I kept trying to make him understand that there had to be a device to take the place of the original concept. And then I just ran out of time. I left the country, and then my dad got sick, so we never did get together. And even if we had gotten together, it would have been a very amateurish thing for us to attempt to work in total concert. Here you have two men who shouldn't really be working together at *all*, trying to weave their two styles and two acts together in some way. Anyhow, we never did work anything like that out, because there was just no time."

"Daddy, can I interrupt a minute?" Mrs. Lewis said.

"What?"

"I don't think you ought to have this air-conditioning on. I think it's too much air for you, darling. It's so cold on your neck."

Lewis asked the driver to turn off the air-conditioning in the back of the car.

"Thank you, Phil," Mrs. Lewis said to the driver. "He's still all wet and it gets too cold for him."

They drove in silence for a while, and then Lewis said, "It's really a strange thing. I was so *confident* tonight, for some reason. I had heard how the audience reacted to Milton during that whole first half, and I said, 'Jesus Christ, they're up, they're high.' And when I walked out, I walked out just like I did in Paris. Very secure and very confident. And the minute I began, I knew I was in trouble. That it wasn't going to work. They're different people. It's a different place and a different audience, and I just—I'm not *right* here."

Lewis shifted in the seat and rested one foot on top of the seat in front of him.

"They just didn't understand some of the things that you were doing," Mrs. Lewis said. "You were too subtle for them. Too quick."

"Well, you can't do subtleties and artistic pieces with this audience," Lewis said. "They aren't used to that kind of comedy or that type of sophisticated performance, the way they are in Europe. Or even the way they are in Las Vegas."

"You did pieces tonight that would get a five-minute laugh in Las Vegas," Mrs. Lewis said. "And here they didn't respond at all. "

"Well, this isn't Vegas," Lewis said. "This is Miami, and I haven't been in Miami in a long time. They haven't seen my style of performance in a long time. In a sense, they didn't recognize me."

The car bumped slightly as it pulled onto the causeway and headed across the bay. Behind it, the carnival lights of Miami Beach were dim and fuzzy in the gray mist, as if the city had been wrapped in wax paper.

"You looked so gorgeous up there," Mrs. Lewis said, smiling at her husband. "So polished and so—well—really performing. Milton wasn't really performing."

"Oh, yes, he was, Momma," Lewis said.

"Oh, not to me, it's not a performance," Mrs. Lewis said. "He just works around the other people he has on with him. Like that harmonica player, that Stan Fisher. He plays beautifully and I really enjoy the music, but it was too much and too loud. It's a drag. You come to see Milton Berle and you see a harmonica player."

"Well, I don't know how long that went," Lewis said.

"He had an awful lot of time, Daddy. Much too much."

"Yeah, Stan might be on too long," Lewis said. "But you can't say Milton wasn't performing, honey."

"No," Mrs. Lewis said. "To me, that's not a performance. I'm sorry, it's something else. I don't know what you'd call it."

"You might call it prejudice," Lewis said.

"No, that's not it."

"You know better than making it a contest," Lewis said.

"I'm not making it a contest, and I'm not saying I didn't enjoy it. I enjoyed Milton. But he was too loose. He wasn't organized. He looked—he looked like he was floundering all over the place. Compared to what I see you do."

Mrs. Lewis reached over and began to rub her husband's neck lightly.

"I knew what the outcome was going to be," Lewis said. "I had a feeling it was going to happen this way. I told you that last night."

"Yes, you told me," Mrs. Lewis said.

"I could just feel that the chemistry was wrong," Lewis said.

"Maybe it would be better if you opened the show," Mrs. Lewis said.

"Well, I told Milton that I'd be prepared to do anything at all to make it work; and maybe that means me performing first. But I don't even know if that's *right*. I think the problem is much more fundamental."

The car turned onto Biscayne Boulevard and headed north. There were no other cars and no other people, and the small single-story houses that were set back on either side of the wide street were quiet and dark.

The limousine turned into the entrance of The Jockey Club and a uniformed guard stepped out of his booth.

"Mr. Lewis," the driver said.

The guard bent over slightly and looked in the back window at Lewis and his wife. "Okay," he said and waved them on.

"Phil, what time is it?" Mrs. Lewis said as they drove through the gate.

The driver looked at the clock on the dashboard.

"Almost twelve-thirty, Mrs. Lewis," he said.

"Oh, Daddy," she said. "It's your birthday already."

Mrs. Lewis put her arm around her husband's shoulders and gave him a kiss. "Happy birthday," she said.

"Happy birthday, Jerry," Jan Murray said. He poured some wine into the glass Lewis held in his hand.

"Here's hoping for many more."

Murray's wife, a beautiful woman named Toni, held up her own glass in a toasting gesture. "Happy birthday, Jerry," she said. "We all love you."

Mrs. Lewis laughed and applauded lightly. "Hooray for the birthday boy," she said.

The four of them sat in Lewis's small backstage dressing trailer. Lewis, who had just finished performing, had his tuxedo shirt pulled out of his trousers and unbuttoned down to the middle of his chest. It was splotched with perspiration.

Onstage, Berle was beginning the second half of the show.

"I heard these two ladies talking in the lobby during the intermission," Berle said, peering out at the audience. "And one lady says to the other, 'Sex gives me a pain in the neck.' The other lady says, 'Well, maybe your husband is doing it wrong.' "

The audience roared and Murray pointed in their direction with the bottle of wine. "Good group," he said.

"Not bad," Lewis said. "Better than last night."

Nobody said anything for a moment, and then Mrs. Murray said, "You look marvelous, Jerry. You keep having birthdays, but you don't look any older."

"Fucking middle age," Murray said, taking a drink from his glass. "I never thought I'd see it. I tell you, Jerry, I never thought of getting old."

"Oh, you're not old, Jan," Mrs. Lewis said. "If you're old, then we're all old."

"I don't mean *old* old," Murray said. "But you begin to get these reminders that you aren't as young as you used to be. Particularly on this fucking condominium route." He took a drink. "But the people are beautiful, Jerry. That I gotta say. They're so warm and receptive. They just smother you with affection."

"You should have seen the reception we got in South Africa," Lewis said. He took the bottle of wine from Murray and poured some into his glass. "Talk about warmth. I've never seen anything like it in my life. See, they don't have any TV in South Africa. None. So when I arrived—when the people heard that Jerry Lewis was going to perform in concert—Jesus Christ, you'd think that Frank Sinatra and the Pope showed up."

"I hear their act is a little slow," Murray said, drinking.

"Tell Jan about the welcome," Mrs. Lewis said.

"We land at the airport," Lewis said, "and we look out the windows of the plane, and the airport is covered with South Africans, with Zulus, and they're all chanting and yelling."

"And you thought they were out to shrink your fucking head," Murray said.

"It was a ceremonial welcome, Jan," Lewis said. "They were of all ages. There were kids in wheelchairs. Jesus Christ, I never saw so many people. And they performed this Zulu welcome just for us."

"Tell him about the drive into the city," Mrs. Lewis said.

"It's eight miles from the airport to the city," Lewis said. "And when we drove in, there were Zulus lining both sides of the road for the entire eight miles, cheering and shouting. And they have a whole series of bridges that you pass under on the way. *Every* one of those bridges had a huge placard hanging from it, saying, 'Welcome, Jerry Lewis.'"

Lewis smiled and then shook his head. "I have that welcome on tape," he said. "It was really something."

"Nothing like that would happen here."

They were all quiet again, and then Murray said, "Are you going back home when you finish here, Jerry?"

"No," Lewis said. "I'm going to Germany."

"*You're* going to Germany?"

"The war is over," Lewis said, smiling. "I'm going to do a show for German TV and I'm going to give a one-man concert. I'm also being given a German film festival award." He pointed at Murray. "For our picture."

"For *Which Way to the Front?*" Murray said. "You're pulling my fucking leg."

"No," Lewis said, shaking his head. "That picture played sixteen first-run weeks in Berlin. With lines down the block."

"That's unbelievable," Murray said. "It's an anti-German film."

Lewis shrugged. "The Europeans think differently about things. They explore and accept film as art. It's a completely different attitude from the way films are viewed here." He finished the wine that was in his glass. "Anyway, the picture was named best picture of the year, from anywhere, and I was named best director. It's my ninth foreign film award."

"That's wonderful, Jerry," Mrs. Murray said.

"It's fucking ironic," Murray said, laughing. "That's what it is. Imagine going from Miami Beach to Germany."

"I'm counting the days, Lewis said. "Which reminds me—"

He took a felt-tip pen from the dressing table and began to write on the mirror. He wrote the names of ten days, starting with Thursday, the day before, and ending with the Saturday after next, the night he was scheduled to close. He crossed off the first two days and put the cap back on the pen.

"Two down and eight to go," Lewis said, stepping back from the mirror and looking at what he'd written. Everybody looked at the mirror expectantly, as if it were going to speak.

"Miami's a toilet," Lewis said finally. "The best thing you can do for it is to pull the chain."

Then, brightening suddenly, Lewis said, "Hey, this is supposed to be a birthday. Where's the fucking cake?"

Lewis stood in the mirrored lobby and waited for the elevator. A lady leaning over the reception desk called to him from across the room.

"How's your father doing, Jerry?" she said. "Is he feeling better?"

Lewis turned and looked at her briefly. "He's much better, thank you," he said.

"We all wish him well," the lady said as Lewis stepped into the elevator.

The elevator gave a lurch and then started up. Lewis looked sideways and caught his reflection in the smoked glass, then looked away.

The corridor was narrow and dark. It had a low ceiling spotted with dim-wattage light bulbs. The apartment doors all had brass-colored doorbell units planted on them like corsages and circular peepholes that stared at one another across the hallway.

Lewis walked all the way to the end of the hall and rang one of the bells. A short woman in a patterned blue housedress and slippers opened the door and put her arms around him. "Hello, Jerry!" she said, kissing him on the cheek. Lewis set down the briefcase he was carrying to give his mother a hug.

"Jerry's here," Mrs. Lewis said, taking him into the apartment. He followed her down a short entrance hall that led into a combination dining area and living room. The hall had a small table sticking out from the wall, with a gold-flecked mirror hanging above it. The mirror was ornamented with color snapshots wedged in between the frame and the glass.

The living room, which was not large, was dominated by a heavy metal hospital-style bed that was made up against one wall. This wall also had a thick fire door leading out to an open balcony that overlooked Collins Avenue, the main street at this end of Miami Beach. Across the boulevard, there was a coffee shop, with a sign flashing the words OPEN 24 HOURS in colored lights.

"Hello, Pop," Lewis said. He crossed the room and kissed his father, who was sitting in a wheelchair not far from the metal bed. "How've you been doing?"

Danny Lewis held his son's hand and smiled at him faintly. He was a painfully weak-looking man, whose body and face had been shrunken by a series of violent strokes. Behind him, on the wall, there was a photograph taken a couple of years before, showing him as a robust, full-faced man, with a broad and winning smile and a full head of hair. Now his hair was thin; his face was stretched and gaunt; and yet his eyes, just as the eyes that looked out brightly from the photograph on the wall, were keenly alive.

"Danny's been doing just fine," said a short, plump lady sitting on one of the chairs in the dining area. "How have you been, Jerry?"

"Oh, Christ, Aunt Jean, are you still here?" Lewis said, turning in her direction. "Ma, I thought you told me Aunt Jean was leaving today for sure."

"Now, what kind of way is that for you to talk to your aunt?" Aunt Jean said from her seat.

"He shows no respect, this boy," Mrs. Lewis said with a laugh. She patted him on the cheek. "Sit, Jerry. Sit down and be comfortable."

She left the room and Lewis took a seat on the sofa, on the opposite side of the room from his father.

"Have you been behaving yourself, Pop?" Lewis said. He turned his head and looked at his father's nurse, a young and pretty Black girl, sitting at the other end of the couch, watching Mike Douglas on television.

"Has he been doing what he's told?" Lewis said to the girl.

The nurse smiled across the room at Danny Lewis. "He's been pretty good," she said. "He doesn't give too much trouble."

Mrs. Lewis came out of the kitchen holding a glass jar. "Let me fix you something to eat, Jerry," she said. "Try some of this."

"What, I'm here two seconds and you're feeding me already," Lewis said. "I don't need anything to eat."

"I bet you haven't eaten anything today," Mrs. Lewis said. "You never eat properly. Here," she handed him the jar, "this is marvelous."

Lewis held the jar and looked at it. "What is it?" he said.

"Herring," his mother said. "Delicious."

"And I eat it right out of the jar?" Lewis said.

"No, dear, you eat it on a plate," his mother said. "I'll fix it up for you. I'll bring you some Ritz crackers with it."

Lewis settled back on the couch as his mother went into the kitchen.

"So when are you leaving, Aunt Jean?" he said, looking at his watch. "You going back to California soon?"

"Fresh boy," Aunt Jean said, polishing her glasses on the front of her dress. "How's your show going, fresh boy?"

"Show's okay," Lewis said. "Milton's rehearsing me every time I turn around, but other than that, okay."

"How is Milton?" Aunt Jean said.

"Milton is Milton," Lewis said. He looked at his father and said, "He wanted to be remembered to you. He said to be sure to give you his best. I think we'll come up someday and see you. After he gets through restaging my whole act."

Mrs. Lewis came in with a plate full of food and set it down on the coffee table. Lewis leaned forward, took a fork off the plate and began to eat.

"What is this stuff I'm eating, anyway?"

"Herring tidbits," Aunt Jean said. "Spiced."

"Delicious," Mrs. Lewis said from the kitchen.

"Jew food," Lewis said, wiping his mouth with a napkin. "This stuff killed more of my people than Hitler."

"No, everybody likes that," Aunt Jean said. "Scandinavians and everybody. In Sweden they make salads with herring. I have the recipes."

"In Sweden you pay nineteen dollars for a portion of smoked salmon," Lewis said.

"Oh, my God," Aunt Jean said. "Who wants to eat that?"

"When you taste it, you do," Lewis said.

"Are we going to eat lunch?" Lewis's father said. His voice was hoarse and strained.

"You had lunch, and you had breakfast," Aunt Jean said, her voice raised. She looked at him over her glasses.

Danny Lewis stopped, as if to think about what she said. "What did I have?"

"You had fish," Aunt Jean said emphatically. "You had that lovely fish that I bought."

"Fish and carrots," the nurse said.

"And mashed potatoes," Aunt Jean said.

"And I had that today?" Danny Lewis said.

"You had that for *lunch*," Aunt Jean said. "Why don't you walk a little bit, Danny? You aren't walking enough."

The nurse went over and helped him out of the wheelchair, then held his arm and guided him into a metal walker. He began to move slowly across the room.

"Hey," Aunt Jean said, looking over at the television, "there's Joe Namath. Everybody makes such a big fuss over him. Do you know Joe Namath, Jerry?"

"Sure," Lewis said.

"What's so wonderful about him?" Aunt Jean said.

"He's a marvelous guy," Lewis said.

"He looks like a nice boy," Mrs. Lewis said. "He's got a cute impish smile. I think he's impish-looking."

"We don't have anything with muscular dystrophy that Joe Namath isn't there to help," Lewis said.

"A dimple in the chin, the Devil within," Aunt Jean said.

Lewis got up and opened the briefcase that he had brought with him. He took out a cassette recorder and began to rewind the tape.

"I think he's going to put you down on tape," Mrs. Lewis said to Aunt Jean.

"Oh, I'll kill him if he does," Aunt Jean said. "I'll kill you if you do, Jerry."

"You know you can't trust him when he carries his valises," Mrs. Lewis said.

"I don't know what he carries in his valises," Aunt Jean said. "Maybe he's carrying extras in there. Whatever that is."

"You're rambling, dear," Mrs. Lewis said.

"So I'm rambling," Aunt Jean said. "Don't dare use that, Jerry."

Mrs. Lewis looked over at her husband and said, "Give me a note, sweetheart."

Danny Lewis sang a soft and raspy note.

"Couple of notes," Mrs. Lewis said. "It's good to use your voice."

Danny Lewis sat and composed himself for a moment; then he began to sing: " 'It's impossible ... ask a baby not to cry, it's just impossible ... .' "

"Perfect pitch," Lewis said to his father, after he sang a few lines of the song. "What key was that?"

"Very low," Mrs. Lewis said. "Maybe a C."

"E-flat," Danny Lewis said in a small voice.

" 'It's impossible .... .' " Lewis began to sing in a high shrieking comic voice, " 'to see goyim in a synagogue, it's just impossible ....' "

"No it's not, not anymore it isn't," Aunt Jean broke in.

Lewis gave his Aunt Jean a look and his mother began to laugh loudly. Lewis punched the Record button on the cassette machine.

"Honey," Mrs. Lewis said to her husband, "give me a real *nice* note, now. Do 'My Way.' "

Danny Lewis did not answer; he sat looking down at his hands, which were folded in his lap.

"Give him the opening words," Aunt Jean said.

" 'And now ....' " Mrs. Lewis began.

Danny Lewis sat still for another moment, then began: " 'And now ... the end is near ... and so I face the final curtain ... .' "

As his father began the song, Lewis turned his eyes away and lowered them to the floor.

" 'My friend ... I'll say it clear ... I'll state my case, of which I'm certain ... .' "

When he came to the end of the song, there was a pause in the room. Then Lewis said, "You hit some pretty high notes there, Dad."

"Did he ever!" Mrs. Lewis said. "Oh, did he go up high! It was beautiful, sweetheart."

"Why don't you sing a song with him, Jerry?" Aunt Jean said.

"Ah, why don't you just butt out, Fat?" Lewis said. "Trying to run everything."

"I don't like you," Aunt Jean said.

"I never liked you," Lewis said. "I was stuck with you. They told me one day, 'That's your aunt. That's a lamp, there's the couch, that's your aunt.' I got rid of the lamp, I got rid of the couch and, Jesus Christ, you're still around."

"So the same thing happened with me when they told me you were my nephew," Aunt Jean said. "So we're stuck with each other."

Lewis walked over to her and gave her a hug and a kiss on the cheek.

"Hey, tell me," he said to his mother. "Incest with an aunt ain't bad, is it?"

"Terrible," his mother said, smiling at him from the couch. "The worst."

When Lewis walked out of the building, the afternoon sunlight was beginning to fade and a bright stream of neon lights had come on up and down the boulevard.

He walked over to his car and got in the back seat. He sat without doing anything for a minute, then he took out his tape recorder and put it on his lap. He punched the Play button and the sound of his father's voice, singing the lyrics to "My Way," came from the speaker.

"Where to, Mr. Lewis?" the driver said, looking into the rear-view mirror.

Lewis did not answer; he just sat listening to the tape recorder.

"You want to go over to the Deauville now?" the driver said. "It's about five o'clock."

"Yeah," Lewis said finally, pushing the button to stop the tape. "Yeah, take me there. And then I want you to go someplace where they have fruit. Gift packages of fruit. I want you to get a basket filled with fruit, and some cheeses, maybe a bottle of booze, and I want you to bring it back to my parents. Get the biggest one they got. Spend fifty bucks or something."

He took a bill out of his wallet and handed it across the front seat to the driver.

"I know just the spot, Mr. Lewis," the driver said. "Real gourmet place. Very high-class."

Lewis nodded and sat back in the seat. "They should have something nice up there in case company comes," he said, rewinding the tape. "It doesn't look good for people to come up and not see anything there."

The driver started the limousine and nosed it out into the stream of traffic. Lewis was listening to the tape of his father's voice once again as the car drove off down the street.

"Miami sucks!" Lewis shouted from the bedroom. He went over and put his head into the living room of his dressing suite in the Deauville. "Sucks!"

Harvey sat on the sofa, drinking coffee and eating pound cake with a fork. "Used to be groovy," he said with his mouth full.

"Used to be, used to be," Lewis said, walking back into the bedroom. "Now it sucks."

He switched on the television and began to go through one of the dresser drawers. "The people here know from nothing. *Nothing* do they know. They know 'shit' and they know 'fuck,' and anything else is out of their league."

He slammed the drawer shut and attacked another. "If you don't open with 'fuck,' you bomb. 'Hickory dickery dock, the mouse ran up the clock; fuck him, let him stay there.' Then you're a hit."

He slammed the second drawer shut and reappeared in the doorway. "Do a routine that starts, 'Two Jews fucked a sheep … ' and then you're home free."

He went back into the bedroom and looked at the television. It was showing a telethon that was being held in the Miami area to raise money for children's diseases. It was being hosted by a local personality, a fat emcee with a leathery tan.

"And I want to make this plea from the bottom of my heart … " the fat emcee was saying.

"The bottom of your heart is in your ass, you local piece of Miami shit," Lewis shouted at the television. "Fucking amateurs. Don't know anything about putting on a fucking telethon. Might as well stay in the fucking bed, for all the money they'll raise."

He went into the living room and walked over to the bar. "You know what pisses me off most about this fucking place?"

Harvey did not answer, just sipped his coffee.

"It's not that fucking stadium we're playing in, with all the empty chairs," Lewis said, pouring himself some wine, "and it's not Milton with all his fucking rehearsing, and his shit-kicking complaints and suggestions"—he drank the wine in a gulp—"but what really pisses me off about Miami is the fucking people. The fucking insensitivity of the people."

"You shouldn't let it get to you," Harvey said. "They don't know any better."

"They should know better," Lewis said, his voice rising. "They're adults. I'm going to punch somebody in the mouth pretty soon."

He poured another drink. "They come up and they grab you. They grab your fucking coat. Did you see that guy in the lobby today? Grabs my fucking arm and says, 'Hey, stay here, Jerry, you gotta say hello to my wife.' I *gotta* say hello to his wife? I told him to take his fucking hands off me."

"There're assholes everywhere," Harvey said. "What are you going to do?"

"There's no excuse for bad manners,'" Lewis said. "There's no excuse for bad taste. They treat you just like an object. They act like you were the Statue of fucking Liberty. Well, I'm not going through that lobby again, that's all. If I can't get on without going through the fucking lobby, then I don't go on. It's Jew-a-Rama down there. Wall-to-wall Jews." He swallowed the rest of his wine. "If I stay here much longer, I'm going to end up sending money to the Arabs."

From the television set in the bedroom, the fat emcee said, "And the phone calls were just not coming in like they should while the Harrington Quartet was performing so beautifully ... ."

"They can't call when they're watching the talent, you fucking fruitcake," Lewis yelled back. "They call after the Harrington fucking Quartet goes off. Jesus Christ Almighty!"

He poured another glass of wine, draining the bottle. He looked at the empty wine bottle a moment, then slammed it against the wall. "I christen this hotel 'motherfucker'!" he shouted. "Pull out the pilings, you sons of bitches!"

He disappeared into the bedroom and came back with a can of lighter fluid. "Here!" he called to Harvey. "Watch carefully."

He poured some of the lighter fluid into a glass ashtray, struck a match and dropped it in. The ashtray went up in a burst of flame. "The Great Super Jew and His Burning Ashtray!" Lewis shouted. "Speak to me. Burning Ashtray!"

Harvey went over to the bar and put out the ashtray with a bottle of Coca-Cola. Lewis was in the bathroom pouring lighter fluid into the toilet. He tossed in a match and the bowl ignited.

"Keep your eyes on the fucking fire!" Lewis shouted. "Anyone who grabs the Super Jew's coat will have to contend with my firepower!"

Harvey went into the bathroom and flushed the toilet. The flames disappeared like a drowning man.

"And now for the greatest feat of all!" Lewis yelled. He sprinkled the lighter fluid in a trail across the bathroom's tile floor. He threw on a match and the bathroom lit up with a roar.

"Aha!" Lewis said, watching the flames. "That's it, burn! Burn, you motherfucker! Burn down the fucking hotel! Burn down the whole fucking town!"

The German countryside appeared suddenly through the clouds, like a rabbit pulled out of a hat; misty, gray-green fields clumped with trees that tilted steeply under the wing of the 747 as it made its approach to Frankfurt's Rhein-Main Airport.

The air on the ground was chilly and damp and beads of moisture splattered across the windows of the plane as it rumbled in a great arc toward the concrete-modern terminal building and came to a stop in the early-morning haze.

Lewis came off the plane wearing a short green topcoat and sunglasses. He was followed by the five members of his staff, all looking tired and rumpled.

They were met by an enthusiastic young man from the airline, a blond-haired German dressed in a navy blazer, who informed Lewis that there was a private jet waiting to fly them to Cologne, where Lewis was performing, but first he would take them upstairs to a lounge, where they could have some coffee.

They took an escalator to the upper level. The young man ushered them into a spacious and pleasantly furnished room.

"Well, now!" the young man beamed. "Shall we perhaps take a seat in here, or, if you would prefer, we can swing on into the leather room." With a gesture, he indicated an adjoining room furnished with leather couches and an enormous bar, which, at eight-thirty in the morning, was deserted.

The Lewis group looked at the young man with tired eyes. They swung on into the leather room.

A pretty, dark-haired girl in a blue uniform left a small desk across the room and went over to take orders for coffee and juice.

The young man from the airline approached Lewis and said that there was a reporter outside from one of the radio stations wondering whether Lewis could spare a few minutes for an interview. Lewis nodded wearily and removed his dark glasses.

The young man brought in the reporter, a massive, dominating man with a great beard. He shook hands formally with Lewis and began to unpack a tape recorder.

The dark-haired girl appeared with a tray. She served cups of coffee and glasses of tomato juice to several members of the group, then went for the rest of the order.

"No ass on that chick," Lou Brown said, watching her walk away. "Nice legs, nice tits." He sipped his tomato juice. "No ass."

Harvey stirred his coffee and smiled across the room at the girl. She smiled back demurely. "So she's shooting two for three," he said. "And she hasn't even suited up yet."

The bearded reporter had started his machine and he squatted on his heels in front of Lewis, holding a microphone.

"Tell me, Mr. Lewis," he said in perfect English, "what I would first like to ask you is whether you think of yourself as having a public face, as in your films, and another separate private face, which the public perhaps does not see."

"Well," Lewis began in a tired voice. "Well, I think that every performer, not just myself, projects a certain special image when he is functioning publicly, as an entertainer, or an actor. This image is an extension of that person's total personality, although the public often sees only a single facet—"

He stopped as the dark-haired girl lowered a coffee cup in front of his face. He looked up at her and then back at the reporter.

"A single facet," he said, then stopped. He rubbed his eyes and looked again at the girl.

"Cream?" she said politely.

Lewis looked from the girl to the man crouched in front of him, holding the microphone in expectation. Then he covered his face with his hand and began to laugh.

The reporter smiled uncertainly behind his thick beard, as if anxious to share in something he did not quite understand. After a few moments, with Lewis still laughing, the smile collapsed like a balloon losing air and the man pushed the stop button on the recorder.

"That was sensational, Jerry!" the director said, walking toward the front of the stage. He came through the wooden chairs and the music stands, and his image bounced onto the half-dozen monitors that were spotted around the subterranean television studio. He was a tall, handsome-looking German, with slightly graying hair.

"Where are you, Jerry?" he called out. "That was magnificent!"

Lewis, dressed in janitor's blue overalls, came through a door and walked over to where the director was standing.

"Sensational, Jerry!" the director repeated. "And on the first take!"

"Yeah, I thought it went well," Lewis said calmly. "Let's look at it and see."

The director called up to the control booth and asked for the tape to be played back. The members of the crew began to form groups in front of the monitors, waiting for Lewis's performance as a janitor conducting an imaginary orchestra in an empty concert hall.

The monitors buzzed, and then Lewis, dressed in overalls and pushing a broom, came onto the screen. The people standing in the back of a group raised themselves up on their toes to get a better look.

The German television crew seemed to find the sketch hysterically funny. They laughed loudly and appreciatively all through the video-tape playback, picking up on every nuance of Lewis's performance, and when it was over, they broke into a vigorous round of applause.

Lewis, who had watched himself on the monitor with his arms folded and no expression on his face, acknowledged the applause with a smile. Then he turned and looked at the director, who was standing next to him.

"Your timing is brilliant," the director said admiringly. "Absolutely brilliant."

Lewis nodded, and then he said, "What's next?'

The reporters gathered in front of Lewis in a large group, holding yellow pencils and folded pieces of colored paper. Lewis sat facing them in a metal chair, with his cassette recorder resting on his lap, his tuxedo tie pulled loose and his shirt unbuttoned at the throat.

It was almost six o'clock in the evening and the taping of Lewis's show had just ended. In the background, there was a hum of German voices as the television crew wrapped up after the day's shooting. A bank of the bright overhead lights was switched off and one section of the studio went dark.

"Mr. Lewis," one of the reporters said, "the European critics, especially the French critics, seem to appreciate your work more than the American critics do. Why do you think that is so?"

"Well, it's not only the critics," Lewis said. He settled himself into the chair.

"It's all Europe, they've all been very good to me. They've acknowledged my work and they look upon it as they look at all cinema. They look a little more carefully than they do in America, that's all. And I've been very fortunate that the European audience has grown for me and gotten larger over time, as the people here have viewed my films and accepted them. The French audience was there first; and now it's happened in Belgium, in the Netherlands, in Italy, in Spain—Spain has become the biggest club of fanatics that I have, of late. And the last film I made took more money out of Germany than any three films of mine did cumulatively in the past. See, I have to come to Europe when my ego gets way down, after the American critics start to pound me into the cement. Three days in Europe and I feel good again, and then I go home."

Lewis laughed loudly and the reporters laughed with him.

"The difference is not in the audience," Lewis said. "I think the American audience is just as good as the European audience. But the critics are something else. I heard that a critic once said the dirtiest words in America are Doris Day, Jerry Lewis, and John Wayne. Now, I really don't know what the hell that means. I guess it's because I won't photograph nudity or make dirty films or whatever—I don't know. But I'm just going to continue to do what I do, without changing my game plan, and I'm not really worried that it doesn't appeal to some people."

"What about the American TV audience?" one man said, "You had your own show, but you stopped it."

"Yeah, No, *I* didn't stop it."

"Really?" the man said. He sounded surprised. "The ratings, you mean?"

"Oh, sure, that's what stops all television. The ratings. Some of the finest shows that we've had on the air went off the air because of the ratings."

"Because they could no longer get sponsorship?" the man said.

"Well, it's almost impossible to explain the ratings," Lewis said. "The ratings go to twelve hundred families, and that's supposed to represent sixty-four million households." He made a gesture of disbelief. "Well, I just can't equate that, you see. I *can* equate the success of a film by the box office receipts, but television has no box office. And they need some sort of a guide, so they use the ratings as a guide. But it's a grossly unfair measure to have to work with, and very frustrating for a creative person. So rather than fight that particular system, I just choose to stay away from television."

"If they would give you the Academy Award, would you accept it?" one young man said with a smile.

"Under a couple—" Lewis looked at the floor and thought a moment. "There would be some conditions."

Lewis looked at the young man and he stopped smiling. "Like what?" he asked Lewis.

"Like changing the Academy Award structure and making it fair," Lewis said. "What bothers me is that there's no category for comedy, nothing that acknowledges my craft or the people who have gone before me, who were the very reason we have a picture industry. At least acknowledge their existence. They got categories in the Academy for the guy who invented a new bulb for the men's room, but they haven't got one for comedy.

"Just think that it took them forty some years to honor Chaplin. Now, that angered me; that was wrong. And when I saw Mr. Chaplin walk out on that stage, not even totally aware of what was going on, all I could think of was, 'Why'd they wait so long?' "

Lewis paused for a moment and watched as several men and women wheeled a piece of scenery across the room. "The Academy," he said finally, "is just very unfair."

"What about your new film, *The Day the Clown Cried?* Is there any comic relief in it or is it a straight drama picture?"

"Absolutely straight," Lewis said.

"Could you give us some details of the story?"

"I could, but I'd prefer not to."

"When will it be released?"

"I'm editing it now," Lewis said. "It's a little difficult to say when it will be released, because I'm being so cautious about how it's going to be handled. I don't want it handled just like the release of another film; it has to be special. And if I can't get the releasing people who can do what I know is right for the picture, then I'll have to do it myself. It's a funny thing about releasing a film. The last picture I made, well—"

Lewis shook his head and laughed.

"Hardly anyone in America saw it," he said. "My own children didn't even see it in a theater; I had to run it at home for them. That was because Warner Bros., the company I made the film for, had another film out at the same time, called *Woodstock*, and they were using all of their energies and resources to push that film. And there was just nothing left over, so my picture died without ever getting a chance. It broke my heart, because I knew I had made a good movie that hardly anybody in my country was ever going to see. Now, that's the problem of distribution. The fate of your work rests in the hands of some distributor or some studio, and if they have some pornographic film they feel they can make more money with, then you just have to take the consequences. So I'm thinking of doing it myself."

"In 1960, when you started to direct your own films, did that also mean, at that point, that you were dissatisfied with the directors you worked with or with your work in general?"

"No, I was very satisfied. I worked with some of the finest directors in the medium. I worked with Frank Tashlin and Norman Taurog and George Marshall—I learned from these men, they were my teachers. But I knew I couldn't always get the director I wanted when I needed him, so I decided that I would have to learn, and do it myself. I certainly wasn't going to sit still and not make films because I couldn't get the best. So I decided I was going to be the best. Which I am not, not yet. But I will be."

Lewis stopped as the reporters all wrote that down.

"Maybe Tuesday," he added.

The driver took the small red Mercedes through the narrow streets of Cologne at top speed and never turned his head to offer any commentary on the scenery.

The weather was cold and the city looked dark and depressing under the heavy, lead-colored sky as it slid past the windows of the car.

The Mercedes hit a puddle and skidded around a corner in a slight drift, shot up a small, cobbled street with heavily barred antique shop windows on either side, took another corner without braking and roared down a slightly wider boulevard crowded with department store shoppers bundled against the weather and carrying wrapped parcels.

"Hey, look, I wonder if those are some of the students they told us about," Harvey said. He pointed out the window toward the sidewalk. Mixed in with the shoppers was a group of young people, walking together in a tight bunch.

"Where are their picket signs?" Harvey said. "Where are their Molotov cocktails?"

The day before, Lewis had gotten word that his ninety-minute one-man concert had been canceled because the city of Cologne had experienced a week of student protests and demonstrations. The German people had been vague as to the exact nature of the student unrest, but it was being described along the same lines as the riots that had occurred in Paris in the late '60s, and there had apparently been several incidents that had approached that state of intensity and violence.

"Did they think these kids were going to toss a bomb onstage while you were singing *Rock-a-Bye Your Baby*, or what?" Harvey said.

"They didn't know what was going to happen," Lewis said, looking out at the sidewalk. "But there were so many dignitaries and political big shots coming to the show that they just didn't feel they could provide adequate security. And you can believe they were plenty worried to kiss away all that money."

"You still getting paid?"

"Oh, sure," Lewis said. "For doing nothing."

"Come sight-seeing in Cologne, folks!" Harvey said. "And now, ladies and gentlemen, if you look to the left of the bus, you will see Cologne's famous student rioters, coming after your ass! Just wait till they put on their brown shirts, then we'll really see some action."

The blond-haired driver raised his eyes to the rearview mirror for an instant, then looked quickly ahead.

The Mercedes looped around a modern-looking skyscraper, a straight shaft of concrete and dark glass, and burst upon Cologne's famous cathedral.

The cathedral was covered with scaffolding for repairs and it resembled the illustrations from *Gulliver's Travels* showing a giant from another world bound with ropes and cables and covered with ladders on which tiny figures scampered about.

The car turned onto a small side street and came to a jolting stop as a large truck backed out of a warehouse into the middle of the road. The driver blew his horn in annoyance, but the truck just sat blocking the way.

By the side of the road, there was another group of young people, larger than the one in the shopping district. They were standing in front of a high brick wall on which several words in German had been written in giant letters with a can of black spray paint. One of the words, not in German, was NIXON.

"What does that say?" Lewis asked the driver. He pointed to the wall.

The driver looked over at the lettering, then back at the truck that was still in the middle of the street. He seemed both embarrassed and annoyed.

"It is nothing," he said, half turning in his seat. "A slogan of some kind."

"Yeah, but what does it say?" Lewis said.

The driver turned his head away and honked his horn again, angrily. He answered without turning back.

"It is a slogan for the students," the driver said. "They are against the Americans and their war. The words say they are murderers."

The young people stood by the wall, staring out silently at the street. They huddled in front of the thick black letters protectively, as if they were guarding them from theft. They didn't say anything to anybody. They didn't talk or laugh among themselves and they didn't call out to people passing by. They just stood and looked.

The driver gave another impatient blast on his horn, and finally the truck started up again and lumbered out of the way with all the solemnity of a Rose Bowl float. The Mercedes jumped forward with a neck-snapping lurch.

Lewis swiveled in his seat and looked out the back window at the group on the sidewalk. As the Mercedes zoomed down the narrow street, the silent students and their guarded graffito fell back into the gathering dusk.

"There she is," Lewis said. "There's the little cunt."

He braked the Moviola with his hand and made a grease-pencil mark on the film. It cut across the face of a beautiful blonde teenage girl.

"Same little cunt who tried to rape us before," Lewis said. "Watch her eyes."

The machine in the Los Angeles studio made a ratchety sound as Lewis backed up the film. He stopped it, started it forward again and cupped his hand against the rim of the small screen to block out the glare from the overhead light.

The screen showed a tracking shot down the length of a barbed wire fence. Crowded behind the fence was a line of children dressed in ragged clothing, staring straight ahead with vacant eyes, standing completely still. The children's faces were all European-looking and they had the same pathetic expressions as the faces found on CARE posters.

The blonde girl stood toward the end of the line. As the camera passed in front of her, an almost imperceptible smile showed up at the corners of her mouth and her eyes drifted over to the side, following the lens of the camera as it moved along. As soon as her eyes shifted toward the right-hand side of the screen, the grease mark cut her face in two and Lewis braked the machine.

"There," he said. "See it? Following the fucking camera."

Lewis turned and looked at Rusty Wiles, his cutter, who sat on a stool with his arms folded, looking at the screen over Lewis's shoulder.

"Bet you didn't see that before," Lewis said.

"Oh, I saw it," the cutter said, nodding. "But that kid right before her had such a good look on his face and he'd have to go, too, if we cut. It's so close."

Lewis backed the film up and looked at it again.

"The sneaky little bitch," Lewis said, shaking his head. "Vamping for the camera. She pulled that same thing in another sequence, remember?"

The cutter nodded. Lewis looked at the girl on the screen for a moment.

"I told her to keep her fucking eyes to the front," Lewis said. "That it wasn't a beauty pageant. On the big screen, those eyes are going to pop right over as big as life."

"Pretty face, though," the cutter said.

"Yeah," Lewis said. "Everybody wants to be a star. Cut her out."

Lewis stepped away from the Moviola and the cutter wheeled himself over on his stool, removed the film from the machine and took it over to a bench to recut the scene.

Lewis went to a small refrigerator in one corner of the room and took out a can of beer. He turned on a portable color television set and sat down in front of it with the beer to wait for the cutter to finish.

"Hey, look, Rusty!" Lewis called out, pointing to the set. "Sherlock Holmes is on the tube."

The cutter looked over his shoulder. He nodded and turned back to the bench.

On the screen, Basil Rathbone and Nigel Bruce stood above the body of an elderly man lying in a pool of blood in a handsomely appointed English drawing room. Rathbone looked thoughtfully at the body and said that it appeared as if Sir George had held something in his hand at the time that he was murdered.

"A matchbook, I should think, by the look of it," Rathbone said, puffing on his pipe.

"Jesus," Lewis said, drinking from the can. "He knows everything, this fucking Basil Rathbone. He'll get the guy by the next reel."

The cutter said that he had fixed the scene and threaded it into the Moviola. Lewis went over and stood next to him and they watched the film.

"Much better," Lewis said when it was over. "Hundred percent better. There's no room for Shirley Temple in a concentration camp. What else have you got for me?" He drained the can of beer and tossed it into a metal wastebasket.

"I've got this sequence with the guard that I shortened a little. It'll take a few minutes to put together." He wheeled himself back to his bench. Lewis sat down in front of the television.

"You know the scene where the guy gets shot?" the cutter said as he worked.

"Yeah," Lewis said. "What about it?"

"Well, when you showed the film last week, a couple of people asked me if I didn't think that ran a little long."

"They didn't say anything to me," Lewis said, getting up from his chair. "What do you mean, 'long'?"

The cutter shrugged. "Just long, I guess. The guy is on the screen a long time. He takes a long time to die."

"Well, Jesus Christ, Rusty," Lewis said, "that scene's going to be an optical. I got faces of kids playing over that scene that I have to put in. It's not even finished yet."

"I know," the cutter said. "I told them you had something planned there."

"People don't even know how to look at a rough cut of a fucking film," Lewis said, his voice getting louder. "It's still being worked on. I still have things to do with it."

"Well," the cutter said, "I told—"

"What if I came up to a guy who was building a house, and he just had the frame up, and I stand there asking him why there aren't any windows in it yet. How fucking stupid can you get?"

Lewis began to pace angrily about the room.

"Everybody's an expert," he said. "There's a fucking genius at every screening. Where were they when the empty pages were in the typewriter? Where were they when we were freezing in fucking Sweden, shooting the film? Too *long*? Jesus Christ!"

"I just mentioned it," the cutter said.

"It has to be long for all the dissolves of the faces," Lewis said. "Besides, it emphasizes the importance of his death. That's a crucial dramatic point, you know that."

The cutter nodded and again began to work on the film in front of him.

"It was the same thing with the dance sequence in *The Patsy*," Lewis said. "And I told them then that they should just wait till it was fucking finished before they go telling me what's wrong with it. Just wait till I'm ready."

Lewis went back and sat down in front of the television. "I don't know who the fuck asked for their opinion, anyway," he said over his shoulder.

The Sherlock Holmes movie went off and a car salesman came onto the screen, standing in front of a tired-looking convertible. Lewis flipped the dial and stopped at Jack Paar's program.

Paar was explaining that he was going to show an exclusive film of the gymnastic team from the People's Republic of China. "It is quite honestly one of the most remarkable exhibitions I think that I have ever witnessed," Paar said.

"Oh, shut up and put on the Chinamen," Lewis said. He got up and went to the refrigerator for another can of beer.

The Chinese gymnasts began leaping through some metal rings, which were so delicately arranged that any body contact at all would knock them over. The men passed through them with effortless grace.

"Big fucking deal," Lewis said. "In and out of the rings. If they could just work on getting the shirts done right, that would be enough."

Wiles turned around to look at the set. "I don't know," he said. "That looks sort of difficult to me."

"Oh, yeah?" Lewis said, opening the beer can. "Let me tell you something. If the rings don't show up, they got no act."

Joseph Lewis, aged nine, stood motionless in deep left field, wearing an enormous glove on his hand and a green-and-white uniform.

"It's a shame he doesn't have more to do," Mrs. Lewis said. "But at least he's playing."

"There's not much going on in the outfield in this league," Lewis said. "But you live to play out the season."

"He looks so small out there," Mrs. Lewis said. "And in that uniform."

Lewis knelt on one of the bleacher seats and squinted through a 16mm camera he had set up on an aluminum tripod in front of him. He panned the camera toward left field.

"I don't know why you brought such a big camera," Mrs. Lewis said.

"I told you I was going to take some pictures of the baseball player," Lewis said, framing Joseph in the viewer.

"I thought you just meant regular pictures," Mrs. Lewis said. "With a hand camera."

"You can carry this camera in your hand," Lewis said, still looking through the lens. "Come on, Joby, do something out there."

Several of the parents sitting nearby stared at Lewis and his movie camera with fascination.

"Momma!" Lewis said suddenly. "He moved! Your kid moved!"

"What did he do?" Mrs. Lewis said, looking out at her son.

"Something with his arm," Lewis said, working the zoom lens. "I got it on film."

After three batters had come and gone, the side was retired. Lewis took movies of his son walking in from left field.

"I don't know what I'm going to do when he gets up to bat," Lewis said. "I don't think I'll be able to watch."

Joseph came to bat with two outs and a runner on first. He stood at the plate as erect and motionless as he had been in the field, and he held the bat directly in front of him, perpendicular to the ground, like a pole-vaulter during the singing of the national anthem.

The first pitch went well over his head and Joseph did not move a muscle.

"Good eye, Joseph!" the coach yelled from the sideline.

"Good *eye*?" Lewis said from behind the camera. "He's scared stiff. He doesn't know what the hell he's doing. I can't keep looking, Momma."

Joseph took two more high pitches without ever moving out of position.

"One more," Lewis said. "Come on, you little bastard, throw one more lousy pitch."

But before the pitcher could go into his windup, the runner on first broke away for second base. The umpire immediately called him out, on the grounds that, in little league, it is illegal to steal a base before a pitch is thrown.

Suddenly, the field was filled with people. The other team, whooping loudly, began to run in for its turn at bat. Joseph's team was on its feet and circling the umpire, protesting the call. The coach argued vehemently that, according to the rules, the runner had only to return to first and was not out. The other coach rushed over, shaking his head.

Throughout all the commotion, Joseph stood exactly as he had before, completely still, with the bat pointing straight up in the air.

"You tell him, coach!" Mrs. Lewis shouted in encouragement. "That umpire doesn't know the rules!"

"Jesus Christ!" Lewis said, following the action with the camera. "My kid's in the middle of a riot. And he still isn't doing anything."

Finally, it was decided that the runner was not out. The opposing team would return to the field and the runner would return to first base. Joseph was still at bat and he watched without blinking as he was thrown a fourth high pitch.

Joseph set the bat down neatly and walked to first base.

"Thank God," Lewis said, panning with him as he took the base. "He got on."

Lewis shut off the camera and sat down with a loud sigh. Mrs. Lewis applauded and waved across the field at her son.

"You did good today, Joby," Lewis said as they went into the house. "You got on base and you didn't get out."

"What's so good about walking?" Joseph asked. He set his glove and cap down on the hall table. "I didn't get a hit."

"Well, that was the fault of the pitcher," Mrs. Lewis said. "He didn't throw you anything that you could hit. Besides, it doesn't matter how you get on base, it's getting there that counts. Right, Daddy?"

"Right," Lewis said. "And tomorrow you and I will go out and practice standing with the bat. A little practice with your old man and you'll be ready for the majors."

"In a year or two," Mrs. Lewis said with a smile.

Lewis told Joseph that he had a present for him and went upstairs. He came back down with a giant assortment of crayons in a flat metal box covered with cellophane.

"I went to the stationery store to get some pens," Lewis said, "and I saw this. I thought you might like it."

Joseph thanked his father for the gift and sat down to open it. The box had a decorated lid that had been removed from its hinge and wrapped against the bottom of the tray, so that the crayons could be displayed through the cellophane. Joseph took both halves of the box and began to put them together.

"Here, let me help you with that," Lewis said, taking the box in his hands. "These are tricky sometimes."

Lewis sat down next to his son and tried to fit the lid onto the hinge. He worked with it for a few minutes, but the lid kept popping loose.

"Just one minute more," Lewis said slowly, concentrating. "This little wire has to slide in there, Joby, see? See the little space? But it keeps coming out."

The telephone rang and Mrs. Lewis came into the room to tell her husband that there was a long-distance phone call for him from Germany.

"Okay," Lewis said without looking up from the box. "I'll be there in a second. Just as soon as I get this put together."

Mrs. Lewis watched him struggle unsuccessfully for almost a minute, and then she said, "Daddy, you better take this call. They might be calling direct."

Lewis nodded and kept working. Mrs. Lewis left the room and came rushing back a few seconds later.

"Daddy!" she said. "They're calling direct! Please come to the phone!"

"My son is waiting for me," Lewis said, as the lid went popping into his lap again. "I have to finish this."

"You can do that later," Mrs. Lewis said.

Lewis did not answer, just kept working with the hinge.

"Lewis!" Mrs. Lewis said finally. "Take the call! Do that later."

"Can you wait a few minutes while Daddy takes this call?" Lewis said to his son. "Then I'll fix this for you, okay?"

"I'll try," Joseph said.

"You'll try and wait?" Lewis said, getting up.

"I'll try to fix it," Joseph said.

Lewis set the box down and went into the next room. Joseph took the box and put it on his lap. He looked at it for a while, then took the crayons out of it and turned it over and looked at it some more. Finally, he picked up the lid and began to work it onto the hinge. After a few minutes, the lid clicked and fell into place. Joseph raised and lowered it experimentally a couple of times and it moved on the hinge smoothly. He was putting the crayons back in as Lewis returned.

Joseph smiled at his father and worked the lid for him.

"Oh," Lewis said. "Did you get it put together, Joby?"

"I put the wire through that bump," Joseph said. "Right there." He held the box out and indicated the spot.

"That's very good, sweetheart," Lewis said. He picked up the crayon box and studied the hinge. "I guess Daddy must have been doing it wrong."

Postscript:

"He was like a character out of a Whit Stillman film," says Stephen Randall, a senior editor at *Playboy* who worked with O'Connell Driscoll on several stories. "He lived in an elegant duplex. The furniture was fussy, not the furniture a young person would have. As was so often the case with many of my successful interviewers, I could never understand why anyone would to want to talk to them. I know I wouldn't, and I liked their writing. But the great ones have an ability to get people to open up and say more than they intended to say."

Driscoll, a Hollywood kid whose father made industrials, got the bug for magazine writing as a high school student when he read Tom Wolfe's first anthology of journalism. As a junior at USC, he found himself on the set of filmmaker John Cassevetes's drama, *Minnie and Moskowitz*. Driscoll observed the entire shoot then wrote an article which he submitted to *Esquire* and *Playboy*. Both rejected the piece though *Playboy* encouraged him to pitch more stories. Which is exactly what he did, to no avail.

Finally, one Saturday morning during his senior year, Driscoll sat in a Beverly Hills coffee shop scanning the *Los Angeles Times* when he read that Jerry Lewis was making *The Day the Clown Cried*, a movie about a clown sent to a concentration camp during World War II.

"I knew where Jerry Lewis lived in Bel Air," Driscoll said. "I wrote him a letter saying I really wanted to write something about him, and drove it over to his house. There was a guard outside and I handed the letter over. He said, 'Oh, he's up in his office now.' I drove home to my parents' place, not that far away, and when I got there, the phone was ringing. And it was Jerry."

"I'd like to speak to O'Connell Driscoll please," Lewis said.

"This is O'Connell Driscoll."

"*Nobody* is named O'Connell Driscoll."

Lewis, on the verge of turning forty-seven, liked the kid. "I was so young," says Driscoll, "and I was so Gentile it just cracked him up. They didn't see me as threatening. The rest was his idea. Going to Europe was his idea. He was like, 'Do more rather than less.' "

"I was aware enough to know that I had a lot of good stuff," he says. "At the same time, I was nervous all the way through. I was always nervous when I was writing. There was only one draft—what I handed in, fourteen thousand words. They were surprised. They'd only okayed a small amount of expenses and I had a huge amount of expenses. But they liked it.

"The editor Arthur Kretchmer said to me, 'Do you have notes?' And I said, 'Yeah, I've got notes.' He said, 'Well, good. Keep those notes because we're going to get sued by everybody.' We didn't get sued by anybody it turns out."

The story put Driscoll on the map—and he hadn't even graduated yet; in true Hollywood style, he had an agent before a degree.

It was a startling piece, nothing but direct scenes of Lewis unguarded, arrogant, and at times—like when he pours lighter fluid in a hotel toilet and yells, "Burn motherfucker, burn!"—downright bizarre. It also showed Lewis's tender side, a kidding, loving side generously on display with his parents, his wife, and his son. But it's Lewis's volatility that made jaws drop.

"I was aware of what I was doing," says Driscoll. "I was aware of the language he used. But there was no way around it. My allegiance was to the story not whether I was going to piss him off or not. I wasn't there to get a buddy, I was there to get the story and make it entertaining. You can't be too self-conscious about it. You gotta let it be what it is. And if they hate you, so be it.

"It's not about you. It's not about the writer. It's about the subjects. I'm not there to make them look bad. I'm there to tell a story about the way that they relate to the world. You want to show them the way they are, but there was never any intention in my mind to be vicious.

"I never heard from him personally. I understand why he didn't contact me. I'm sure he was upset by some of it. But he got a lot of publicity out of it and there's no such thing as bad publicity. Years later, I felt—I don't know if guilty is the right word—but I certainly felt the responsibility that these were real people, and I was writing and showing them as such. But it was most controversial with Jerry Lewis because of the language."

It was the start of Driscoll's career. He would never again have it so good.

SAGGY QUINN

When the *Washington Post*'s Style section was the bellwether for cheeky but reliably probing feature writing, Sally Quinn (1941-) occupied the profiler's throne a few daunting steps higher than any of her competition. The proof was right there on the page, in her gimlet-eyed style, and nepotism had nothing to do with it—she made no apologies for being the paramour (and eventual wife) of legendary *Post* editor Ben Bradlee.

Quinn came out of nowhere, journalistically, an army brat raised partly overseas, she began to find her footing when her father moved the family to D.C. and the rounds of embassy parties began.

She joined the *Post* in 1967 at age twenty-eight, and highballed from party coverage to features. The Rudolph Nureyev with whom she would stage a journalistic assignation in 1974—was a wildly talented, absurdly beautiful man-child who was the star defector from the Russian oligarchy that conservative DC saw as our key global enemy. The piece is a classic example of Quinn's work, a bit apart from some of the prickly *Post* gems, the lunch chats gone sideways in which the reader has a sense of watching a nature video of a tigress hunting a gazelle. Here Quinn finds the famous dancer's forthright elusiveness entertainingly deft. When she confirms his fears by asking, "How's your sex life?" She describes for us an elfin charmer with a certain maturity at thirty-six. She'll end by telling him he's revealed nothing. Leave it to the tell-it-like-it-is Quinn to state seven sentences in, "He has a fabulous behind."—FS

NOT ONLY IS HE BEAUTIFUL, BUT HE CAN DANCE TOO

The Washington Post, 1974

Rudolf Nureyev seems so much smaller in real life than he is on the ballet stage. Everybody says so. He is about five feet, eight inches and weighs 150 pounds. But he is beautiful.

He has those high Tartar cheekbones, the slightly slanting eyes, the full cruel mouth slashed by an old scar, the taut muscular body, strong but gentle hands, tousled brown hair, and a provocative half-mischievous, half-soulful look in his eyes. And, of course, there is his behind. He has a fabulous behind. Women follow him around and stare at his fanny as blatantly as some men would stare at a woman's bosom.

There is no doubt that at thirty-six Rudolf Nureyev understands the full extent of his animal magnetism. If pressed, he will admit to an interviewer, with a half-smile and a teasing sincerity, "I know I am beautiful."

He strides with a sense of confidence, a confidence he has gained with the years. He has shed his legendary arrogance, an arrogance he developed, probably, out of a sense of insecurity and perhaps fear. What may seem like arrogance now could be a sort of reverence he has for his own body, which is, after all, the instrument of his craft.

At a Kennedy Center rehearsal, upon entering the room, he walks to the mirror and looks at himself. He falls instantly into a posture of shyness, almost as if he were a teenager meeting someone for the first time who he thought was terribly attractive. It is not offensive. He seems objective about his own subjectivity. He is straightforward about himself. He has a good sense of humor, though somewhat childlike in its simplicity, possibly a holdover from his peasant childhood in Siberia.

There is a strange regal quality about Nureyev, especially considering his lowly origins, though he says he is not a Russian peasant but a Tartar. The dictionary defines Tartar as an "unexpectedly formidable person." One is reminded by this regal simplicity of the king in *The King and I*. Indeed, when he first defected he wanted badly to dance for Balanchine. But Balanchine wouldn't have him and reportedly said, "Rudolf, when you are tired of playing the prince, come to me."

He is playful and he can laugh at himself. Talking to him one has the feeling of playing with a lion cub: you don't want to go too far for fear of making him angry or annoying him. He does, as everyone who has followed him knows, have quite a reputation for an erratic temperament.

In 1964 at the Spoleto festival, Nureyev arrived for a dinner at composer Gian Carlo Menotti's and reportedly ordered one of the guests to get him a plate. Told everyone was to serve himself, the dancer allowed as how, "Nureyev never serves himself. He is served." And he smashed his glass on the floor and stomped out.

Later, when a photographer was trying to take his picture he announced, "I give you three minutes, photographer, and I start counting now." He wouldn't stand next to Margot Fonteyn or lean toward her. "Everyone leans toward Nureyev."

One morning earlier this week the press was invited to watch a Royal Ballet rehearsal by Rudolf Nureyev and Merle Park. Television cameras, reporters, and photographers gathered in rehearsal hall four and waited for the Big Star to appear.

Suddenly the door creaked open and a small face peeked around the corner, the head covered in a heavy wool ski cap, the body swathed in thick hand-knitted peasant sweaters, the feet wrapped in knit stockings and peasant clogs. The person smiled a bit reticently, then unprepossessingly entered the room, shook hands with everybody, answered a few questions politely, then went over to Merle Park to prepare for the rehearsal.

As they began to dance, cameras clicked and cameramen and reporters hovered over the two, making noise, shooting pictures, and staring, until they couldn't concentrate any longer. Shortly afterward, he quietly asked to be left to dance privately and he smiled as everyone cleared out of the room.

"Are you sure that was Nureyev?" one reporter asked outside.

In 1964 during Lyndon Johnson's inaugural, when Rudolf Nureyev was in Washington with Margot Fonteyn to dance for the inaugural, he was approached by a reporter. "Get away from me," he ordered. "I never talk to the press."

One night last week, after his opening performance, Nureyev was to appear afterward at a black-tie function in the Kennedy Center Atrium. He was quite late getting there. Finally arriving, he was besieged by women asking for his autograph, gushing over him, staring at him, firmly nudging each other aside for a good head-to-toe look, grasping his arm to get his attention. He smiled, answered their questions politely, signed autographs, and got himself an omelet. He was friendly and warm and correct for more than an hour.

"Are you sure that was Nureyev?" one woman asked another.

Nevertheless, Nureyev did not want to be interviewed. And when he finally agreed several days later, he asked a PR woman and several others to come along. "I wanted her as a witness," he said in his soft Russian accent. "She is supposed to interrupt, to barge in there and protect me from difficult questions. There are always questions I don't want to answer."

It was midnight and the lights were dim at the Watergate Terrace. A small party arrived shortly before closing to precede Nureyev, who was changing after his performance of *La Fille Mai Gardee*.

"We will want," said the PR person from the Royal Ballet, "one thick rare steak, done on both sides for two minutes and warm inside. So please take it out of the fridge now."

"Madam," said the maître d'hôtel, "we never keep our steaks in the fridge."

A few minutes later, out of the shadows of the room, appeared Nureyev, in a dark wool Yves St. Laurent jacket. He was shivering.

He sits down, puts on a fur Dutch cap, and hugs himself. "This air-conditioning," he says, "I hate it. I like the cold but not air-conditioning. All you Americans love it. I have to wear a sweater all the time to keep warm."

The waiter comes over to take the order. "Okay, five minutes if you want anything to eat," he barks.

"I think," says Nureyev. "I will have a soup."

"Onion?" says the waiter. "No." "Gazpacho?" "No." "Vichyssoise?" "No. I will have turtle."

"We don't have turtle."

Then he reiterates his first order.

"I will have a steak, *bleu*, cooked two minutes on each side. And not cold inside."

"Well, what do you expect, it'll be cold if you want it that rare," said the maître d'hôtel. He obviously doesn't know who Nureyev is. Nureyev doesn't care. He shrugs and pours himself some wine. It is California wine. Too sweet. He asks for imported wine. They bring it.

"I should have eaten in my room," he says. "I have my driver who cooks."

A question is asked that he doesn't like. He laughs and answers, "You are on a wild-goose chase." He seems pleased with that expression. He says it again. And again. "You are chasing wild gooses." He smiles triumphantly.

He makes no attempt to carry on a conversation and will answer questions politely if succinctly, constantly on his guard. His English is fluent, his accent is not heavy, just heavy enough to make him seem mysterious. He doesn't mind long silences.

Nureyev talks first of his life in Russia. Of being a peasant child with nothing to eat. The scar on his lip, he explains, he got when he was thirteen. "We were only allowed a ration of so many grams of bread a day. I gave mine to my dog. When I leaned down to hug him, he tore my mouth open."

He ran away from home when still young and went to Leningrad where he quickly became the star of the Kirov Ballet. But on a tour of the West in 1961 he defected, one of the first of numerous Russian artists to do so.

"I don't see my friends from Russia very much when they come to the West," he says. "We have grown apart. We have nothing really to talk about. Everything is so different. Because I am not involved in politics. I don't care about American politics or Russian politics. You cannot be a dancer and care about it and I devote myself to my art. I think it can be dangerous. Like in Russia. If you are not involved you are out of it."

Nureyev admits to having less training and to starting later than most dancers. But, without modesty, he will admit that he has something special that "nature gave me. I had a talent, a gift. I was talented, I knew I would be a dancer from the beginning … but, you know, everyone in any field who becomes great has to overcome something, a major defect or flaw."

What was Nureyev's major defect?

"Secret," he says solemnly. Then breaks out in a grin. "I will never tell you. Nobody will ever know."

But once one overcomes the major defect, the flaw, and one has achieved success, that's the worst part, according to Nureyev. "It is terrible to be a success," he says. "I mean that. Because once you become a success you have to maintain your excellence. You don't compete with anybody else anymore. You compete with yourself. It is exhausting. You are tired all the time because the hardest thing is maintenance. And there are always people coming up behind you. People who are good and who want to be as good as you. So you must be as good as you were. Not the same. But a lot of young people don't understand that it is a long way from the rehearsal hall to the stage. For me it was a short way. Because I had the strongest driving ambition. Dance is everything for me. I knew what I wanted."

Nureyev knew, too, that what he wanted would be hard. "Ballet is a very hard life. But it is a good one too."

He rewards himself for his energies with a Mercedes, a villa in the south of France, an enormous record collection, a wardrobe designed for him by Yves St. Laurent, and the company of people like Jackie Onassis and Lee Radziwill. But ask him what kind of people he likes to hang out with, who are his friends, and he stiffens, then laughs defensively.

"What do you want me to say," he asks warily. "You are closing in for the kill. I know. You are not interested in the dance. You are interested in the man."

The answer, carefully reflected upon, is "people who are involved in the arts."

Nureyev seems shocked at a distinction between art and entertainment. He does not consider what he is or his personality or his mass popularity as anything like "show biz."

"I don't bring ballet to their level or tastes, they come to mine. If it is because I have the personality or the character to attract people then that is good. It happened in Russia, it happened in London and it happened in America. If I made ballet popular then that is good for other dancers too because they will come and see them. If it's me, that is good for me, but if it hadn't been me, it would have been somebody else."

In the early years of his career, Nureyev tended to be temperamental. But now, a new Rudolf (he hates to be called Rudy) has emerged. Now, everyone seems to agree that he has changed, mellowed, calmed down. He is nicer to deal with and delightful to work with, though members of the company say they have no idea where he lives or what he does. They say they know nothing about him at all. He is remote.

"Having a temperament is part of the ballet," says Nureyev. "It is part of being a star. To sign autographs, have your picture taken, accept compliments, that all takes time. Before I never had the patience. It bored me and I didn't like it. I used to be difficult, rude and temperamental. But I have found now that it is easier than not to be polite. It takes not so much time as I thought. I am older. I learn by time and experience."

He is on his third glass of wine and he is beginning to giggle.

He begins to talk about the movies. He left immediately after a performance the other night to catch a flick downtown. He is a movie freak. He says he goes to more movies in New York than ballets. "Paul Newman is my favorite movie star," he says.

Some people think Nureyev looks like Warren Beatty. He's not too crazy about that. "He's a nice boy," Nureyev says and dismisses that subject with a shrug.

Nureyev stays up until 3:30 or 4 a.m. when he's in New York, watching the late and the late-late shows. "I saw *Anchors Aweigh* with Gene Kelly and Frank Sinatra last night," he says. "I love to watch Gene Kelly dance but Sinatra is my favorite."

He turns to the waiter and asks for a cup of tea.

"I think I am getting drunk. I want to be able to think straight. This interview is so acid it's good we didn't have vinegar with the salad." He laughs.

"I want to be sober when you drop the bomb question, when you do a Hiroshima on me," he giggles again.

Well, then, Mr. Nureyev, how's your sex life?

"I knew it, you see, there it is," and he clasps his hands and throws his head back and laughs with Slavic glee.

"Sporadic," he announces.

Well, tell us more. The ladies will be disappointed with that little morsel and nothing else.

"The ladies will just have to remain tense," he says sadistically.

He leans back smugly, ponders his own words, then leans forward and asks with real earnestness: "This is a city of politicians. How am I doing in this interview? Am I as good as the politicians?"

When told he has revealed absolutely nothing of himself, that he is still a complete mystery, that he is impenetrable as an interviewee, he beams like a Boy Scout receiving a medal.

"Now we must go," he says, his success complete. "We will pay the bill, then you will feel guilty and your conscience will make you write nice things."

And he gets up from the table and stalks triumphantly out of the restaurant, as though he is taking bows for a magnificent performance.

Postscript:

Sally Quinn remembers really liking this piece even though Nureyev never responded. "Everybody else did," she says today, with a laugh. "Friends and readers. Ballet aficionados. That piece got attention. I came to it with a certain reputation: I got people to talk. That's to say, I got them to say things they wished they hadn't said, though nobody ever accused me of making things up. There was a famous Henry Kissinger line who said that the gossip columnist 'Maxine Cheshire makes you want to commit murder. Sally Quinn makes you want to commit suicide.'

"Fame and power are always interesting to me. Fame often comes with power. It's just fascinating to me how some people can handle it, and some can't. I wrote it the way I saw it. I wrote what they said. I would say ninety percent of the pieces were favorable but those are not the ones people remembered. I always went into an interview without preconceived notions and got interesting interviews because of that. A lot of time, I was favorably surprised. It was always fun.

"I never used a tape recorder at that stage of my career. I had a notebook with me and took notes during the conversation. I don't think it was anything I wore. I tried to dress how they would dress. If I was interviewing a farmer, I'd wear jeans and a jacket, if I was interviewing a Park Avenue hostess, I'd dress up. That had everything to do with my upbringing. I was an army brat. I never lived in a place longer than a year-and-a-half. I constantly had to integrate to the culture, people, style of dressing. Tacoma, Washington, where the girls wore poodle dresses and angora sweaters and black and white shoes. We didn't have a lot of money. We'd go to Government employee's merch to get clothes. McMullan blouses with circle pins and Madras skirt and loafers in prep school. I learned very quickly how to fit in—whether it was Greece, Japan, Germany, or Alabama.

"I was lucky I had the advantage to travel around the world. It helps you to be sympathetic and accepting. And curious. My mother was having lunch with her friend once, and her son was there and I was asking him a ton of questions and he said, 'Gee, you're nosy!' That's stuck with me all these years. I wasn't nosy, I'm just curious about other people. I still am."

MARK JACOBSON

The child of New York City school teachers, Mark Jacobson (1951–) grew up in Flushing, Queens, but lit out for seismically changing America after high school. College was just one thing competing for his attention. He attended the University of Wisconsin, San Francisco Art Institute, and the University of California at Berkeley and hitchhiked across the country seventeen times before returning home in the early '70s. Encouraged by *Village Voice* rock 'n' roll columnist Richard Goldstein, Jacobson, who eked out a living as a taxi driver, wrote about the burgeoning disco scene taking place in downtown lofts. *New York* magazine bought the piece and quickly put Jacobson on staff, giving the aspirational uptown biweekly a needed dose of downtown nerve, and hip intelligence. For Jacobson, who really wanted to work at the *Voice*, it was a weird miracle.

Jacobson flourished. His 1974 depiction of cab drivers was the basis of the TV show *Taxi*; later, his unforgettable piece on Harlem gangster Frank Lucas became the basis for the Denzel Washington vehicle *American Gangster*. Jacobson's admiration for the performing arts, and his ability to comment with taste and style, is evident in early profiles of comedians Freddie Prinze and Richard Pryor. It's also there in this 1975 profile of Pam Grier at her height as the 1970s blaxploitation movie queen.

"There's no secret about any of this stuff," says Jacobson. "I want to write a magazine piece; they want to be more famous. It was probably weird for her to hang out with a guy like me. She was so removed from the effect she was having on her audience." Jacobson isn't afraid to slip on a banana peel, making himself the brunt of a joke, to get a laugh, as you'll see in the ending on this story. "I saw her once later," says Jacobson. "She said, 'You know I think the ending was kind of funny.' It's supposed to be funny! Gee whiz, I mean, come on."—AB

SEX GODDESS OF THE SEVENTIES

New York, 1975

Pam Grier peered around the corner of Seventh Avenue and Forty-Second Street, squinted at the row of movie theaters, and quivered her upper lip. Across the street two small-fry superflies in rainbow shoes and felt felony hats had recognized her. They started to snake between the taxicabs, and Pam's panther body stiffened. She clutched her Gucci pocketbook and seemed to grow a few inches. As they got to the sidewalk, she wheeled on her boot heel, lowered her voice a couple of octaves, and asked what she could do for them.

It almost knocked those cats off their platforms; they hung there like vinyl Jell-O. Pam jabbed her aquiline nose into the air insistently. Finally the dude with the fake fox collar meekly asked her for her autograph. Pam loosened a little and signed. *"OOOO-eeee,"* the other guy said, "you are dangerous. What would happen if I tried to get next to you?" Pam squinted again and sent a look that said, "You can *try* me." With that, the dudes got themselves lost under the marquees.

It was just like a Pam Grier movie, except nobody got shot in the groin. When people try to get next to Pam Grier, they usually wind up being very sorry. In a long series of films that will never be reviewed by John Simon, Pam has made a living out of beating up men. She gun-butted them in *Black Mama, White Mama,* cast voodoo spells over them in *Scream, Blacula, Scream,* ran them through with spears in *The Arena*. In *Coffy*, Pam was at her most outgoing: she blasted a pusher's head off, stabbed a kinky hit man in the eye with a bobby pin, ran a mafioso over in a Dodge, and blew away three different sets of genitals with a double-barreled shotgun.

Like the dude said, this lady is dangerous. She might even shake up a few preconceptions about Blacks and women in today's movies. For one thing, those funky films she's been making have raked in prodigious amounts of money. *Coffy* has grossed more than $8.5 million (it cost about $700,000), and *Foxy Brown*, another nut-cruncher, has done almost as well. Pam Grier is now spoken of as a "bankable star," the only Black woman around who fits that description.

The vast majority of the White audience doesn't know much about Pam. That's because, until now, she has been doing her "tough mama" number in what White reviewers generally call "blaxploitation movies." "Tough mamas" have been the thing in Black movies for a few years now. There has been *Cleopatra Jones*, with Tamara Dobson; *Savage Sisters*, with Gloria Hendry; and also *TNT Jackson*, with Jeannie Bell. "Tough mamas" do much the same things as "mean street brothers": bust up slews of lowlife black hustlers, then stick it to the white baddies who really run things, getting laid a lot along the way. It's mostly comic book stuff. But after the roles Black women have traditionally played on the screen, it's got to be a step forward. No one would ever call Pam Grier a victim, not to her face at least. At twenty-five, she's the toughest mama.

Since *Coffy*, in which she can be seen reading *Ms.* magazine (open to the Lost Women section), Pam Grier has become a heroine. More specifically, a Black woman's heroine. She talks street self-sufficiency and attacks the macho's last refuge, his muscles. I saw one woman in a Forty-Second Street theater smack her boyfriend's arm as Pam was icing half the Roman army in *The Arena*. The woman said, "See, fool, I'm going to get myself together like her, so next time you think you're Superman, watch out." Pam herself says, "It makes sense that strong women would come out of Black films. The woman has always been the strength of our family. Because if one thing has always been true, it is that Black boys are terrified of their mamas."

In her beige suite at the Regency on Park Avenue, physically a long way from Forty-Second Street, Pam sits with her leather pant legs crossed, eating twelve dollars-worth of fresh strawberries and talking about power. "Look," she says with a voice that seems to wrap around your windpipe, "I read a lot of scripts these days and most of them are terrible. Really bad. Or maybe the script isn't so bad and they mess it up in the production. Like *Sheba, Baby*. They get some guy to direct it who doesn't know what he's doing. I knew I could have done a better job, but they told me to sit down, you're only the actress, don't tell *us* what to do. So right now I'm setting up my own production company. I know I can do it. I read the trades, I know I'm big. I can get investors. And I'm going to make movies the way I see fit. No threatless, mindless women. No dumb situations. I know I have to go slow. But I'm going to sneak up on them little by little and then I'm going to create a monster. This girl isn't just another body for their cameras."

Her message comes hard and fast. She's learning everything she can about film by taking cinema courses at UCLA. She's been having long discussions with her friend and mentor Roman Polanski. She will pay her young screenwriters out of her own pocket so she won't owe anyone anything when the films are made (the first one being due "within a year"). She plans to become the first Black woman to direct a major film.

Listening to Pam Grier is easy; trying to get next to her is harder. If you change your seat, she'll change hers. We've been jockeying around this hotel room for hours. Even though she isn't as overwhelming as she seems in the movies—about five feet eight and an almost skinny 121 pounds—she still looks dangerous. Her eyes are electric, dark, and smoldering, but she hides them behind bubble sunglasses; she won't let you get lost in them. Her skin is light caramel. It looks five inches deep, and you want to roll in it. But that might not be too smart. Her body, which looks so supple in her films, is all sharp angles and athletic steel from her daily martial arts practice. And her nose, easily her best feature, juts away from her face defiantly—a warning, or a dare.

Pam says she just likes to "have her own space," but you get the message that she isn't the trusting type. She grew up on U.S. Air Force bases in Europe, maybe five or six of them, with her mother and father, an NCO who said "positive" and "negative" instead of yes and no. Eventually the family settled in Denver, where the English accent Pam had acquired on a base in London made her appear like a snot to her classmates. She remembers being teased and beaten up regularly. Later her boyfriend, whom she hoped to marry, volunteered to fight in Vietnam; he died there. Still in mourning, she was spotted at a Colorado beauty contest (she was the only Black) by an agent who invited her to Hollywood. She ran the American International switchboard for a while, listening in whenever producers called to talk about young actresses. "You should have heard what they said ... it was like ordering meat in a butcher shop. Pretty disgusting, really."

In her first few months out West she depended on her cousin, Rosey Grier, the former football Giant turned actor, to show her around. But Rosey, she says, was too busy trying to project a slimmer image and wasn't much help. He did, however, introduce her to Kareem Abdul-Jabbar. Kareem and Pam lived together for a while, until his Muslim religion got in the way. Kareem expected Pam to leave the house when his friends came over because Muslim men cannot tolerate the presence of women when they are discussing the affairs of the world. One day Kareem came home in a rage and screamed at Pam for wearing a bikini on the beach. That was enough.

The roles she began to get didn't do much for her self-image, as a woman or as a human being. She mostly played "things." Her first part was an anonymous piece of flesh in Russ Meyer's *Beyond the Valley of the Dolls*. She played leopard women, Nubian princesses, and lesbian prison guards before she got a chance to be "a person" in *Coffy*. During this time, she was at the artistic mercy of men like Sam Arkoff, president of American International, whom Pam speaks of as "someone who can't see past the cash register, someone who has a peanut brain."

It sounds as if Pam plans to blast her way through the motion picture industry as easily as she brings a mafioso to his knees in her movies. But there are parts of her that don't seem to fit the quicksilver image. A hard-bopping feminist, she can't stop talking about all those beauty contests and who is pretty and who's really a dog. Also, the tough street mama doesn't want to go outside the Regency. Forty-Second Street makes her nervous. She looks down the street and asks if it really is true that "down there" is where her films make their money. This morning Pam jogged up and down Park Avenue; her friends in LA told her Central Park was full of muggers.

Pam has other worries too. Her image is about to be transformed. Now she's beginning to look on her "tough mama" movies as part of her "film adolescence." She's more interested in doing things like *Alice Doesn't Live Here Anymore* and *A Woman Under the Influence.* Starting with her next picture she is changing her name to *Pamela Grier.* " 'Pam' was all right for those action pictures," she says, "but I can't spend my whole life wrestling." But breaking into "the general audience market" is touchy for a Black performer, especially an independent woman. Everyone is telling Pam she's going to have to tone herself down. "They want me to be a noble slave or a doormat," she moans. "I can't end up like Sidney Poitier, he's pure Saran Wrap."

For a star, Pam's got a dumpy hotel room. You'd figure a big moneymaker would at least have a view of the avenue. Pam sneers at the wall outside the window, blames it on American International, and says she's restless. But she's in town only for interviews, has never spent any time in New York, and doesn't know anybody. Finally we decide to go to the Hollywood, a discotheque on West Forty-Fifth Street that some of Pam's LA friends talk about.

The Hollywood has seen better days. Its clientele has always been young and gay, but now the place has lost its glitter. The music is loud, so we dance—there's nothing else to do. Pam is the whole show. She's changed her clothes and is wearing a slinky knit dress that clings. Her hair rises in a great wave away from her unlined forehead. Her nose cuts through the cigarette smoke. Her dance style isn't flamboyant; it's close and clipped, more athletic than sensual. She's not interested in holding hands.

The floor is filled with gay white men. In her four-inch heels, Pam is one of the tallest people in the place. A towering, gorgeous Black woman surrounded by a hundred men with skinny behinds. After a couple of tunes she asks if we can leave. On the way out a squat man in a black leather jacket and a tiny fedora stops us. He looks like one of the Sicilian heavies Pam throttles in her films. He says he's got a piece of the Hollywood and wants to take Pam's picture and put it on the wall. His eyes are plastered to Pam's breasts the whole time he talks; she pretends not to notice.

In the limousine, Pam lets out a deep breath. She slouches and tells the chauffeur to drive up and down the avenues. She looks exhausted. She's been on tour to promote *Sheba, Baby* for about a month now. It was part of her contract and she's doing her best even though she hates the film. But now all the hotel rooms and limousine rides and acting tough to the superflies who want to steal a kiss are beginning to take their toll. Her backbone, which has been starched all day, is folding against the velvet of the limo seat and she feels like talking.

"You know," she says wearily, "I really only started to think about things about a year ago, I mean really think. Right now I'm just scratching the surface. I think I'd rather just make movies for Black people. You know, just be satisfied with what I'm doing. But I can't. I'm too ambitious. I want all the acclaim. That bothers me. I think if I weren't an actress, I'd be a doctor by now. I'd have to, because I'm the first generation of moneymakers in my family, and I can't blow it now."

After nearly fifteen hours together, Pam and I are almost friends. We've played Pong in the arcades and had footraces in Central Park. She says I must be "from the Bronx or something" because my questions are "intellectual." She's sitting, almost curled into a ball, on one of ice cream-colored Regency couches, looking very tender. She takes off her sunglasses and invites further discussion. I tell her about the Brooklyn graffiti artist who has been writing, "That's good for her, what about the rest of us niggers!" on the glossy subway ads for *Sheba, Baby*. She doesn't want to hear that. She starts to tense again. "Everyone thinks I have an Eldorado. Well. I don't have an Eldorado.

I have a Jeep. Eldorado's are for fools; they waste too much gas." Then she says the guy ought to get an education so he won't spend time writing on walls. I ask her about a *Ms.* magazine piece that asserts that much of the violence in her films only serves to separate women by assuming that Black women are athletically superior to white women. Now Pam is pissed off. "What do they know?" she rails. "They're just a bunch of rich bitches. What do they know about my problems?"

I can see it was a mistake—one hassle too many—and try to change the subject to her nose. I like it a lot, I tell her. "Yeah," she says tersely, "they used to call me hawk in school. You want to come over here and punch it?" I say I was only kidding, but it sounds like a dare, so I do it. I stand in front of her, legs spread, menacing her flared nostrils with a clenched hand. It is the closest we've been to each other since we met. Suddenly her mouth twists. Before I realize it, a fist is heading toward my groin. I try to block it, but it is too late. As I stumble across the thick Regency rug, Pam Grier says, "See, see what I have to do to defend myself?"

Postscript:

Mark Jacobson's first assignment for *New York* came about when he drove a taxi. That's how he learned about the underground discos blossoming downtown. After the piece appeared, says Jacobson, the editors at *New York*, "had me as the White guy who could talk to Black people. Which I was happy to do. But it was kind of gross. They didn't have any Black reporters. I was the only street guy they knew. Everyone else was buttoned down.

"I think it was my idea to do Pam Grier. It was early on, within the first eight or nine pieces I had published. I like doing profiles because at least back in the day they would give you unlimited access. I spent an enormous amount of time with Richard Pryor when I wrote about him, at his house, in the car, we went to the movies. Ali was fighting a Japanese wrestler. We went to dinner at Musso and Franks and ate dinner with Jim Brown and two guys from the Dallas Cowboys and then went to the see the fight. He liked me enough to let me come along. There were no PR people. Maybe they made the original introduction, then they just dropped out of the scene.

"It was a big deal to have someone come from a national magazine and do a big piece. It was an accepted idea that you as the writer were going to be around, and this was sometimes going to be a two-to-three-week process, sometimes longer. You were going to be there because the magazine pieces were mini biographies. This was before everyone hated the media. I feel very grateful and blessed to have functioned in my job at a time when magazine journalism was *it*! It was the place you wanted to be. I managed to buy a house in Park Slope and send three kids to college without being anything but a magazine writer. This is the great accomplishment of my life."

ROBERT WARD

Robert Ward (1943-) writes like a man who doesn't care if he gets invited back. In a postscript to his 1977 profile of Reggie Jackson included here, he described himself, with only a little irony, as "a tough-guy reporter, who really would print anything no matter what the fuck anyone said to me." Notably, Ward never abused this privilege.

Nonetheless, while he approached his subjects with unflagging curiosity and respect, if someone chose to make a fool of themselves in his presence, he never turned a blind eye, especially if that person had already spent ten years in the major leagues, which leaves plenty of time to learn how to keep your mouth shut in front of a reporter.

As a journalist, Ward was attracted to talented people—actors and athletes mostly—who were a puzzle to themselves, forever trying to reconcile the job, the public's perception, and what they thought of themselves at 3 a.m. He published his first article in a national magazine in 1974—about the cops in a small upstate New York city—while he was still teaching college English. He'd grown up in working-class Baltimore, and started out trying to write fiction. By the time he began teaching college in his mid-twenties, he had already published one novel. But teaching just paid the bills, and as soon as he found out he could pay those bills by writing for magazines, he quit teaching and turned pro.

Serendipitously, Ward got into journalism just when it was most receptive to stylists and provocateurs able to go 20,000 words without getting winded. It was a milieu made for his talents, and he took full advantage with a string of enduring stories, notably his defining profiles of Lee Marvin and Larry Flynt. If anyone ever got more out of either man, they kept it to themselves. In the early '80s, when the magazines where Ward had found a home began to dry up, he moved to Hollywood and began writing for *Hill Street Blues* and then writing and producing *Miami Vice*. He still writes for television, and he has never stopped writing fiction, including the acclaimed novel *Red Baker*.—Malcolm Jones

REGGIE JACKSON IN NO-MAN'S LAND

Sport, 1977

Oh, golden, yellow light shimmering on Reggie Jackson's chest! Yes, that's he, the latest member of the American League Champion New York Yankees, and he is standing by his locker, bare-chested, million-dollar sweat dripping from his brow, golden pendants dangling from his neck. God, he looks like some big baseball Othello as he smiles at the gaggle of reporters who rush toward him, their microphones thrust out, their little ninety-eight-cent pens poised, ready to take down his every word. But somehow, it's hard to ask the man questions ... certainly not such standard ballplayer questions as "How's the arm?" or "Toe hurt?" ... for not all ballplayers are Reggie Jackson, whose golden pendants catch the sunlight filtering through the steamy Fort Lauderdale clubhouse windows and reflect dazzlingly into your eyes. What are these priceless reflectors? Well, first, there is a small golden bar with the word "Inseparable" on it, a gift from Reggie's Norwegian girlfriend, and gyrating next to that memento is a dog tag—the inscrutable Zen koan (though slightly reminiscent of the Kiwanis Club), "Good Luck Is When Hard Work Meets Opportunity." And, finally, there is the most important bauble of all, an Italian horn that Reggie tells a reporter is supposed to keep the evil spirits away!

Evil spirits? Egads. What evil spirits can be following Reggie Jackson? The man has been on three World Series Championship teams (Oakland A's 1972–1974), has led the league in RBIs (1973: 117), home runs (1973: thirty-two, 1975: thirty-six) and was the American League's MVP in 1973. Since then he has topped his on-the-field-feats by playing out his option under Charles O. Finley, and refusing to sign with his new club, the Baltimore Orioles, until they gave him a gigantic raise. Finally came the *coup de grâce*: signing with the New York Yankees for three million big ones. Reggie is expected to be the biggest thing to hit New York since King Kong. So where are the evil spirits?

"No evil spirits, actually," Reg says, answering a newsman's question. "Just in case, you know? Hey, could you move that mike out of the way? Shoving it up my nose like that is *sooooo* uncomfortable ... ."

The little man yanks his mike back.

"I am not merely a baseball player," Reggie says to another reporter, who nods gravely. "I am a Black man who has done what he wants, gotten what he wanted, and will continue to get it.

"Now what I want to do," he adds, "is develop my intellect. You see, on the field I am a surgeon. I put on my glove and this hat ... ."

He picks up the New York Yankee baseball hat. Itself a legend. Legendary hat meet legendary head!

"And I put on these shoes ... . " Reggie points down to his shoes. "And I go out on the field, and I cut up the other team. I am a surgeon. No one can quite do it the way I do. But off the field ... I try to forget all about it. You know, you can get very narrow being a superstar."

Reggie removes his cap. "I mean, being a superstar ... can make life very difficult, difficult to grow. So I like to visit with my friends, listen to some *fine* music, drink some *good* wine, perhaps take a ride in the country in a *fine* car, or ... just walk along the beach. Nature is extremely important to me. Which may be just about the only trouble I'll have in New York. I'll miss the trees!"

Then, in his quiet, throaty voice, Reg politely says he must be off to the training room.

"Terrific," a jaunty reporter says as Reggie leaves. "He's so terrific. He's the kinda guy you don't want to talk to every day ... because he gives you so much. It's like a torrent of material. He overwhelms you!"

"Yes," I say. "But how do the other guys on the Yankees feel about having a tornado in their presence? I heard Thurman Munson and some of the others gave him a chilly reception."

"No problem," says the reporter. "All that stuff about problems on the team is just something somebody wrote to sell papers. Hell, Reggie hasn't even been here for a week. There hasn't been time for resentment yet!"

The next day after practice, Reggie Jackson is once again standing by his locker, once again surrounded by reporters, who ask him to reveal his "personal philosophy of life."

I look down the seats before lockers and see last year's Yankee stars sitting like dukes around the king. Next to Jackson is Chris Chambliss. Remember him? He hit the home run that won the pennant for the Yanks. But no one seems much interested in this instant (though brief) hero's developing intellect or his reflections on recombinant DNA, which happens to be the subject Chambliss is discussing with Willie Randolph. And down the line a little farther is old gruff and grumble himself, Thurman Munson. Today he rubs his moustache, and stares at the floor, looking like Bert Lahr in the *Wizard of Oz*. Folks aren't rushing to ask him about the philosophical questions that are addressed to Jackson, yet Munson is the acknowledged "team leader."

And across the room is Catfish Hunter, the wise old Cat, and businesslike Ken Holtzman. Their combined salaries are enough to send up a space shot to Pluto, but no one is asking them if they like to recite Kahlil Gibran. It's strange, a little dreamlike. There is the Superteam, but if this first week is any example, Reggie Jackson has taken over so totally that it's almost as if the other players were rookies who had yet to prove themselves to the press.

Now, Jackson says goodbye to the reporters, and tells me he is going outside to sign a few late-afternoon autographs. Would I like to come? Certainly.

And so we stand out by the first baseline while the fans crowd around, pushing and shoving and holding up their cameras.

"Smile, Reggie," says a woman with a scarf on her head, tied up so she looks like she has two green rabbit ears.

Reggie produces a semi-smile.

"You have such white teeth," she says.

Jackson turns to me and raises his eyebrows, then moves along signing scraps of paper and baseballs when a man on crutches is pushed precariously close to the edge of the stands. Jackson stops signing and demands that the other fans help the crippled man. The fans do what he says.

Finally, after Reggie has signed endless signatures, a young boy says, "Thank you, Mr. Jackson."

Reggie stops, looks up at me and says: "You sign a million before anyone ever says thank you."

On that perfect exit line, Reggie does a perfect exit. He picks up a loose ball and flips it to the crowd, who cheer and applaud. Waiting for Jackson to get his rubdown, I ask Sparky Lyle, who is seated in front of his locker: "How's it going?"

"Great," says Lyle. "I may be leaving tomorrow. We are only about two hundred and fifty thousand dollars away from one another."

Perhaps not the best time to ask him about the new three-million-dollar superstar. But duty must be done.

"I don't think we need him," Lyle says. "Not to take anything away from his talents, but what we really needed was a good right-handed hitter. A right-handed superstar."

Jackson comes strutting into the room. Not a self-conscious strut. Just his natural superstar strut. He can't help it if he is bigger than all indoors.

Lou Piniella strides across the room and says, "Hey, Reg, How you doing?"

"How you doing, hoss?" Reggie says affably.

"I'm not the horse, Reg," Piniella says, with a good deal of uncertainty in his voice. "You're the hoss ... I'm just the cart."

Jackson smiles, trying to pass the remark off as a joke.

Jackson and I enter the Banana Boat Bar, and he undoes his windbreaker just enough to reveal the huge yellow star on his blue T-shirt. Around the star are the silver letters that spell out superstar! At the bar, he discards the jacket. All around us people start staring and the waitresses start twitching in their green Tinkerbell costumes.

We order Lite beers, and Reggie gives me a pregnant stare and says, "If I seem a little distant, it's because I got burned once by *Sport* magazine. They wrote a piece which said I caused trouble on the team. That I have a huge ego. That I only hit for a .258 average. That I wasn't a complete ballplayer. They only say that kind of stuff about Black men. If a White man happens to be colorful, then it's fine. If he's Black, then they say he's a troublemaker."

I tell him that I have no intention of showing him as a troublemaker. As far as I'm concerned the league could use fifty more Reggie's, and fifty fewer baseball players who sound like shoe salesmen.

But almost before I'm finished, Reggie has forgotten his fears. "You see," he says, "I've got problems other guys don't have. I've got this big image that comes before me, and I've got to adjust to it. Or what it has been projected to be. That's not 'me' really, but I've got to deal with it. Also, I used to just be known as a Black athlete, now I'm respected as a tremendous intellect."

"A tremendous intellect?" I say.

"What?" says Jackson, waving to someone.

"You were talking about your tremendous intellect."

"Oh, was I?" Jackson says. "No, I meant ... that now people talk to me as if I were a person of substance. That's important to me."

I mention Jackson's reportage on the Royals-Yankees pennant playoffs last year for ABC, saying that most of my friends felt that Reggie had done a much better job of analyzing the motivation of the players than Howard Cosell. What's more, he did it in the most hostile atmosphere imaginable, with Cosell constantly hassling him and chiding him for defending Royals's centerfielder Al Cowens on a controversial call.

"Well, that is part of my problem," says Reggie. "I do everything as honestly as I can. I give all I have to give. But I don't let people get in my way. Cosell was insecure. He thought I was trying to put him down, make him look bad by correcting him. He made quite a stink about me to the big people at ABC, but they took up for me. I really wasn't trying to compete with him. I was just being myself and it got me in trouble."

Jackson smiles, sits back and folds his arms over his superstar chest. A second later we are joined by Jim Wynn, who at thirty-five is trying to make a comeback with the Yankees: Once a tremendous long ball hitter known as "The Toy Cannon," Wynn has been faltering, and certainly he can't have more than a year or so left. He orders a drink, and then Reggie and he begin to talk about hitting in Boston's Fenway Park.

"You are gonna love the left field fence," Reggie says.

"I know I will," Wynn says. "If they play me, you know I'll hit some out."

But he doesn't sound convinced. There is a lull in the conversation and then Wynn looks over at Reggie, and says, "You know, Reggie, I hope my son grows up to be like you. Not like me. Like you."

Wynn smiles in awe at Jackson, and I realize that for all their professionalism, the Yankees are just as subject to the mythology of the press as any fan. Just by showing up, Jackson has changed the ambiance of the locker room. And no one yet knows if it's for good or ill.

As I ponder, two of the original mythmakers appear at the Banana Boat—Mickey Mantle, now a spring batting coach, and his old crony, manager Billy Martin. Soon they are settled into drinking and playing backgammon, and when they are joined by Whitey Ford, Jackson hails a waitress and sends them complimentary drinks. The waitress comes back to Reggie and says, "Whitey Ford appreciates your offer of a drink, but says he would rather have your superstar T-shirt."

Jackson breaks into a huge smile, peels off his shirt, and runs bare chested across the room. He hands the shirt to Ford, and then Ford, in great hilarity, takes off his pink cashmere sweater and gives it to Jackson. A few minutes later Reggie is back at the bar, the sweater folded in his lap.

"That's really something, isn't it!" Jackson says. "Whitey Ford giving me his sweater. A Hall-of-Famer. I'm keeping this."

He smiles, looking down lovingly at the sweater.

On the Yankees the old-timers still retain their magic, even to the younger stars like Jackson. In a way it is easier for him to relate to them than his own teammates. For they were mythic, legends, as he is … . In fact, their legends are still stronger than Reggie's, coming as they did back when ugly salary disputes didn't tarnish both players and managers.

This becomes even more apparent when Jackson moves to the backgammon table to join the crowd watching Mantle and Martin play one of the most ludicrously bad, but hilarious, games in recent history. Both of them beginners and slightly loaded, the two men resort to several rather questionable devices. The object of the game is to get your men, or chips, around the board, and into your opponent's home, then "beat them off the board." The man who gets all his men out first wins. (You throw a pair of dice to decide how many spaces you can move.) Martin rolls a seven and quickly moves nine spaces. Jackson and Ford laugh hysterically. Mantle rolls his dice, moves the properly allotted amount, and then simply slips three of his men off the board and into his pants pocket. Martin, busy ordering drinks and taking advice from Reggie, misses Mantle's burglary, which gives Mickey a tremendous advantage in the game. Martin's next roll lands him on two of Mantle's men and sends them back to the center bar. Mantle rolls the dice, orders another round of drinks and, while Martin chats with the waiter, takes four more of his chips off the table and puts them under his chair. Mantle chuckles as Martin, unaware of what has happened, rolls the dice. Reggie tries to control his laughter—unsuccessfully—the mirth bursting out of him. And now everyone is laughing, Mantle so hard that tears are streaming down his face. Martin suddenly notices that Mantle, despite weaker rolls of the dice, already has fewer men on the board.

"You bastard!" Martin shouts. "Where are all your chips?"

Mantle protests his innocence with great vigor but Martin reaches down and pulls out the evidence from under Mantle's chair. Mantle screams in mock surprise, and then throws up his hands. "Hell, Billy," he says, "you were beating me even though I was cheating."

"You bum," says Martin, "You bum. I'm just too good. I'm a winner."

"Nobody can beat Billy," Mantle says as he beams at his old buddy.

Reggie is still laughing, shaking his head, and I can't help but feel that he has missed something. Mantle, Ford, and Martin have a kind of loyalty and street-gang friendship that today's transient players don't have time to develop. Soon Mantle and Martin are involved in another humorous game, and Reggie goes back to the bar. Alone.

Minutes later I join him and try to gauge his mood. What did he feel watching Mantle and Martin? In a second I have my answer, for Reggie starts talking about how he is less the showman. He seems to be talking directly from his bones:

"You know," he says, "this team ... it all flows from me. I've got to keep it all going. I'm the straw that stirs the drink. It all comes back to me. Maybe I should say me and Munson ... but really he doesn't enter into it. He's being so damned insecure about the whole thing. I've overheard him talking about me."

"You mean he talks loud to make sure you can hear him?"

"Yeah. Like that. I'll hear him telling some other writer that he wants it to be known that he's the captain of the team, that he knows what's best. Stuff like that. And when anybody knocks me, he'll laugh real loud so I can hear it ... . "

Reggie looks down at Ford's sweater. Perhaps he is wishing the present Yankees could have something like Ford and Martin and Mantle had. Community. Brotherhood. Real friendship.

"Maybe you ought to just go to Munson," I suggest. "Talk it out right up front."

But Reggie shakes his head. "No," he says. "He's not ready for it yet. He doesn't even know he feels like he does. He isn't aware of it yet."

"You mean if you went and tried to be open and honest about it he'd deny it."

Jackson nods his head. "Yeah. He'd say, 'What? I'm not jealous. There aren't any problems.' He'd try to cover up, but he ought to know he can't cover up anything from me. Man, there is no way ... . I can read these guys. No, I'll wait, and eventually he'll be whipped. There will come that moment when he really knows I've won ... and he'll want to hear everything is all right ... and then I'll go to him, and we will get it right."

Reggie makes a fist, and clutches Ford's sweater: "You see, that is the way I am. I'm a leader, and I can't lie down ... but 'leader' isn't the right word ... it's a matter of PRESENCE ... . Let me put it this way: no team I am on will ever be humiliated the way the Yankees were by the Reds in the World Series! That's why Munson can't intimidate me. Nobody can. You can't psych me. You take me one-on-one in the pit, and I'll whip you ... . It's an attitude, really ... . It's the way the manager looks at you when you come into the room ... . It's the way the coaches and the batboy look at you ... . The way your name trickles through the crowd when you wait in the batter's box ... . It's all that ... . The way the Yankees were humiliated by the Reds? You think that doesn't bother Billy Martin? He's no fool. He's smart. Very smart. And he's a winner. Munson's tough too. He is a winner, but there is just nobody who can do for a club what I can do ... . There is nobody who can put meat in the seats [fans in the stands] the way I can. That's just the way it is ... . Munson thinks he can be the straw that stirs the drink, but he can only stir it bad."

"You were doing it just a few minutes ago over there with Martin, weren't you?" I say. "Stirring a little."

"Sure," says Jackson, "but he has presence too. He's no dummy. I can feel him letting me do what I want, then roping me in whenever he needs to ... but I'll make it easy for him. He won't have to be 'bad' Billy Martin fighting people anymore. He can move up a notch cause I'll open the road. I'll open the road, and I'll let the others come thundering down the path!"

Jackson sits back, staring fiercely at the bar. A man in love with words, with power, a man engaged in a battle. Jim Wynn resumes his seat next to Reggie and watches him with respect. An ally.

But, I wonder—are there any others?

Billy Martin is sitting in his office at Yankee Stadium South. He is half dressed and his hair is messed, but for all that he still has what Jackson called PRESENCE. Now he runs his hand through his hair and laughs: "I couldn't lose to Mantle, could I?" he says.

"You had him psyched."

Martin laughs again and nods. "And he was trying to act like he wasn't mad."

Mantle comes in the door sipping coffee and looking about two years older than the night before. "You know," he says, "I woke up this morning, and I had me a whole pocket full of them white things!"

After we finish laughing, I ask Martin if he thinks there will be any problems having Reggie Jackson on the team.

Martin, who as Reggie himself said is "no dummy," smiles and asks, "What kind?"

"Like team leader problems?"

Martin shakes his head. "Not a chance. We already have a team leader. Thurman Munson."

I walk into the locker room and sit with Catfish Hunter in front of his locker and talk about Reggie. Catfish shoots a stream of tobacco juice on the floor, and shakes his head slowly, philosophically. "Reggie is a team leader," he says. "The thing you have to understand about Reggie is he wants everyone to love him."

For a second I think Cat is going to elaborate on this theme, but he holds back, chooses a new path—a safer one. "I mean," he says, "he can get hot with his bat and carry a team for three weeks. He's always ready to go all the time."

Hunter squints at me as if to say, *"That's all, my friend. I'm staying out of this one."*

Chris Chambliss's locker is right next door to Reggie Jackson's. The men literally rub elbows when they dress. Yet when I ask

Chambliss how he feels about Reggie, he says, "I haven't had a chance to talk to him yet. I think he'll help the ball club. Most of the rumors you have heard are untrue. Still, we do have a lot of personalities on this team … things could happen. I doubt it. But they could."

I catch Thurman Munson as he comes in to practice. An hour late. I wonder if he isn't having some kind of psych battle with Jackson. Which star arrives on the field the latest? Gruffly, he declines to talk to me until after practice, and then he declines again for some thirty minutes. Finally, he nods me over and I ask him about Jackson.

"What are you asking me for?" he says. "Why does everybody ask me?"

"I'm not singling you out," I say. "I've asked quite a few others. But there has been talk that you two will have problems competing as team leader."

Munson shakes his head, makes a face. "No. No way. And what difference does it make if I'm not 'team leader'? There are a lot of leaders on this team. We've got a lot of stars. They are all leaders. As far as Reggie goes, he's a good player. He'll help the club. Has a lot of power."

"How about jealousy over his salary?"

"No," Munson says, "I don't care about that. He signed as a free agent. I hope he makes ten million dollars. Is that all?" Munson turns away and begins to talk to a businessman about a shopping center they hope to build in Florida.

It's late in the afternoon and Reggie Jackson is taking extra batting practice. The only people left on the field are Thurman Munson and Chris Chambliss. And a young pitcher, a rookie who is new to me.

Jackson fouls off a couple of pitches, and Chambliss looks at Munson and says, "Show time!" There is a real bite in his kidding. "Hey," says Munson, "are we out here to see this?"

Jackson digs in and fouls off a few more.

"Some show!" says Munson. "Real power!"

Jackson tries to laugh it off, and finally connects on a pitch. It falls short of the fence, and Munson and Chambliss smile at one another. Munson steps into the cage, but Jackson hurries into the locker room.

I am about ready to leave, and I thank Reggie for his cooperation, but he seems disturbed by my going. "Listen," he says, "I'd like to know what the guys thought of me. You talked to them. How about telling me?"

"Okay," I say. "I'll meet you back at the Banana Boat."

An hour later, at the Banana Boat, I tell Jackson that Lyle had said the team didn't need him, that Lyle said it was nothing personal, but the Yankees needed a right-handed hitter more. Then I tell him that Munson had denied there was any problem, and I mention that Chambliss had said, "I haven't had a chance to talk to him yet."

"Yeah," says Jackson. "You see it's a pattern. The guys who are giants like Catfish, the guys who are really secure … they don't worry about me. But guys like Munson … . It's really a comedy, isn't it. I mean, it's hilarious … . Did you see him in the batting cage? He is really acting childish. Like the first day of practice he comes up to me and says, 'Hey, you have to run now … before you hit.' You know he's playing the team captain trying to tell me what to do. But I play it very low key. I say, 'Yeah, but if I run now I'll be too tired to hit later,' and Munson says, 'Yeah, but if you don't run now, it'll make a bad impression on the other guys.' So I say, 'Let me ask the coach,' and I yelled over to Dick Howser, 'Should I run now or hit?' and Howser yelled, 'Aw, the hell with running. Get in there and hit.' So that's what I did. It really made Munson furious. But I did it so he couldn't complain. Listen, I always treat him right. I talk to him all the time, but he is so jealous and nervous and resentful that he can't stand it. If I wanted to I could snap him. Just wait until I get hot and hit a few out, and the reporters start coming around and I have New York eating out of the palm of my hand … he won't be able to stand it."

Jackson delivers all this with a kind of healthy, competitive, and slightly maniacal glee. It's as if he has said to himself, "Okay, they aren't going to love me. So I'll break 'em down. I'll show them who's boss." And he might. I can't help but think that the situation would be a lot healthier if the other Yankees had come to him.

"How has Chambliss been treating you?" I ask.

"Standoffish. They all have. You see Piniella in there yesterday? He said that stuff about me being the horse and him being the cart. That's how they feel. But at least he talked to me. That was a kind of a breakthrough. That and the thing with Whitey, with the sweater. That was good too."

"Maybe you are overreacting," I say. "It is a new year, and everyone has heard about your legend, and they feel like they can't be the ones to come up to you and try to break the ice because then it will look like they are trying to kiss your ass, and they'll feel embarrassed and self-conscious."

Jackson nods hopefully. "Yeah, it could be that. I know it could be. Say, did you talk to Billy Martin about me?"

"Yeah," I say. "He told me that the Yankees had a team leader."

"Yeah? Who?"

"Munson."

Reggie laughs ruefully.

"But maybe he's gotta say that," I say. "It wouldn't look good to say you are the team leader this early. It would hurt Munson's pride."

"That's right," Jackson says. "I just want you to know that [coach] Elston Howard came up to me today and said, 'No matter what anybody says, you are the team leader.' So I think there is some real heavy stuff going on. But it is weird. You know, up until yesterday Martin had hardly said two words to me. But he has made me feel I'm all right. Still, I don't understand it."

"It could go back to your verbal ability," I suggest. "I mean, a lot of athletes are suspicious of people who can talk well. It makes them feel dull and stupid, so they resent the other guy and get hostile toward him."

"Right," says Jackson. "That's true. I've been through that one before. But you know ... the rest of the guys should know that I don't feel that far above them ... . I mean, nobody can turn people on like I can, or do for a club the things I can do, but we are all still athletes, we're all still ballplayers. We should be able to get along. We've got a strong common ground, common wants ... . I'm not going to allow the team to get divided. I'll do my job, give it all I got, talk to anybody. I think Billy will appreciate that ... . I'm not going to let the small stuff get in the way … . But if that's not enough … then I'll be gone. A friend of mine has already told me: 'You or Munson will be gone in two years.' I really don't want that to be the case … because, after all is said and done, Munson is a winner, he's a fighter, a hell of a ballplayer … but don't you see … .'"

Reggie pauses, and opens his hands in a gesture that seems to imply, *"It's so apparent, why can't Munson and Chambliss and all the rest of them understand the sheer simplicity … the cold logic?"*

"Don't you see, that there is just no way I can play second fiddle to *anybody*. Hah! That's just not in the cards … . There ain't no way."

Postscript:

From his 2012 anthology, *Renegades*, here's Ward with more:

It was a hot summer day in June 1977, and I was on the Long Island Railway coming in from my house in the Hamptons. For the past month I had holed up in this old red-shingled house on the bayside just a few miles south of Montauk. Jann Wenner had come over one night to tease me about not having a house, or a compound, like he did on the ocean side. But the truth was I loved it where I was. Tall grass, swans that swam up to the beach every night, and plenty of room for my dog, Byron, to run around chasing rabbits. My girlfriend, Robin, loved it too and it had been a wonderful month, writing my screenplay, *Cattle Annie and Little Britches*. I wanted and received no phone calls. This was, of course, before the days of the computer so there were no emails, no phone machine, and no one had my number. I didn't want to be bugged by my magazine editors. The truth was I was kind of burned out interviewing endless people and now that I was making money writing scripts that seemed a better way to go. (Little did I know I would have another eight years of struggling before I cracked Hollywood. It's a good thing we don't know what lies before us because if someone had told me I would be looking forward to eight more years of living hand to mouth I might have turned to a life of crime instead).

So there I was with my typewriter, perfect sunsets, swans, Byron and on weekends gorgeous Robin, who had a job at Ballantine publishing. Everything was fine and dandy. I never once gave a thought to Reggie Jackson.

Why? Because in those days magazines, like *Sport*, had a three-month lead period. That meant you handed the piece three months before it was going to be published. In fact, I had done three or four other pieces after it for other magazines, plus my screenplay, and some short fiction. Reggie Jackson was the last thing on my mind.

One day, however, I wanted to go into the city to see some of my friends. I was getting a little cabin fever writing all day and night, and I wanted a little city-action. So I took the train into town and got off at Penn Station. I was headed to a cab on Eighth Avenue when I happened to see the sports page of the *New York Post* on the magazine rack. The headline was in big bold letters.

It read: "furor on the Yankees!!"

I walked over to the magazine stand and picked it up. As I read, my heart beat faster and faster. I don't recall the exact words but the gist of it was: "A bomb exploded in the Yankee clubhouse today due to an article on Reggie Jackson written by Robert Ward of *Sport* magazine ... ."

"Holy shit," I said, and ran for a pay phone. I called Berry Stainback; he wasn't in. But Dick Schapp was.

"Robert," he said. "Where the hell have you been? The whole goddamned world wants to talk to you!"

"They do?" I said. I'd had some violent reactions to my writing before but nothing like this. Dick then listed five radio shows and three TV shows that wanted me on. Not to mention every newspaper in the country.

"It's great," Dick said. "We haven't had a story like this in a long time!"

"Right!" I said. "Great!"

"Why don't you come up here now and we'll plan on what we're going to do first!"

"Is it okay if I get to my apartment and change clothes first?"

"Yeah, sure," Dick said. "But get over here. The Yankees are going nuts. I talked to Phil Rizzuto about twenty minutes ago."

The thing was, even though I was a tough guy reporter, who really would print anything no matter what the fuck anyone said to me (and especially if they threatened me), I was still an all-American kid, who had always loved Phil "Scooter" Rizzuto. The idea that I had done something that would make him hate me really bothered me. I mean, hell, I had his baseball card!

"So what did Phil say?" I said, buffering myself for the shock.

"He loved it," Dick said. "Phil's just like all the old Yanks. They can't stand Reggie."

That was only a partial relief. I didn't want people to hate Reggie. The truth was, I kind of felt sorry for him. And did the old Yanks hate him because he was Black and smart? Or was it because they couldn't take his big ego, his fur coats, and all the rest? Or were they just jealous of him because it was his time in the sun and theirs was over?

That was one problem with journalism that I never got over. You stirred up a hornet's nest, but then left to do other pieces and never really knew what the real answers were.

Ah, well, I told myself, you should feel good about it. You've only done one piece on the New York Yankees and it's become world famous.

Such are the small victories of freelance writers.

Jacqueline Trescott

Even before Jackie Trescott (1947-) became a high school gossip columnist she was surrounded by newspapers. Her grandfather bought each New York daily and her father collected out-of-town Black papers such as the *Amsterdam News* and the *Pittsburgh Courier*. But it wasn't until she attended St. Bonaventure and spent two years (1965–1966) as a proofreader for the *Newark Evening News*, that she considered a career in newspapering. Trescott attended graduate school at NYU, then got her start at The *Washington Star*, an afternoon paper that for years was the biggest in DC. After the usual initiation on the police and fire beats, Trescott landed at Portfolio, the paper's revamped women's section. She moved on to the *Washington Post* Style section a few years later and found a dream beat, covering the Black Arts Movement. The *Post* had a sizable Black readership, and the task before Trescott was to write for that audience while including White readers. "It was a very exciting time," Trescott says. "I got to interview incredible artists like Alice Walker, Toni Morrison, Debbie Allen, Phylicia Rashad, and Stevie Wonder."

Add to the list Donna Summer, grappling with the suddenness of her fame as a sex symbol. In smart, inquiring fashion, and faced with the space limitations of a daily newspaper, Trescott paints a memorable picture of Summer's vulnerability. She delivers what we always want from a celebrity profile—to somehow feel as if we're in the room with the star and to see the frailty and humanity of the person behind the artist.—AB

DONNA SUMMER INTIMATE AND UNTOUCHABLE, TRYING TO COOL HER IMAGE

The Washington Post, 1978

Donna Summer, the torrid singer whose name and moans have steamed up disco for almost three years, has sung ten songs. There have been few grunts or grinds. She has shown this audience, as she vowed to do in her first American tour, that she is not a heavy-breathing novelty but a versatile performer. To demonstrate, she has just ripped the lid off "The Way We Were."

The people in the audience respond well but are still anticipating what they hope is underneath Summer's modest covering of billowy chiffon and sequins. Slowly the layers of chiffon vanish, slowly the audience starts to steam. Forty minutes into her show, the slow beat of "Love to Love You Baby" begins. The seventeen-minute disco version with its twenty-two orgasmic gasps has made her a Phenomenon and earned her the title, "Sex Queen of the '70s." Now the gray eminence with his blonde companion is grinning, the cats from Baltimore are calling louder, the gays are jumping up to dance.

Now Summer, down to a dancer's black skirt and sequined vest, has an icy, forbidden-fruit look on her long face. With the makeup she looks like a Barbie Doll. She is moaning. She is massaging the microphone stand, moving her hips. She is doing things that would make Blaze Starr blush. She is doing all the things in public your mother forbade you to do in private. The audience is manic.

She doesn't smile, she hardly responds. That's part of the act, being simultaneously untouchable and intimate, but it's part of her ambivalent feeling about her image. She is tired of being only erotic.

"That's an image I have been plagued with," she says later. In a breathless, fast voice, she explains how she almost couldn't deal with the public Donna Summer. "When I came back from Europe I walked into this commotion. ["Love to Love You" was already number one.] I didn't watch the song climb like other artists; I got off the plane and there was all this frenzy. I didn't understand it, I was shocked and I almost had a nervous breakdown."

It's time for her encore. She chooses "A Song for You," which she winds up with "Thank you Jesus, Moses and Abraham/I was just singing my song for you." The crowd roars.

Ten minutes later, the spontaneous Donna Summer is inside her suite at the Painters Mill Music Fair, again, stressing that she is the normal, twenty-nine-year-old, down-home, Capricorn sister.

She is tidying up the room. "Domestic? No, not really, I just can't wait," she says, cordially. Then she launches into a description of her curtain- and canopy-making marathon for her new home in Los Angeles. After eight years in Munich, she has landed in America's glitter, dream factory with her daughter, Mini, 4; from a marriage to an Austrian actor.

Finally, she stops cleaning, smiles at the motion picture distribution man, who hasn't seen *T.G.I.F*, a film in which Summer stars as a Los Angeles disco lady. It will be released in May.

Next, her wide-eyed gaze falls on the entourage from Casablanca Records, who are all smiling back because they like her and because she, along with Kiss, has made that company. (Summer has sold more than twelve million records in less than three years.) Then Summer smiles at the press. She knows to smile, a big, open-mouthed grin, temporarily outlined in scarlet.

She has plopped a tweed cap on top of her monstrous, curly wig and is now wearing an oversize T-shirt with a picture of her current boyfriend, Bruce Sundano, a singer with the Brooklyn Dreams. It's inscribed "Here's My Mugger." The girl has a sense of humor.

When her group traveled all day Easter Sunday, she dressed up as a bunny and distributed candy on the plane. But right now she wants to work off her nervous energy. She talks, nonstop.

"That was my first experience in a theater in the round," she starts, unprompted. "You know I don't smoke pot, don't take any drugs. Out there I inhaled something from the audience and, wow, I missed a note. Did anyone notice?"

Why had she waited so long to do an American tour? Instantly, her tone is emphatic. "I wanted to stand on my own first. I couldn't allow the public to catalogue me on just a minimum of my talent," she say.

In Europe, where she lived for eight years, Summer was a different kind of star. "Clean-out, funny and not at all suggestive," she says. In 1967 she went to Europe for the European production of *Hair*, stayed, sang with the Vienna Folk Opera and had some hit records. When Neil Bogard, president of Casablanca, heard "Love to Love You Baby"—it was bombing Europe—he wanted it revised to be as sexually explicit as possible, and brought her back to the states.

Summer's "Love to" fit neatly into an explosive trend, orgasmic rock, which started with the mildly provocative "Let's Get It On" by Marvin Gaye and graduated to the explicit "Do It 'til You're Satisfied."

Preachers, teachers, and parents debated the lyric's decency, but the music captured fifteen percent of radio airtime. Summer simply provided the ultimate fantasy.

Even before Summer returned in late 1975, she was being hailed as the hottest thing since Ma Rainey brought the blues to the city, since Josephine Baker took off everything but her bananas.

Summer pushed all the other disco queens to the background. But the packaging was so perfect that some people doubted its authenticity. She was haunted by rumors that she was a transvestite, which she denied. Then she was attacked on moral grounds by folks like Rev. Jesse Jackson, who campaigned to rid the airwaves of sex and drug lyrics.

If she didn't like it, if it was causing her so much pain, why didn't she stop the sex goddess hype earlier? "I was part of the machinery, the album cover, the promotion. But I was prepped to be a part of that, because I wanted to be a success. Now I am in better control and I can show what else is there," she says, smiling and disappearing into a cream-colored Rolls-Royce.

She didn't know how, but Summer knew she was going to be a success the day she stood up in Boston's Grant A.M.E. Church and sang "I Found the Answer" by Mahalia Jackson and her father cried.

"I discovered right then that God had blessed me. I had a talent. I knew I was going to be great," says Summer. She was then LaDonna Andrea Gaines, one of seven children of a butcher and a schoolteacher. As she grew up listening to Dinah Washington, the Supremes, Dionne Warwick, and Janis Joplin, all Summer wanted to do was sing. In high school, she joined a group, "Crow." She shakes her head, "I was the only Black and my mother said it would never make it with that name. She was right."

With only a month to go in high school, she auditioned for *Hair* and departed for Europe. She missed the King assassination, the riots, the Vietnam protests, much of the women's liberation move-ment, as well as the gay movement.

"When I came back I was in shock. It was a cultural shock, but also an amazement at how I was perceived, and the intensity," says Summer. "Basically the song that created the image was an accident. I found the image to be stunting, too small. But I was also shocked at the new environment, being a star, having servants. Also, there was too much luxury. I wanted to do my own shopping and I couldn't."

The ulcers got worse. Everything came too fast. "I felt like I was going up, when I was going down. I couldn't relax, sometimes I had to go to the hospital for a week. I have an acute memory and I couldn't remember my name. I was petrified," says Summer. "But," she adds, "I did learn how much I could take and when to draw the line. That's important in this business."

Summer's successful tour of Italy last fall, the upcoming movie, a couple of planned television appearances, and the success of her last two albums have all boosted her confidence. "I love the notion of people trying, people growing. I want people to see that in me. I'm out here and I have learned that what is out here has to work for me."

She has talked to her astrologer in Chicago. She has taken some white medicine for her ulcers, chased down with a Coke. She turns to her three sisters, all tall like her, and gathers them into a group. The folks chanting outside in the darkened theater don't know it, but their sex queen is backstage, praying before she goes onstage.

Postscript:

"One thing you realize about famous people in the arts is how hard some of them work," says Jackie Trescott. "It's not the cushiony life you expect. That covers political celebrities as well as the cultural ones. I remember interviewing Shirley Chisholm, carving out an hour to talk was a real feat for her staff. Interviewed Patti LaBelle once, in a hotel room. She was exhausted, but she was a trooper, willing to talk. Some people put a lot into their lives, not only what they give back in performances, but they do a lot of things that take up all their time. They are not in a spa.

"Some people were just very stiff with the media so you didn't get to do your fandom thing. But some people were very relaxed. Stevie Wonder is a very relaxed person so you can sit with him and talk and talk and talk. It was friendly. It wasn't antagonistic. There wasn't a lot of fawning going on. I don't understand people being intimidated or hesitant about interviewing celebrities. I think everyone sees it as part of the job. The person who had agreed to it saw it as part of their job. You knew what common ground you had went from there.

"I was the second generation of Black reporters who worked for daily newspapers. There was a whole host of people in the '60s, scattered all over the country who really broke the barriers. I belong in the second group. I define myself as someone who did help shape interpretations of the Black arts movement at that time, in the '70s and early '80s. Then when I went on to do the hard news scene about the art institutions. I was one of the few people in the country who was paying attention, day after day, to what was going on with the Endowment for the Humanities.

"My approach is to be open and people would recognize that. I wanted to hear what they had to say. I didn't come in with a preconceived notion. Just that kind of friendly, relaxed approach would make people comfortable. A lot of these folks did not like reporters even though they agreed to do an interview. So there was some tension when you first start. I defused it by being prepared. I was not always asking the obvious question. You prepare so you ask them something that surprises them. My style doesn't hit you right over the head. After the interview just thinking about what had surprised me the most or what I really thought was an eloquent response to a question and then working around that."

JOHN ESKOW

John Eskow (1949-) was a sixteen-year-old speed freak who earned his nickname "the Littlest Yippie" when he befriended Abbie Hoffman. He tagged along with Hoffman and counterculture demigods Jerry Rubin and Paul Krassner for the march on the Pentagon in 1967. Five years and incalculable acid trips later, Eskow found himself with an MFA from Columbia in poetry. Hoffman, then the most wanted fugitive in America, called Eskow to help him write one of a series of autobiographies, this one titled *Soon to Be a Major Motion Picture*. "I had a severe terror of working in a real job," says Eskow, "and I'm not trying to be funny. The idea of working in an office or having a regular job was a claustrophobic nightmare. I knew I had to do something that got me out of that world."

Eskow divided his energies between performing in rock 'n' roll bands and writing. When he got involved with a woman less than thrilled by the prospect of his opening for ZZ Top 250 nights a year, Eskow started writing a novel about being in a rock band, met an editor at *Hustler* magazine, and got an assignment to write a piece about evangelists. Next, Guy Flatley, the articles editor at *Cosmopolitan*, took Eskow to a lavish lunch at the Russian Tea Room. He presented the young writer with a binder of story subjects and said, "Pick one." Eskow chose NFL star O.J. Simpson and his brief magazine career was up and running. He delivered meaty profiles to *New Times*, *Rolling Stone*, *Playboy*, and *Sport*. Then he pushed on to a lucrative stint in Hollywood writing scripts for Clint Eastwood (*Pink Cadillac*) and Mel Gibson (*Air America*). Although not long for the world of magazine writing, Eskow grasped the form, a natural storyteller. As the son of a college administrator and frustrated novelist, Eskow knew something about the heaviness between fathers and sons, which informs this lively, haunting portrait of Hank Williams Jr. trying to emerge from his famous father's shadow.—AB

OEDIPUS ROCKS

New Times, 1978

Karl Wallenda plunges to his death, and the man beside me booms out "Gawd!" In the slow-motion TV replay, Wallenda's last-second grab for the wire seems to sum up everyone's will to live in one gesture. Then he falls. It's a horrifying sight, but my host—a tall man in a Stetson and black shades—feels it more deeply than I do: Hank Williams Jr. knows about falls.

We're sitting in his den in backwoods Alabama, where he's unwinding after a grueling tour of California. Like his father before him, Hank is a singer, and even his speaking voice borders on song. He commands a range of Southern vocal tricks, from a playful falsetto crack to a sage-like *basso profundo*, with separate controls for drawl, speed and irony: Each story becomes an aural roller-coaster ride. The one he tells now is especially bumpy.

It was August 8, 1975. He'd just recorded a landmark country-rock album, *Hank Williams Jr. & Friends*, that signaled his emergence from his father's shadow. Climbing a Montana mountain with a guide and his son, he stood at the Continental Divide and looked out.

"It takes a while to get up to 9,000 feet. We were lookin' over at Salmon, Idaho, right by a brass stake that marks the Divide. We were on Ajax Peak, which is like a knife edge—you've really got to climb around to get there.

"We're lookin' for mountain goats, way up past the tree line. And finally we started back down, crossin' some pretty rough terrain. And I stepped in the guide's footprint, but it had loosened, and I got caught in a snow slide.

"It was just like fallin' out an airplane—straight down. So down I went, slidin' headfirst on my back. Emotionally, I just froze inside. No feelin'. Just shock. And I thought: You're dead. You're just gonna splatter on the rocks.

"Then, after that thought got out of the way—all this is goin' on within seconds—I flipped over so I was slidin' headfirst on my stomach, and I tried to get that .44 out of my shoulder holster, tried to dig that long barrel into the snow, to try and break the fall. 'Course that was a joke.

"Then I swung my feet down under me as I felt the first little rocks hittin' me, and I decided that the first boulder I hit, I'd just kick out with all my might. Bump, bump, bump, I felt the rocks gettin' bigger, I was bouncin' across 'em. So I drew up my legs and kicked out.

"Dick [the guide] was watchin'; he said it looked like a guy comin' off a ski jump. Then it was a free fall, with me flippin' over. As I'm fallin', I see this huge mountain lake, and I said, 'I'm gonna try and land in that lake.' 'Course that would've killed me right away.

"Finally, I hit that snow like a swan dive. There was a boulder stickin' up through there, and I just hit it straight on, headfirst. It just literally split my face in half. It started right at the top of the hairline, split me right exactly between the eyes, down the left side of the nose—stopped at the chin, although that was broken too … .

"Came to a rest slumped over in a sittin' position. First thing I done was to look at my hands—you always look at your hands, for some reason—and I couldn't see anything wrong! I thought, hell, I've made it! And I started gettin' my hands up into my head, and I don't have any nose, any teeth—I don't feel any *head*. It's just all a hole, and I'm puttin' my fingers up in it. Just a hole from the lip all the way up, and I'm puttin' my hands inside it … grabbin' hold of my brains and all this gobbledygook.

"And Dick gets down there—course there was a lot of snow, retardin' the bleedin'—he starts tearin' my hands away. I'm sayin', 'What is it, what is it?' And he says, 'It's your *nose*, it's your *nose*.' He said it was all he could do to keep from throwin' up. And I saw that he was cryin', and he's a pretty tough old boy.

"Then I jumped up, with this big surge, and I said, 'I'm walkin' out of here, let's get to the Jeep.' Then, of course, the blood came out in torrents, just like turnin' on a water hose, pumpin' out with every heartbeat. And my right eye's hangin' out. And Dick keeps sayin', 'It's your nose ... .' Then I just made two or three steps and piled up. So Dick grabbed all this stuff hangin' out and just shoved it back into place, and it made a terrible sound—all this flesh and bone crunchin' up. Then he tore his shirt off, ripped it up, and wrapped the stuff in place as best he could. No tellin', no way to describe what he seen.

"Now I'm gettin' cold—real cold—so he made a rock enclosure around my head. Now the little boy gets down there, and 'course he's cryin', cause he's seen this terrible fall, and he wants to go for help. But Dick just grabs him and shakes him and tells him to just keep me talkin', kick me in the back now and then to get that junk out of my mouth. And Dick goes lookin' for help.

"Now I'm alone with this boy, and he's stunned. That's when the bad period set in, the give-up period, when I just knew that I was dyin'. And I'm lyin' there, lookin' out with one eye at this great scenario, these beautiful snowy mountains—very peaceful, if you weren't in my situation ... . And I thought: This is death.

"And I said to the Lord: I've wanted to die a lot of times. But I wanted it to be *onstage*, or an overdose in a car—you know, some nice *musical* death. Not like this, alone in the snow with a little boy chatterin' on beside me.

"By now he's talkin' a blue streak—his coon dog's the best coon dog in the world, and he's gonna win a prize at the fair, and he loves to go fishin' ... . And I'm thinkin' about my own little boy, and about Becky, and the guys in the band, the bus, my mother, my grandfather—the whole thing ... .

"But then all that's gone, and it's just *here comes death, whatever it is*.

"Now for some reason my eye—the one still in my head—caught sight of these two rings on my hand, the H and W, my initials. And for some reason, seein' those rings made me think I could live. And I started poundin' my hand in the snow, poundin' with every heartbeat. When they finally got to me, I'd dug a crater two feet deep in that snow. Two and a half hours went by that way.

"But now the boy's still ravin' on, and I'm tryin' to answer him—couldn't understand me 'cause of the gook in my throat, but I said, '*I'm not givin' up here, I'm gonna fight this thing.*'

"Now his daddy's at the foot of the mountain. And he yells up to the boy, 'Is he still talkin'?' And I wanted to jump up and holler, 'Hell yes, get up here!' I could see him down there, and he looked like a giant—some muscles in my brain had been strained, affectin' my sight in the eye that was workin', and everybody looked like a giant to me. Dick looked like he could just reach up the mountain and carry me away himself.

"He hollered up, 'The helicopter's coming!' Now he'd found a forest ranger, by pure luck. Otherwise he'd have had to drive to the ranger station, which was twenty-seven miles away.

"Then the medics came, and it was in with the Demerol, in with this and that. Wrapped my head in bandages. And these rescue guys had this cocoon-like stretcher, and they had to carry me.

"And it's hurtin' now. Bad. And then I realize I'm goin' on the *outside* of the chopper, it's a one-man machine. And my cocoon is clamped to the outside. Up goes the helicopter, and I'm right out there in the wind, on the struts. And I'm wonderin' if I'm gonna die in this cocoon hangin' off a helicopter.

"But it didn't take long before we set down on a ranch. They got me right into this Cessna, did some more work on me there, and off we go. We've still got this 100-mile trip to make.

"We land in Missoula, and it's right into another helicopter. This is nearly five hours after the fall. They've got bottles and needles hangin' over me. And we set down on the helicopter pad, and we're inside the hospital.

"I never lost consciousness the whole time. The doctors said that had a lot to do with me livin'.

"And they started cuttin' off my clothes, my shoulder holster, and they went to cut off the cross I wear around my neck. I started yellin', 'No! Don't cut that cross!' And that's the last thing I remember before I went under. And later I had all that stuff—clothes, holster, and cross—sewed back together.

"Four doctors operated on me for seven-and-a-half hours. And as soon as I woke up in that hospital bed, I thought: *The hard part's over. Now the healin' can begin.*"

To be born Hank Williams Jr. in 1949 was to be the namesake of a god. His father was—and still is—adored with fervor throughout America. His first hit, "Lovesick Blues," established him as the greatest draw the Grand Ole Opry ever had. Through his songs—"Your Cheatin' Heart," "Jambalaya," "I'm So Lonesome I Could Cry"—he became the down-home poet of hell-raising and grief. Add a death at twenty-nine from speed and alcohol, and you have all the ingredients for an instant myth.

The last few years of his life were a boozy fog, marked by a divorce from his wife, Audrey. Although still idolized, he was increasingly tormented by the forces that shaped his lyrics. His one sustaining joy was Hank Jr., who was three years old the night his father died in the back seat of a new '52 Cadillac.

When asked what he remembers of Hank Sr., the son at first responds with a brusque "Nothing." Then he ponders the question for thirty seconds. "Wait—just a snapshot image in an airplane, once. And backstage at the Opry—I knocked something over … ."

But if his memories are vague, there were always thousands of people to fill him in. The Hank Williams legacy was his, whether he wanted it or not.

He was raised on the belief that loneliness was in his bloodline, along with music and alcohol. As if the "lovesick blues," like black lung, was a disease linking the generations.

When he was eight years old, he was thrust into a career as a professional specter, playing his father's songs for crowds of necromantic drunks. Red Foley, the Opry star, would sit backstage with the child and tell him: "You're a ghost, son, nothin' but a ghost of your daddy." His mother would hold him close and say virtually the same thing.

For months at a stretch he would tour the honky-tonk circuit, rooming with legendary wild men like Johnny Cash and Jerry Lee Lewis. He'd watch Cash stuff cherry bombs down motel toilets and rig booby traps for the maids; he'd serve as mascot for troops of stoned musicians; and he'd steal every show because his name was Hank Williams.

Then he'd go home for a while and sit in class with the other third graders.

"It was a *bit* schizophrenic," he says with a wry smile. "At first, I thought bein' Hank's boy was the greatest thing in the world—a ghost of this man that everyone loved. They think I'm daddy—how wonderful. Mother's smilin', she's happy, money's rollin' in, manager's happy—seemed ideal. Then, round about my teens, it all hit me at once."

One can only try to imagine how adolescence hit Hank Williams Jr. When he was sixteen, he had a number one record on the C&W charts—"Standing in the Shadows," a recitation set to music. MGM, his record company at the time, had him overdub his voice onto Hank Sr.'s songs, and released two albums that featured a living teenager harmonizing with his dead father.

A heavy drinker since his mid-teens, he embarked on a nonstop bender through his early twenties.

"It was the whole country-music syndrome. I got to where I didn't have any more hangovers—woke up drunk, went to sleep drunk." During this period he also costarred in a movie, *A Time to Sing*, with Ed Begley, did the soundtracks for several other films, and married for a second time.

He was rich, sweet-faced, and an idol by proxy. But in addition to his Jack Daniel's habit, he'd become addicted to Darvon. He seemed bent on replaying his father's melodrama—live hard, die young, and be played by George Hamilton in a cheesy film biography. (The movie, *Your Cheatin' Heart*, has grossed millions over the years; Hank Jr. did the soundtrack.) With a myth for a father, and a classic stage mother, he was caught in a Freudian squeeze play.

In 1973 he snapped. "Booze, sleeplessness, pills, depression, it just got to be too much." Just as his father had done twenty years before, he began missing gigs, acting crazy, inching closer to ruin.

"I was still havin' to do shows as daddy. I'd sit home listenin' to Chuck Berry and Fats Domino, thinkin' of musical concepts myself, but I'd still have to play those lonesome songs of Hank's—and they were hittin' pretty close to home. Marriage bustin' up—I was supposed to be this big success, but where were the friends? Where were the lovers? I guess it all ganged up on me. So I tried the check-out route."

In a 1974 song, "Getting Over You," he describes his attempted suicide: "I got some pills from an old doctor friend;/The bottle said one every twelve hours for the pain./You know this pain I feel ain't small,/That's why I took them one and all./It was something I had to do/To get over you." (To get over whom? He says it's addressed to his first wife, but the lyric makes sense as a message to his father too. In any case, friends got his stomach pumped in time.)

After his suicide attempt, he sought help from a Nashville psychiatrist, not an easy step for a man trained in macho loneliness.

"Well, I'd been huntin' with him, so I trusted him as a man. And it was pretty much life-or-death at that point."

The psychiatrist diagrammed a deadly triangle that had kept Williams trapped and depressed: his mother, widely described as a hard-drinking, haunted woman who exploited her son; his manager, who resisted Hank's creative impulses; and the city of Nashville. All conspired to keep him a ghost.

"The doctor said, 'You'd best get the hell out of this town. Ain't no good times for you here.' So I did—moved down to Cullman, Alabama. Started havin' some fun. Realizin' that self-pity is bullcrap.

"Pain is somethin' you get to leanin' on. I fell into that trap of thinkin' I had to suffer to create. Finally I realized: Hell, I don't need it *that* bad. No matter how good the songs that might come of it, *nothin's* worth that kind of pain."

After listening to numerous writers who treasure their hard-earned angst above all else, and who constantly quote the old Rilke saw, "I don't want to exorcise my demons, for my angels might leave too," it's a pleasure to hear the cult of despair ridiculed—especially by a writer as gifted as Hank Williams Jr.

"Hank is as fine a songwriter as you'll find in country music today," says Michael Bane, editor of *Country Music* magazine. "Like Willie Nelson—his only equal—he's got that intuitive poetry that makes you think, I've *been* there, and it happened *that way*."

That poetry comes from a struggle—to carve a selfhood from a block of legend, to deal with pain without self-pity.

"Look at some of these rock stars, throwin' TVs outta windows to show how *artistic* they are," Hank snorts. "It's the difference between *actin'* crazy for publicity, and *bein'* crazy 'cause you just can't help it. Well, I figure I've put in my time. Let somebody else sing the blues."

Friday night. A redneck civil war rages in the Palomino, L.A.'s country music venue. Roughly half the patrons are bouffant-and-sagging-jowls types who've come to hear a séance, a slavish evocation of Hank Williams Sr.; the other half are spaced cowboys who want Hank Jr., rock, blues, and all. The schism widens as the band moves into a signature tune of Hank Sr.'s, "You're Gonna Change (or I'm Gonna Leave)."

It's the old lyric, all right—a typically Williams mix of plaint and whimsy—but it's done in a grinding, Chicago blues adaptation that strikes a bouffant next to me as sheer heresy.

"Shoot, he's got it all niggered up," she whispers in disgust to her husband. Meanwhile, the cowboys are stomping and yipping their approval.

Hank's voice is a wonder—it hits a high, keening note and holds it for eight bars, then nosedives into a cavernous bass without hesitation. As a pure instrument, his voice far surpasses his father's; few white singers can compete with him. (One voice teacher has compared his singing to opera star Luciano Pavarotti's.)

He does Lynyrd Skynyrd's "Sweet Home Alabama" as a tribute to several of that band's members who died in a recent plane crash. It's a fittingly rowdy eulogy, with Hank ad-libbing and the band rocking out.

Hank sings with his head tilted back, sunglasses dazzled by the baby spotlights; he looks, and sings, like a blind man. (Since the accident he's worn a Stetson to hide a dented forehead, and shades to hide eyes that don't match.)

Mayday, mayday—there's danger at a table right in front of the bandstand. Two drunken couples are passing their multicolored drinks around like joints, with predictably bad results. They're alternately shaking with the music and slumping in their chairs, fixing Hank with the hopeless fish-eye stare of the truly wasted.

As he finishes "Stoned at the Jukebox," a great outlaw anthem from the *Friends* album, one of the women springs back to life. "Hank!" she screams. "Play 'Cheatin' Heart' for Hank and Audrey!" With this, she digs a crumpled twenty from her purse and flings it onstage. Hank ignores it, but more bills come sailing up from the crowd, many with requests scribbled on them. Napkins inky with requests fly onstage. *People* with requests fly onstage.

"Gawd, I hate that shit," Hank says later. "Sometimes I kick the damn bills off the stage, hopin' to head it off. And sometimes I just stop and lecture 'em. I say, 'Look. At one point in my life I was programmed to be my daddy. But my daddy's career is doin' pretty good, so how 'bout lettin' me work on my own?' If that don't work, there's usually a few cowboys in the crowd to make the loudmouths shut up."

This time, however, he responds to the shower of twenties with poetry—his most poignant song, "Living Proof."

> *I'm gonna quit singin' all those sad songs,*
> *'Cause I can't stand the pain—Oh, the life I sing about now And the one I*
> *live is the same.*
> *When I sing them old songs of Daddy's,*
> *Seems like ev'ry one comes true. Lord, please help me, do I have to be*
> *The living proof.*

His voice, rich and sonorous, coaxes extra syllables from "living" and "proof," drawing more rebel cries from the aficionados. The bouffant next to me pouts in silence.

> *Why, just the other night after the show*
> *An old drunk came up to me.*
> *He says, "You ain't as good as your daddy, boy,*
> *And you never will be."*
> *Then a young girl in old blue jeans*
> *Says, "I'm your biggest fan";*
> *It's a good thing I was born Gemini*
> *'Cause I'm livin' for more than one man.*

When he reaches the last line, both factions—his father's and his—suddenly roar in unison.

Hank Williams, also known as Luke the Drifter and Old Lovesick, fathered Hank Williams Jr., aka Luke the Drifter Jr. and Bocephus.

As far as Hank Jr. can remember, "Bocephus" was the name of a hillbilly comedian's puppet in the Grand Ole Opry. In 1951 and 1952, during Williams's greatest stardom, little Hank would sometimes watch the wild shows at Ryman Auditorium. He was entranced by the dummy. So his father, having already named him after himself, renamed him after a puppet.

It's best to cast a wary eye on symbols when you're dealing with real people's lives. Bocephus might also be, Hank Jr. says, "just some silly hillbilly name."

Now the band's warming up the crowd, beginning the second set. Chris Plunkett, the bass player, sings a country-rock call-to-arms, "The South's Gonna Do It." He sings it with deep conviction, and the crowd hoots him on, never suspecting that this drawling Johnny Reb is a jazz composer from Asbury Park, New Jersey.

After three songs they introduce Hank. Back onstage, fighting a high fever and flu, he starts out ferocious. He's got that hell-raising mania that punk bands counterfeit, a roadhouse urgency that precludes slickness.

It's so easy to milk pathos in C&W bars—all it takes is a few songs that Hank describes as the "my-darlin'-left-me-so-I-got-drunk-drove-home-and-ran-over-someone's-little-girl" kind. For the most part, he resists this temptation, going after ecstasy instead. He seems to want to squeeze his whole body through the microphone, into some wilder land. Sometimes his lip, permanently numb from the fall, actually curls around the mic, and he has to pull his face away.

And sometimes he falters. Never scrupulous about tuning his guitar, he's capable of playing an entire song in the key of X, loud. And when his energy sags, the act deflates instantly, as it does now in mid-set. Three or four tunes drone by in a stupor. Hank's major problem as a performer is also his strength: Like all instinctive artists, he leads with his subconscious. But in an era when music is market-tested, shrink-wrapped, and sold like deodorant, a few dull stretches and discordant notes seem a small price for authenticity.

By the end of the set, he's got his grin and élan back in place, and he's singing with the power of a Ray Charles, rocking through "Jambalaya"—"Son of a gun, we'll have big fun on the bayou." The band rips into the last descending chords, and Hank's already moving through the crowd as the ovation begins.

A would-be groupie jumps up and grabs her idol in a half nelson.

"Ah'm gawna put somethin' on yew *alcohol* cain't rub off!" she wails. Hank staggers a few steps with this doped-up albatross around his neck, then gestures to Albert, his road manager. It takes all of Albert's considerable strength to pry her loose.

At the front table, the drunken foursome is still yelling for "Your Cheatin' Heart," even though the band's already packing up and scanning the floor for loose waitresses.

Welcome to the Motel California: Howard Johnson's in North Hollywood. In a working year, Hank spends 150 to 200 nights in motels like this—a toilet on perpetual flush, Art Drecko lamps with switches hidden in unlikely places, elevators where the air is so denatured that it's like riding in a giant menthol filter.

We meet first on neutral turf, his manager's room. Becky, his wife of a year, and several associates are there to run interference: After twenty-five years of being grilled about his father, he's initially nervous at interviews.

"Say Jawn," says J.R. Smith, his manager, "y'all bein' a writer, y'all must know this Paul Schrader fella?"

Schrader, who wrote *Taxi Driver* and directed *Blue Collar*, has conferred with Hank Jr. about doing a new film biography of his father.

"That'd be a *real* good lick," says Hank. His enthusiasm is understandable: How would you like to remember your father as played by George Hamilton?

Without seeking it, we're into the father-son question. "See, the record companies tell me I'm writin' too *personal* when I talk about my relation to daddy," he says. "But every town we play at, some young person comes up and says, 'I had the same routine with my father.' So it seems like it's pretty universal."

Outside, the blond canyons look down at the sea. Hank's wearing his gray high-rise Stetson and denim, a cowboy in a long black limo, cruising L.A. The sun glints off the diamond clef above the hat brim, gleams on the ever-present shades.

We're headed for Nudie's, the Paris of redneck couture, the Hollywood shop that's draped rhinestones around everyone from Elvis Presley to Elton John, by way of Dolly Parton. Albert and Becky shift uneasily as we approach—Hank's been known to buy outfits he doesn't need at Nudie's, and they're wondering what new extravagance he's got planned.

(One point about Hank Williams Sr.: In addition to the long shadow he left for his son, he also left Hank Jr. a share of his royalties—something like $250,000 a year.)

Nudie himself greets Hank at the door. Nudie, at seventy-five, is American weirdness at its zenith—both larger than life, and smaller. A wizened Brooklyn-born Jew in a Stetson of his own, wearing one black cowboy boot and one yellow one, he clearly revels in the role of Crusty Old Bastard.

He greets Hank like a beloved nephew, which, in a sense, he is. Hank Sr. was a close friend of Nudie's and bought all his outfits at the shop; his skeleton now reposes in a Nudie burial suit. Nudie remembers "little Hank" from his crib days.

"I made that boy his first rhinestone suit when he was two," he says, ordering an employee to dig up a photo. "Yes sir ... they used to send his daddy out to me for drying out. Sometimes we'd just both get wet."

Among the 2,800 photos on Nudie's walls, a somber oil painting of Old Lovesick occupies a prized space. Nudie sits down facing it and takes an ancient mandolin out of its case. Hank sits under his father's lean face and takes the guitar someone offers him.

There's mandolin talk and reminiscing as they tune up. Nudie starts to play an old hill ballad, "Ramona," a haunting air with its Scotch-English roots still audible. Nudie plays his mandolin—two centuries old—with great tenderness and very little skill and sketches the melody with a timeworn voice.

Next they drift into "Blue Dream," another mountain lament; a dozen customers gather around. Nudie's an old man recalling a woman and a river, recalling much that is gone, and the eyes of a matron across the room begin to fill with tears.

"Darling," Nudie recites, "I can still feel your kiss on my lips ... won't you come back? Won't you, just once? You won't? Then FUCK YOU, YOU LOW-DOWN BITCH!"

The timing is George Burns/Julius Erving perfect, the jump from heartbreak to profanity made in one nimble move. Our laughter is sudden and uncontrolled: Nudie's just placed the two crucial elements of country music, mourning and outrage, face to face.

Hank, who rarely wears anything more gaudy than Levi's, is suddenly enchanted by a jumpsuit—skintight and spangled with purple butterflies—that Elvis Presley ordered just before his death. As Becky and Albert exchange helpless glances, he goes to try it on.

Alone with Nudie in a corner of the store, I ask him about Bocephus.

"I've known that boy all his life. He's a helluva man, a helluva singer, and let me tell you something from the bottom of my heart—I seen him gettin' laid when he was *seven years old*."

(Later, when I read the quote to Hank, he roars and shakes his head. "Naw," he smiles. "I was eight.")

Hank comes back, decked out in butterflies. He buys the suit for $1,200—only, it seems, because of its connection to Elvis. (Five days later he decides he doesn't really want it, and has it shipped back to Nudie.)

After visiting a few guitar shops, we return to Nudie's for a photo session on the roof. Hank's mood, dampened by flu and medication, has been slowly warming as we drive.

His size and manner and history conspire to make you forget his age. Until now, he's shown no sign of being twenty-eight, but clowning on the roof, with the L.A. skyline behind him, he becomes a young man.

"Hello," he intones, in a perfect imitation of Lorne Greene on *Bonanza*, "this is the Ponderosa, and these are my people ... some of 'em are a little *weird*, but they're all I've got. This here's my horse Fag ... ."

Once he gets started on Wild West shtick he reveals a little-boy side. He's a passionate fan of Yosemite Sam, the Mel Blanc cartoon sheriff. He even got Blanc to record the message on his phone-answering device—"All raht, you ornery varmint, leave yer name 'n' number or ah'll plug ya fulla holes, ya big galoot!"

Hank's sense of humor is a hybrid—sometimes it's backwoods mock-dumb ("They're gonna have another drought in L.A., 'cause all this rain's washed the water away"), and sometimes it's downright black. (At one point at the Palomino, when his amplifier began to squeal, he said, "Sorry, I'm gettin' some feedback from these wires in my head.")

But the humor vanishes as quickly as it appears, as Hank stares down at Los Angeles.

"Gawd," he sighs. "Sometimes it seems I've been on the road forever."

It's Saturday night at the honky-tonk, with all that that implies. A 300-pound behemoth in worsted picks a fight with a scrawny long-hair, a tattoo artist covered with his own handiwork chats with a woman in leather, John ("Gentle on My Mind") Hartford is called onstage to play a remarkable solo.

"*Git rowdy*," someone hoots, as someone always will. This is the Temperament Exchange: For the price of a draft you buy the rights to a stranger's psychosis, or a night's feigned intimacy ... GIT ROWDY! IT'S SATURDAY NIGHT, GODDAMMIT!

Becky Williams, with her seraphic face and calm intelligence, is probably the least rowdy person in the place. She talks in a Louisiana accent thick as gumbo, with that lilting question mark at the end of each sentence.

"I first met Hank just a week before his fall. Next thing I knew he'd fallen off that mountain, and they told me he'd never look the same again. Only thing that worried me was that, with the plastic surgery, his face might not seem … real. But it did. And he seemed like the same person too."

In C&W circles, of course, the "good-hearted woman" is the traditional Rx for the blues. Becky Williams is certainly that, but she's quite a bit more. She graduated from Louisiana State University with a major in music, and she's one of the few people who can read serious novels in crowded motel rooms.

"I'm damn lucky to have that woman," Hank says when she's out of earshot. "She stood by me and never flinched a bit. Not only that, she's a pretty good hunter. We can share things … I looked at her in the hospital one day, and I thought: If it's this good through the bad times, think what the good times will be like. And let me tell you, they've been *good.*"

By now the Palomino crowd is screaming for him. Tonight there are fewer death-cultists in the audience, a few more true fans. It's a war of attrition, but it's slowly being won.

"Ladies and gentlemen, let's hear it for the one and only BOCEPHUS … MR. HANK WILLIAMS JR.!"

"I woke up the next evenin' in intensive care, and my jaws were wired shut. 'Course there were no teeth. I'm runnin' my tongue around, feelin' nothin' but brass wires. Tubes down the throat, the whole bit. I rolled my eye around and looked around: Everything was so lily-white in the room, and I saw the mountains out the window covered with snow, and then I was out again.

"They said, 'If he makes it eight days, he'll live.' But they didn't expect me to. They figured my brain had to be infected, from me touchin' it and the wind cuttin' through it.

"And my head's a basketball, all shaved too, with stitches and wires all over it. But I couldn't see myself.

"Next morning I asked the nurse, 'Is this my nose?' And she said yes. I said, 'Are you *sure* it's not a plastic nose?' And she said no. See, it was just flapped over there, like you took a flap of cloth and peeled it away, and they just hooked it back in there. So it *was* my nose.

"Then I started noticin' the sounds—everything was too loud! The blips on the oscilloscope were like hammer blows! They were soothin', for what they meant, but too loud.

"But now I'm gettin' better, better, takin' liquid through a straw, but the pain is gettin' worse, so I'm takin' a lot of Demerol too.

"Then I caught myself callin' for Demerol when I didn't need it. Johnny Cash was in my room, and he'd been through his pill thing, and he said: 'Hoss, don't let me catch you buzzin' for that Demerol when you don't need it—'cause it's *real good*, ain't it?' And I said, '*Uh huh!*' But I remembered that, and I caught myself.

"On the eighth day they gave me a whirlpool bath, and that was the most fantastic sensation you can imagine. By now I could take little steps on my own, and I had to go to the bathroom, so they let me go myself.

"Well, they'd forgotten there was a mirror in that bathroom. I looked in that mirror and it was ... *bad.* Much worse than I'd expected. Just this tremendous, swollen head, a monster's head—one eye screwed way off to the side, like an involuntary thing, the other eye black, jaws wired together, no teeth—it's got a grotesque look to it. There's a hole in my forehead where the bone's sunken in, and you can see the heartbeat pulsin' in my forehead. Terrible green and blue colors, stitches down the middle of the face, unbelievable weight loss, bony limbs, ribs stickin' through flesh. Muscles gone. That was a downer. I figured I'd get some Frankenstein roles. Or some leftover Jack Elam parts.

"That's when I resolved myself that music was over. I thought, hell, there's no way to get past this stuff! And I'd told God many times I didn't want to sing, so this looked like the deal goin' down that way. I went into a rejection period.

"Next day they brought a guitar down there, into the rehabilitation unit. I knew I could move my hands, but ... it was a pretty quiet moment. Then I started, real slow at first, and soon I was rollin' along! Then it almost turned into Request Time. Cash was there, and he'd sing a song and I'd tinkle along. And that was a rush.

"Better and better and better. So I asked 'em if I could hunt in October, which was two months later. They said, 'No, you'll be here at least six weeks.' Fifteen days later I left.

"Dick's wife, Betty, said, 'You've been left here for some purpose.' It seemed that way. Shuffled outta that hospital and up to Dick's house. Stayed there for a month, readin' every Indian book I could find. Bought a guitar and started playin'. Bought a big hat to cover the hole in my skull, sunglasses to cover my eyes. And blue jeans— Gawd, that felt good, to wear blue jeans!

"I'm still wired together. Couldn't see too good, but I'd watch the Yosemite Sam cartoons at three-thirty. Progressin' along.

"Then I had to go back to Missoula to get the wires out. Doctor sat me down in a chair and said, 'Hold on, this is gonna hurt a little bit.' By now they'd given me so much pain killer they couldn't give me anymore, so it had to be done without it. And he said, 'This wire is coming from just behind your eyeball,' and he got hold of it and just yanked it clean out through my jaw. And it hurt, all right. 'Cause it was wire through bone.

"Then he took the other one out. Well, my jaws have been wired for a month. So when we got back to Dick's house I had Betty make me up the most beautiful tuna fish sandwich. And I took this big bite, so excited to be eatin' again—and there was nothin' but a wet circle on the bread where I'd bitten. See, all the muscles were gone. Freaky. So I threw the damn sandwich and bounced it off the wall.

"Well, I could eat, but not that stuff. So Betty started makin' spaghetti, casseroles, stuff like that. Man, I was *really* doin' good, then I eat a lot anyway, and I thought: This is great!

"Also, I could start to sing now. Plus I took my .45, to see if I could sight with one eye, and I hit the damn bull's-eye first time. That really turned me on.

"Left Montana in October with my big Alabama hat pulled down low. Got home, started drivin' the pickup, shootin', feelin' good. Then the doctor told me the jaw was healin' wrong. Swung over to the left. This was two weeks after I'd started eatin', and he said they'd have to wire the whole thing over.

"Now this was a bummer.

"Back to the hospital, back on the table, pop, pop, break the jaws again. Take a knife and cut the gum away. Bring it over there, line it up right, I'm wired up again. And they worked on the nose—the nose is headin' east, lookin' pretty bad. Come back to Cullman, wired up. Went huntin' that season, like they said I wouldn't do, killed a deer. Go back to Nashville and they yank the wires out again. Nose is better, eyes a little better.

"Mother died right about then, and at the funeral I guess I looked a little weird. The papers said, 'Williams looks like death himself.' Big funeral—George Wallace came down, a bunch of other folks. All the Black people linin' the streets, and White people, heads bowed. It was a rough time.

"Then oral surgery, takin' metal out of the roof of my mouth. Then we need a forehead plate to get the brain covered better, 'cause it's just skin still, no bone. This was March. April we started playin' shows again.

"Got this funny toupee on my head, along with the hat and glasses.

"Then we had to go to this eye doctor, get the orbit of this eye built up. We get it done, leave the hospital, the eye looks a little bit funny.

"We go down to Becky's folks' house for Thanksgiving. And we're sittin' around the table and everybody's givin' me some mighty strange looks. So I go into the bathroom—somethin's come loose, and this whole implant has rotated up, and this eyeball is stickin' out—it's red, it's blue, it's terrible, it's runnin'. Had to go back for another implant.

"See, all these operations—you're lookin' forward to each one. Each one's a step. Each one moves you forward ... ."

The "den" is generally a dumb name for a room with a TV, recliner, and Parcheesi set. Williams's den, however, houses a grizzly, a timber wolf, an owl, and a bobcat—all stuffed, of course, but so artfully that they seem to be sizing each other up.

We're sitting in the midst of this silent animal face-off, drinking Jack Daniel's and watching the news. But Wallenda's death has spooked Hank a little, and he's itchy to move downstairs, to the shop where he works on his guns.

Guns have been a lifelong passion for him. He owns several hundred, including many rare models, and he is an expert hunter and gunsmith.

Today he's retooling the grip on Becky's .45, adjusting the trigger alignment, doing it all by feel. As I watch him work, his six-foot-one-inch frame bent over a table, he looks like a medieval craftsman.

When he's finished with Becky's gun, he suddenly decides it's time I fired some "real weapons." He ponders the choices, then reaches behind a loose ceiling panel for a long khaki bag. Slipping on a pair of ear protectors, he motions for me to follow him outside.

The Alabama woods are quiet in the twilight, but you can see firing lanes set among the trees—rows of stumps honeycombed by shots, spent cartridges, massacred tin cans. As we stand before the widest lane, Hank unzips the khaki bag and takes out ... a machine gun.

"Listen, Hank—is a *machine gun* a good thing to start on?"

"Gawd, yes. It's like in the movies."

And he's right. It's crazy—the trigger senses every vague impulse to fire, and you're barely conscious of your finger's intervention. I'm wounding the cans and stumps at random, amazed by the ease of it all.

"Now hold 'er sideways and spray it," he says, and, as in the movies, it happens. The weapon trembles as bullets dig a trench in dry earth.

"Kind of a rush ain't it?" Hank grins.

It's a rush all right. Machine guns are hooked so well into the subconscious—you could wipe out a whole family as an afterthought.

But that's a city kid's rush. There's no homicidal edge to Hank's love of guns; he doesn't have enough hatred for that.

Hank Williams Sr. was known, in freaky moments, to ventilate motel rooms with gunfire; but just as Hank Jr.'s learned to control his melancholy better than his father did, he's also more circumspect about when and where he shoots. And he always keeps the first chamber unloaded, just in case.

After shooting, we stroll around to see his dogs and smell the spring air at dusk. Tennessee is the last green hill on the horizon.

Silence grows around the house in abundance, like a crop, as darkness falls.

When it's time to leave, he offers the use of his pickup truck and a bottle of Jack Daniel's—we're in a dry county. Driving through nighttime Alabama that way, I feel, surprisingly, half at home.

Hank Williams is often called the "father of modern Nashville": It's true economically as well as spiritually. Although his own style was relentlessly down-home, he was the first country songwriter to have his work "covered" by many pop artists. Tony Bennett, Polly Bergen, and Andy Williams all scored early successes with saccharine versions of Hank Williams songs, and the blend—earthy sentiment and windy string arrangements—made Nashville rich.

So when Hank Jr. finally left Nashville in 1975, he was leaving the house of his father, perhaps for the first time.

Now the plates on Hank's beige Fleetwood read Alabama Governor's Staff—he's an honorary deputy of the state, a post he takes fairly seriously. Considering he also extols dope-smoking and drinking in a dry county, an observer from the North sees a paradox.

It won't be resolved. Hank has no discernible politics beyond a love for his birthplace and an allegiance to his pleasures. He loves Black music—but what musician doesn't? The closest thing to political awareness in Hank is a populist streak that you can also find in characters as disparate as George Wallace and Thomas Paine.

On my last day in Alabama, Hank visits the dentist. One of his false teeth is too sharp and must be filed down. When he's finished in the chair, the dentist comes out into the foyer with him, beaming.

"It's on the house," he says, clapping Hank on the back.

"Hey," says Hank, unsmiling, "I'll tell all my friends to come up here. Free dentistry."

"Just for you," the dentist laughs nervously.

Outside, Hank is fuming. "*On the house* ... Gawd, next thing some poor bastard'll walk in there in agony and he'll charge him $35 just to look. Gawd, I hate that shit."

For politics, that will have to do.

Williams's home is 140 miles south of Montgomery, where his father lies buried. A ritual visit to Hank Sr.'s grave is the C&W equivalent of communing with Keats at his graveside in Rome—hundreds of songs have been written about it. Hank Jr. sings the best of them, "Montgomery in the Rain," written by Steve Young. "I'm gonna go out to Hank's tombstone, and cry up a thunderstorm chain ... ."

Hank adds a chilling line at the end of Young's song: "You all know me well by the songs on the cemetery wind ... ." And he pronounces it *"winnnnnd,"* so it whistles through the room. When he sings it, you're not sure if you're hearing a voice from the grave, from a living son, or from some ghastly fusion of the two.

"The pure products of America go crazy," said William Carlos Williams. If that's true, we might be grateful that nothing is pure anymore. Hank Williams's voice mapped out an America of unyielding farms and open skies, bad luck and long railroad trains; and his son was supposed to live in it. But it was a smaller America, without Motown bass lines and Eric Clapton guitar licks, and to keep a child/man there was to freeze him in time. So Hank Jr.'s story has been a long catching-up, a fight to be his own contemporary.

It's been a story rife with purity and craziness. Pain alternates with gross comedy—at his mother's funeral, Bob Harrington, the "Bourbon Street Preacher," stood over the open coffin singing "Hey, Good Lookin' " to the deceased. Blood ties loosened and tightened—a Southern gothic sense of predetermination—and at the center, one human, who somewhere found the sanity to say, "I don't want to be a legend, I just want to be a man ... ."

As a kid, he was subject to a terrifying force: indiscriminate love. Sometimes he'd try desperately to alienate a crowd, only to find they still "loved" him. Loved his chromosomes. Loved the fact that his father died young.

As a man, then, he seeks respect for what he does. This has seriously hurt his career. These days, he plays far too many junior high gyms and roadhouses, when with a little honing of his act and a change in focus he could be packing showcase rooms in New York and L.A. Sales of his latest album, *The New South*, have been somewhat disappointing; as the country proverb has it, he's hiding in plain sight.

It's frustrating, of course, for those who admire him, but at base he just doesn't care that much. Having been packaged since infancy, he won't be packaged again. So he indulges himself, sloughing off the demands of the commercial world. He rejects the blind love that most singers court.

But he knows what *he* loves: music, Becky, food, guns, solitude, pickup trucks. When asked what got him through the fall and the months of recuperation, he said: "I had just learned how to relax, to enjoy life. And I thought: *I want more of this.*"

Postscript:

"I pitched Hank Williams Jr. to *New Times*," says Eskow. "They were New York intellectuals, but they liked the idea and flew me to L.A. where Hank Jr. was playing at the Palamino Club, which no longer exists. I didn't write very many profiles but what made me good at that gig was that I was good at The Hang, I knew how not to be an asshole, and I knew how to communicate to suspicious dudes like O.J. Simpson, Carl Yaztremski, and Hank Williams Jr. that I was not there to hurt them but to be fascinated by them. And they picked that up. I was allowed to follow them around. I sat at a comfortable distance, not judging but absorbing. Within an hour, Hank Jr. considered me a pal. We were about the same age, and I couldn't believe the life he had lived compared with mine. 'Well, John,' he said, 'I've just had a few more oil changes than you've had.' Good line. He'd had a lot more oil changes.

"We hung out for four days in L.A. The trust extended, continued when we went back to Cullman Alabama, where he was living then. We drank so much Jim Beam and smoked so much weed. I don't know what else he was doing. But that's what we did together. There's a part in the story when we were shooting machine guns. Then he brought out the bazooka and we blew up a row of trees. So I put all of that in the story, of course.

"I came back with endless reams of tape that all needed to be transcribed. I was a little nervous. I had so much good material I didn't want to screw it up. This was my first important piece—they put it on the cover, which at the time, was a big deal for a country star in that kind of publication. The deadline was such that I ended up writing the piece in a whoosh. Woke up at 5 a.m., wrote until midnight and handed it in. Never did that before or since but again, deadlines are what they are and you do the best you can with the time you've got. I felt inspired, that's not too lofty a word.

"About a month after the story came out, Hank was in New York playing down at the Lone Star Café. His publicist called me up and said that Hank really loved the piece and 'he'd love you to be his guest at the Lone Star tonight.' I went down with my wife. Hank had me come up and sing background on 'Amazing Grace.' Later on, we're drinking, and he said, 'John, I loved the story, it was great. There's only one problem I had but it's a serious fucking problem. About a week after it came out, I got a visit from the boys at BATF—The Bureau of Alcohol, Tobacco, and Firearms. They said, "Hank, machine guns are a no-no." They said I need to be a little more discreet.'

"My firearms adventure with Hank included the bizarre experience of firing a freaking *bazooka*—something few living people have done, other than Vietnam vets. At that moment we graduated from firing practice to pretty much deforesting large stretches of land. I self-censored the bazooka detail, because I was worried it might bring The Heat down on him, but I left in the machine guns."

ANNE TAYLOR FLEMING

The child of Hollywood actors, Anne Taylor Fleming (1950–), grew up with a keen appreciation of both the allure and limitations of fame. As children, she and her sister were posed just so in movie magazine photo shoots. Her father, Don Taylor, played Elizabeth Taylor's groom in the original *Father of the Bride*; he was charismatic and ambitious but starring parts proved increasingly elusive and his marriage to actor Phyllis Avery ended in 1955. "The downside of fame was apparent," says Fleming. "Don't chase this. This is a false value. If they fawn today, they won't tomorrow."

Fleming's interest in journalism began when she was eighteen and met Karl Fleming, *Newsweek*'s Los Angeles bureau chief, then in his forties. They married four years later, and she began freelancing for *Newsweek*, *Ladies Home Journal*, and *Redbook*. Fleming's big break came at twenty-eight when the *New York Times* assigned her to profile Truman Capote. Though Capote's best writing days were behind him, he was still very much of a celebrity. In truth, he'd suffered a public fall from grace after alienating the women of New York's high society with a series of slightly fictionalized articles for *Esquire*. These were not lucid days for Capote, and he likely underestimated Taylor, who delivered a clear-eyed portrait of a man who'd sold his soul for fame. Curiously, the profile stands as somewhat of an aberration in Fleming's long career, where she is best known for smart radio commentaries for CBS and TV essays for PBS, as well as writing novels and a searing book about motherhood. This is one of the few magazine profiles she wrote. It's a pleasure to read and catches Capote, the ultimate celebrity writer, exposed.—AB

THE PRIVATE WORLD OF TRUMAN CAPOTE

The New York Times Magazine, 1978

I had to be successful and I had to be successful early. The thing about people like me is that we always knew what we were going to do. Many people spend half their lives not knowing. But I was a very special person and I had to have a very special life. I was not meant to work in an office or something though I would have been successful at whatever I did. But I always knew that I wanted to be a writer and that I wanted to be rich and famous.—Truman Capote

Truman Capote is fifty-three. He has been famous since he was twenty-three, when his first novel was published. He always wanted fame. He coveted and curried it, calculatedly at first, then instinctively almost, needing it even more than he wanted it. He wrote a handful of precocious short stories in his late teens and early twenties, then a handful of books, slender, basically sentimental novels like *Other Voices, Other Rooms* and *Breakfast at Tiffany's*, and finally brought forth his much-imitated "nonfiction novel," *In Cold Blood*, which solidified his literary fame. And all the while, he was finding fame in another way, as an entertainer-gossiper, on television, and in the salons of society's rich, to which his literary fame gave him access. In his public appearances, he was gay in both the old and new senses of that word, outrageously so, a man who looked in love with the success he wore like a second skin. There were small signs along the way that underneath that skin, all was not well. He was aging not quite easily, his eyes were sometimes bloodshot, sometimes hidden behind dark glasses, his rounding middle not hidden. Then, in the fall of last year, Truman Capote, round, weary, obviously intoxicated, walked off the auditorium stage of a college near Baltimore, saying he was an alcoholic. This is the first time since he walked off that college stage that he has talked openly about what happened to him. As it turned out, he himself, with that odd blindness born of desperation, had damaged the fame it had been his life's work to secure.

Through the years, Capote had made a number of very smart career decisions, but then in 1975 he made one which, while it might have seemed smart at the time, was finally disastrous. Ten years after *In Cold Blood*, Capote was suffering a sort of writer's block and thought that publication of a few sections of his long-overdue novel, *Answered Prayers*, would help get him back to work. The publication of the second section, "La Cote Basque, 1965," in *Esquire* magazine in November of 1975 quite simply changed his life. In it he named real names and told real stories about his high society friends, some of whom were lost to him forever; other friends were lost indirectly around the same time, rather like canoes being tipped over in the wake of a big boat. Instead of being famous he became infamous, and for a while they must have seemed like the same thing. He was still on talk shows and in all the newspapers and magazines, but it was not the same. Something had been lost in the transition: friends, well-born women whose soft rooms and high style— Capote's favorite word—he had loved, even envied. And something had been gained: a drinking and pill problem, a longtime habit at last grown serious. Looking back a few years, all the bad things get jumbled up: the book, still unfinished, for which Capote had taken, in a three-book deal with Random House, a $750,000 advance in assorted stocks from which he is drawing yearly dividends; the drinking; the defection of real friends; the death of a Black woman, Myrtle Bennett, housekeeper at Capote's Palm Springs, California, home and his major West Coast confidante; a near-fatal automobile accident on Long Island; a $1 million lawsuit filed by Gore Vidal over a story Capote had told about him in *Playgirl* magazine, and a brutal four-year love affair with a married man, Capote's official reason for the suicidal sadness from which he is now surfacing. But looking further back, looking at the boy he must have been, the slender, pretty, high-voiced boy, a spiritual orphan in Monroeville, Alabama, the very small town his mother had come from and where she left him with relatives when she moved North, looking at that boy who wrote from the age of twelve the prettiest prose, it seems easy to see, too easy maybe, how the kind of fame he coveted would someday become too heavy.

"How was I?" Capote asked. We were standing on the street waiting for a cab. He had just finished taping *The Dick Cavett Show*, slipping again, easily, into his time-honed media persona: the small feisty down-home sophisticate with, in the camera's eye, an almost prenatal head, round, soft, oddly photogenic, caricaturely "homosexual" hands brushing often one eye or the other, his tongue resting between sentences at different places in his mouth, looking, in fact, as if it had got temporarily stuck; and a laugh to keep the world at bay and a charm that's complete and compulsive and scary almost in its effectiveness and in its need.

"You didn't really like me on the show, did you?" he asked again. Standing on the street looking at the back of his head with its businessman's shaved-neck haircut and at his loose green glen-plaid suit and his fuzzy pea-green golfer's shirt and his proper heavy shoes, I said yes, of course I had liked him, wondering why he cared, because he genuinely seemed to. I wondered, too, why he, a serious writer, even did these shows year in and year out, and whether or not he was gearing up for another round of publicity, not to promote the book, because the book still wasn't finished, but to convince himself, meanwhile, that he was alive, to get a fix. And I wondered, too, if I were part of that round, and did not care because I liked being with him. I did, despite his having begun the day by telling me—to declare his turf I guess, to be, as small men often want to *be*, unsettling—some quite suggestive gossip about some very well-known woman and my husband.

At night his media manner dropped away when he was safe in his apartment on the twenty-second floor of the United Nations Plaza. It is an apartment full of complicated fabrics, Persian objets d'art, miniature animals, and many photographs, many of an early Capote of whose delicacy the older Capote is still protective, proud. Wearing a billowy short-sleeved pink shirt, slippers and—in a momentary resurgence of impishness—a white laminated cowboy hat, Capote seemed weary of the effort of his own charm. He drank a bit, becoming, as his friends say he does with drink, sadder, more introspective, a man very hard to pry out of himself. At the base of the sadness, always, is the mother who left him in Monroeville when he was about four, leaving him earlier, too, and more indelibly, when they were still together and she locked him in their hotel room many nights when she went out. "I pounded and pounded on the door to get out, pounding and yelling and screaming," he said. "That did something to me. I have a terror of being locked in a room—of being abandoned; I have a great fear of being abandoned by some particular friend or lover."

His mother was a Southern belle, a one-time Miss Alabama with beautiful eyes and great style—his word again—but an eccentric, too fragile, a woman who herself turned to drink when she could not have the children she wanted with her second husband; then he strayed—leaving her with what Capote calls a hysterical jealousy that finally drove her to commit suicide when Capote was twenty-nine.

He says his mother hated his father the minute they were married, and she married him merely to get out of Monroeville. A bounder and a cad, Capote calls him, a man who talked a good line—clichés offered with amusement, not malice—a lawyer who never practiced, Capote says, but got involved in a steamship business in New Orleans where Capote was born. His parents divorced when he was four and his mother left him with family in her hometown,

Monroeville, when she went to New York City. She remarried and sent for him five years later when she understood, after a series of miscarriages, that he was to be her only child.

The years in Monroeville, so few out of a lifetime but so celebrated by Capote in what many think are his best works, his best kind of works—things like his story, "The Thanksgiving Visitor," and his novel, *The Grass Harp*, works about simple people, as was, in its way, *In Cold Blood*—those early years in the South stamped Capote, or at least stamped his storytelling muse. He himself said: "I like my writing to be very clear and simple as though you were sitting by the fire on a cold night and I were telling you the story."

In Monroeville he was lost, lonely but for the friendship of an odd, sturdy girl named Harper Lee, who would later write one book, *To Kill a Mockingbird.* "She's a lawyer, a recluse," Capote said. "Every single person who's really been close to me in my life has been a recluse. I can't imagine why I'm attracted to them when my attitude is, 'Let's go to a party.' "

The love Capote had in Monroeville came from his elderly relative, Miss Sook Faulk, the archetype of the aging innocent, the best of the simple people with an inarticulate wisdom and a childlike capacity for joy and strange imaginings. They lived, the young boy and the old woman, in the womb of their joint imaginations in which delights and demons cohabited, demons which later haunted Capote's first stories, causing critics to call him a writer in the Romantic-Gothic tradition. "Aunts, cooks, strangers," he wrote in "A Tree of Night," published in 1943, "each eager to spin a tale or teach a rhyme of spooks and death, omens, spirits demons. And always there had been the threat of the wizard man: stay close to the house, child, else a wizard man'll snatch and eat you alive! He lived everywhere, the wizard man, and everywhere was danger. At night in bed, hear him tapping at the window? Listen!"

Though there was Miss Sook and their communal spooks, Capote felt in those years in Alabama "like a turtle on its back. You see, I was so different from everyone, so much more intelligent and sensitive and perceptive. I was having fifty perceptions a minute to everyone else's five. I always felt that nobody was going to understand me, going to understand what I felt about things. I guess that's why I started writing. At least on paper I could put down what I thought."

Precocious about sex as about most things, Capote said he was eight when he started "going to bed" with the older boys in school and that he "never had any problem about being homosexual. I mean, look at me. I was always right out there. The other kids liked me for that. I was really quite popular. I was amusing and I was pretty. I didn't look like anybody else and I wasn't like anybody else. People start out by being put off by something that's different, but I very easily disarmed them. Seduction—that's what I do! It was: You think I'm different, well, I'll show you how different I really am. So it was layers of this thing building, this persona, and I didn't even realize I was doing it. I was totally self-created."

He left the South when he was nine, returning summers until he was sixteen. The big old house in Monroeville finally felt lonelier than the apartment at 1060 Park Avenue where his mother and stepfather lived, an apartment that was his home base for the next five years. His mother gradually became, for her young son with high imagination, a tragic heroine. It was to be a lifetime habit, that of seeing women as heroines in their own lives, heroines of varying degrees of tragicness whom the older Capote would help to shape as if they were characters in a novel of his.

He went to school in Manhattan, to Trinity, then briefly to a military boarding school, St. John's Academy, at thirteen. Capote had one big romance from the time he was fourteen until he was eighteen, with a boy a year older whom he had met in the public high school in Greenwich, Connecticut, where his parents had moved from New York City. "We had this big falling out on my sixteenth birthday," he said. "He gave me this very expensive present with a very cruel note and I cried for two days. It was the first time I'd been hurt, like that. I've been hurt all my life. We had lunch just last week —he's married, a businessman—and asked him why he'd done it. And he said, 'Because I cared too much about you and you hurt me.' And then he blushed."

Matters of sex, his own sex, he relates this way, if at all, reminding one that the persona he created was based on or based against, really—not only his exaggerated sense of abandonment but also on his young boy's sense of small-town propriety which he carried with him from Monroeville. He has always hated vulgarity and loved, as a grown man, pretty, soft things and other men, one at a time for a long time. Though his public came to perceive him as a sophisticate, a man familiar with the low life as well as the high, he was and is conservative in many ways. He falls in love with square men with crew cuts and ties, married men, often churchgoing, often with children; he falls in love, too—cut of an odd mixture of apology and jealousy—with their wives and children, so that he inherits not only the lover but the family he feels he never had. With his acquired family, he is tender, shepherding, a good uncle figure, trying not to flaunt the thievery of the man from their lives.

When Capote hit the New York publishing scene, a high school dropout and literary debutant of seventeen in 1942—the year *Story* magazine published "My Side of the Matter"—his persona, he said, "was totally intact. I knew damn well I was going to be a famous writer. In fact, I considered myself so at the time. I would sashay down the corridors of *The New Yorker*, where I'd gone to work at the age of seventeen, in these natty three-piece Brooks Brothers suits and little moccasins outraging a lot of people."

Those who knew Capote in his early days in New York smile at the memory of him, this delicate-looking boy all dressed up—a present to them somehow—with a street toughness and an intransigent charm, part Hemingway, part Fitzgerald. He was the kind of man or boy who could, and did, literally leap, one day in a crowd in Bloomingdale's, onto the chest of a man he did not like, humiliating him by shouting into his face, "I love you, I love you," but who could just as easily cower in child's game.

The friends Capote made in the '40s are the friends he's kept. Leo Lerman, longtime *Vogue* magazine editor, writers like Christopher Isherwood and Donald Windham (most recent book: *Tennessee Williams's Letters to Donald Windham, 1940–1965*), and Windham's companion, actor turned author, Sandy Campbell. To this list would be added, in the '50s, John Knowles, author of the novel *A Separate Peace*. They were men who knew about writing, his writing, knew that it was his center just as later they could sense when he wasn't writing and was drinking. He tried to hide the drinking from them, these forever friends whose affection he could not shake, who became small consciences in a sense, tender like parents about Capote's exaggerations. In his 1957 *New Yorker* profile of Marion Brando, "The Duke in His Domain," Capote rhapsodized about stumbling upon the brawny, sleeping figure of Marlon Brando at a rehearsal for *A Streetcar Named Desire*. It was, in fact, Sandy Campbell who had come upon the sleeping star, a quietly erotic moment he had described to Capote in full detail and which Capote then described in print as if it had been his own. Campbell was amused by the appropriation. A few years later, in *In Cold Blood* days, when Capote was living in a basement pied-à-terre in set designer Oliver Smith's elegant house in Brooklyn Heights, he invited Campbell and Windham to dinner with some people from Kansas. He told the people the house was his, that he had designed and decorated it, and he showed them around it proudly. "How did he know we wouldn't say anything?" Campbell said with a slight shake of the head and a smile.

"There was something so childlike about him that what might have been freaky was somehow reassuring," Christopher Isherwood said. "A skin has grown over his personality through the years, but he had an extreme power in those days a quality that can only belong to a very young person or perhaps to a saint."

Capote stayed at *The New Yorker*, where he sorted cartoons, for two years, writing short stories at night, stories like "A Tree of Night" (1943) and "Miriam" (1944), delicately styled stories full of outer demons that were really inner demons, and full of characters that seemed not to know that. They were characters who, like Capote, invented themselves and lived in fantasy worlds, however strange or evil, half raw, half-wily children who, fearing abandonment, abandoned the world first. They were, after all, Capote's children—rather, the children of his own childhood. Many, like critic Malcolm Cowley, think those early stories—though not quite at the top with Faulkner's and Eudora Welty's, Cowley cautions—are Capote's best works, which left him, then, with most of a life to live up to them.

Capote left *The New Yorker* to finish a novel, *Summer Crossing*, which he did not finish, writing instead, in a rented room in New Orleans. *Other Voices, Other Rooms*, which was published in 1948, making him famous in another way. The book was equivocally reviewed, praised for its prose, criticized for its shadowy story. But on the back jacket was a photograph that no one ever forgot. Stretched out on a chaise longue, part puppy dog, part potentate, Capote was the quintessence of camp seduction. The only thing that comes near it in memory, in its plaintive sexuality, is the calendar picture of Marilyn Monroe. "I think what Truman wanted to be more than anything in the world," a friend said, "was a woman of beauty."

Capote said the use of the photograph was inadvertent, that it was sent to Random House by the man who had taken it, Harold Halma, a friend, when Capote was away somewhere. Be that as it may, Richard Avedon, who took Capote's picture shortly after Halma, and many times thereafter, said that Capote knew then what he was doing. "He always thought of photography in the same way he thought of the press," Avedon said, "as something to be used for the purposes of public relations. He was very inventive: he always had an idea for every session, if it was only a new hat."

And now always there was a lover, the one part of his life he kept for himself. He never shared it until much later, sharing that part only when it went sour and he could not stop himself from sharing it any longer; and he lost friends that way at the same time he was losing them in others. But early and for a long time, that part of his life was warm, stable. He loved, after his first big romance, a Harvard English professor, the first man he had taken away from a wife, inviting thereby the envy of both women and men. He lived for four years with the professor, a man who introduced him to the books of Willa Cather and Sarah Owe Jewett, writers whom to this day—out of conviction laced with loyalty—he will cite as his favorites. Then about 1948, Capote met two people with whom, in different ways, he fell in love: a woman, Babe Paley, wife of CBS chairman William Paley, and Jack Dunphy, a thirty-three-year-old Irish Catholic novelist from Philadelphia; and it was the woman who finally broke his heart, cleanly, in a way no man could ever do.

But that came much later. His life at twenty-three became a life with Dunphy, the only man, he said, with whom he has ever been in love. They have been together for thirty years, the first fifteen of which they were lovers.

Jack Dunphy gives the impression of having been cut cleanly from the space around him. Lean, fading the way redheads fade into a sort of soft amber, he has a certain fastidiousness, not just in dress but deep down. There is an intentional degree of difficulty about him that is strangely appealing. What he has to say about Capote has not been published before, a silence born of pride and privacy. Talking about Capote he talks about himself, lurching garrulously through non sequiturs and literary-Biblical references, with the irreverence of the seriously religious. Jack Dunphy never misses mass.

They lived in Europe, on and off, for many years, quietly, writing during the day. The only shadow over their early love was that of Dunphy's ex-wife. "When I met Truman, I was still very much attached to her," Dunphy said. "I think it weighed on him a lot. But we never talked about it. We don't break down things with one another that way. That's very unmanly." They moved a lot, both restless by nature, looking to a new place for a new peace—"doing a geographic," Capote calls it—moving on again, always one step ahead of the wizard man. In 1951, Capote published *The Grass Harp*, a slender, very autobiographical novel; reviewers found it less pretentious than *Other Voices, Other Rooms*, and tenderly effective.

Capote never established a habit of writing. He wrote, and writes, in bouts, fevered months followed by a sabbatical, writing, when he does, in lined notebooks in an immaculate pencil scrawl, each page rewritten to perfection, publishable, before he goes on. It was seven years between *The Grass Harp* and *Breakfast at Tiffany's*, a book which did not receive the unqualified praise of its predecessor. Reviewing both the book and Capote's public decade, Gordon Merrick wrote in *The New Republic*: "There is nothing here for anybody in search of a 'major' novelist, but at his best, Capote is very, very good ... Truman Capote is no genius, despite the manner of his presentation ten years ago, but his music, when in tune, is clear and lovely ... "

In one's memory, of course, all of Capote's works received raves; moving through a media blitz of interviews and talk shows at the time of each publication, Capote, a master of promotion, left the impression, each time, of unparalleled success. He works on the publicity campaign for a given book for months, lining up the reviews and interviews so that all his exposure happens within two weeks of publication.

Between the two novels, there was an extended *New Yorker* piece, "The Muses Are Heard," about an acting troupe touring Russia with *Porgy and Bess*, a detailed, satiric but not unsympathetic piece of nonfiction, the genre in which Capote would finally have the massive writing success for which he had been in preparation.

Meanwhile, he was earning fame in another way, there had to be a backup as a social butterfly. During the years with Dunphy, Capote was widening his circle of women friends, women with names like Agnelli and Vanderbilt and Guinness and Guest, and Paley. He loved these women's lives, and their husbands surely liked him because he was clever and amusing and a famous author and because he didn't threaten them. He was an amateur affairs counselor; soft and sweet and deliciously bitchy about one woman to the other, he would sit on the ends of their beds in his robe and ask them if they were happy and tell them which was the best moisturizer to use. And he knew. In the venom of his gossip, which swelled proportionately to his sadness, in his need to tell tales even about his best friends, there was not so much meanness as a child's need to matter. And for a long while, it all seemed like great fun to everybody. The women gave Capote stories and he gave them advice. Those who knew what to read he told how to dress; those who knew how to dress he told what to read. Proust if they could manage, books on royalty if they could not, his own stories always. "I knew they were no Mary McCarthys or Simone Weils," he said, "but I didn't want to socialize with the other intelligentsia; that was like talking to myself. At least they were elegant—it's whatever pleases your eye, just like furnishing a room."

All the while he was listening, gathering anecdotes like Easter eggs for the books about them which, as early as 1955, he meant someday to write. And all the while he was on their yachts and in their homes, Jack Dunphy, by choice, stayed at home or went skiing. Capote told everyone that Dunphy was a scholar and a recluse.

Dunphy says: "The thing I was amazed at with him was the strange immaturity of the people around him. But he's very immature in certain ways. He's startled by flash and brilliance and power. He never read Shakespeare. If I were going somewhere, I wouldn't go out and buy something special. He'll go out and buy drawerfuls if he knows he's going somewhere there are going to be butlers. Truman has these beautifully articulated toes; at least those crazy Italian shoes haven't ruined them.

Capote says he is sometimes sorry that he and Dunphy could not share friends. "But if we had," he said, "he would not have been the man I love. Jack has the most integrity of any man I know. He is my family. Jack would never abandon me."

Dunphy, who spends a large part of every year in a house of Capote's in Verbier, Switzerland, said, "Now, it's a friendship in every sense. We're proud of our past, a terrific past we've held on to and don't talk about. We traveled all over the world and stayed young for a very long time."

In 1959, Capote took a sharp life turn, a turn that would be the beginning of his greatest literary achievement, but also the beginning of the slide from which he has never quite recovered. Like many fiction writers in the '60's who were attracted to writing about real events, out of a feeling that the times demanded bald truth-telling and not storytelling, Capote went to Garden City, Kansas, to begin work on a book that would be called *In Cold Blood*. Listing further away from fiction and from the sentimentality that had characterized that fiction, Capote was drawn to the cold-blooded murder of the wholesome, Middle Western Clutter family. It was during the six years that he was in and out of Kansas that Capote began to take the tranquilizers to which he later became addicted. Capote's sympathy—from the way he talked about it, his almost sexual sympathy—was severely pulled between one of the killers, short, dark, thick-trunked Perry Smith, and the head of the investigation, Alvin Dewey, also dark, nice-faced, soft-faced, the quintessential family man. These were tense years, not unhappy, but very tense. He exhausted all his charm to get his story from plain people who by all rights should have shuddered at the sight and sound of him. Which he knew.

He worked hard, and everybody loved him. His friend Sandy Campbell was, by then, a checker of facts for *The New Yorker*, which was serializing the book, and he spent time with Capote in Kansas toward the end. In his diary entry of Oct. 26,1964, Campbell wrote:

Truman calls Alvin Poppy, and Alvin calls Truman Coach .... It is certainly extraordinary how he fits here in this small Kansas town with these simple Kansas people. They all like him, that's obvious, are all at ease with him.

Richard Avedon also joined Capote in Kansas for a few days and he saw the Hemingway charm in action. "I expected to find him in blue jeans and blue-jeaned shirt like every other farmhand out there," Avedon said, "but there he was in a fancy brocade vest. He was not going to be invisible. They would know he was there and deal with it. One day we walked into the courthouse and there was a handful of sheriffs sitting around, very tough-looking strong men in their late fifties. And Truman said in his highest voice, 'Oh, you don't look so tough to me.' And one of these guys stood up and put his fist right through the courthouse wall. It was a terrifying moment. Then Truman threw his hands over his head and hopping from one side to the other said, 'I'm beside myself, I'm beside myself.' And everybody broke up. That's guts."

By the time Perry Smith and Dick Hickock, after multiple stays of execution, were hanged on April 14, 1965, Truman Capote was taking a lot of tranquilizers and had developed twitches. It was not just sympathy for Perry—sympathy, he says, no crush, just a deep-seated, there-but-for-the-grace-of-God-go-I sympathy (though Perry was in love with him, he says, told him so a few years earlier and then, for the last time, an hour before he was hanged). It was also the reporting effort, the amassing of facts, which, said Campbell, were all correct. They were correct despite Capote's personal penchant for exaggerating and despite the fact that he reported without pad and pen, sitting down instantly after each long interview to recreate it from memory. Campbell said he had never seen such an accurate account and that whatever the fiction veneer, *In Cold Blood* was a scrupulous nonfiction report. Capote kept his masses of index cards tied with ribbons in those lovely robin's-egg blue boxes from Tiffany's.

Capote attended the hangings at the request of Perry and Dick. A few days before, at home on Long Island, he had roared into the driveway of his friend and neighbor, Mary Gimbel, fairly spitting, she said, with laughter. He had just got a card from Dick saying he was giving up smoking because it was unhealthy. But on April 14, after his own efforts and those of others had failed to halt the execution, Capote had little laughter left. From the diary of Sandy Campbell:

Alvin [Dewey] and all the K.B.I. [Kansas Bureau of Investigation] men were there. Everybody behaved wonderfully. When Perry went up to the gallows, he stopped in front of Truman, kissed him, and said, "Adios, amigo." The Times said each man was left 20 minutes hanging. Truman said the ritual of it was like a high-school graduation. When Perry was dead and taken away, the warden came up to Truman and gave him an envelope. "Mr. Smith wanted you to have this," he said. It contained all the money Truman had sent Perry of the five years. Truman burst into tears.

He cried then for two days, trying to tranquilize his tears, his book editor holding his hand all the way back to New York. Capote was later flamboyantly criticized by British critic Kenneth Tynan for not having done enough to save Hickock and Smith, a criticism some labeled as moral sniping and that Capote labeled jealousy. The book was published at the end of 1965 and was an instant success, called by some the finest crime book ever written in America. To Capote's claim that he had created a new art form, the nonfiction novel, a combination of "the persuasiveness of fact" and the "poetic altitude fiction is capable of reaching," critics were lukewarm, saying that many novels were nothing more than thinly poeticized facts. The only real critical cloud that hung and hangs over it, in a minor way, is the complaint about oversentimentalizing the killers. Most reviewers, however, saw the book as an equal-handed treatment of killers and killed—Rebecca West, one of the most eloquent, urged everyone to read "Mr. Capote's grave and reverent book." To date, 335,000 copies of *In Cold Blood* have been sold; the paperback rights went for half-a-million dollars, as high a price as had been paid for any book to that time. From the *In Cold Blood* movie royalties, and his combined book royalties, Capote still draws about $80,000 a year, money with which, as with all his moneys, he has been extravagantly generous, to himself, to friends, to relatives, to lovers and their families.

When the book was done, Capote, to give himself a treat and fend off what he called a severe postnatal *tristesse*, took up his social life where he had left off, a social life that culminated in the black-and-white fancy-dress ball he gave in November 1966 for 540 of his friends. They included, always, his early friends, men like Sandy Campbell and writer Donald Windham, whom he painstakingly introduced to the immaculate beauties and their moneyed men, as well as to the stars and starlets. He worked on the party as if it were a book, laboring over flowers, colors, seating, food—which alone cost $12,000—scrawling details in a notebook in his tiny hand. People who were not invited left town that weekend; others tried to bribe their way in. The woman for whom the party was given had never made her face up before. Katharine Graham, then forty-nine, the inheritor of *The Washington Post*, and Capote's neighbor in the United Nations Plaza, needed cheering up, Capote said, so he gave the party, already in the offing, to her.

"It was like Cinderella," she said. "I called Kenneth's [the hairdresser] to get an appointment and they said, 'Oh, Mrs. Graham, we're so busy, there's a big ball next week.' And I said, 'You won't believe it, but it's being given for me.' It was seven-thirty the night of the party after Marissa Berenson had had dozens of fake curls put on that I finally got into Kenneth's. The party for me was like an odd, overaged and gray coming out party."

He liked that, doing that with women; he was, in the words of Mary Gimbel, a sort of pint-sized King Kong, tender but very proprietary about his charges to whom, like a fish in the seas, he was attracted when they were wounded. "He gets you in the moment you're vulnerable," she said, "and massages your life, pulls the strings a bit. He gives birth to the idea of people: it's like writing fiction in three dimensions. It's like what he did with Lee [Radziwill]—trying to make her into an actress. But he enhances life in a heidey-ho way. Everyone wants a Truman in his or her life."

He is not as much in Mary Gimbel's now, because on a trip with Capote out West a few years ago, she received a number of long-distance telephone calls from a man whose name she would not share. Capote, wounded, she says, feeling an intrusion, started telling indiscreet things about her and finally Gimbel heard from a friend that Capote read her telephone messages to find out who the man was. "I was no longer his," she said. "It was that simple. It's all about power, isn't it? Once I was at a horse show. Everyone had been there all day. It was hot and dusty and all the fat mothers had dirt in the wrinkles of their necks. Suddenly, coming down the driveway was Truman with the wife and children of his then lover, all spotless, all dressed in white with little polka-dot belts. The sun was on them and they were semi-blinding. And I turned to a friend and said, 'What's that?' And she said, 'Well, he has six to control instead of one.' But that didn't mean she didn't want him in her life. We all did. Later, on Long Island, he'd come often unannounced like Queen Bess making a pass through the hinterlands, and you'd have to stop what you were doing and sit and listen. Sometimes I'd hide, but he'd come creeping up the stairs and say in that little voice of his, 'I know you're in there.' "

This was when things were already beginning to be bad. He had published a book of essays, *The Dogs Bark*, in 1973, but *Answered Prayers* was already five years overdue. It was seven, going on eight years since *In Cold Blood*—the book he called the book of a lifetime—had come out and Capote was moving in a world that demanded accomplishment in lieu of money, a world in which, however long he had been in it, he was a visitor, not a court jester, never that, but a visitor who in some way had to sing for his supper. "You were always aware of that," said Paley former son-in-law Carter Burden. "Truman couldn't just come for the weekend and sit in his room. He had to amuse; he had to be happy."

Now he was trying to write about a world, "their" world, in *Answered Prayers*, his masterpiece, he hoped, his American version of

Remembrance of Things Past. He had taken, in 1966, a $750,000 advance in assorted stocks for this book and two others. Entangled in what he himself calls an obsessive perfectionism, he would redo thirty pages to change twenty words. He went months without writing at all. "As hard as I work, and I really do," he said, "I feel as though my talent was given to me and I'm trying my best to see it as I can. I always liked Sinatra saying he took no pride in his singing because he felt it was a gift he'd been given. I feel the same way. That's why when I don't work I feel so guilty. I'm a pretty humble person. Jack [Dunphy] once said to me, 'If you get any more humble, you'll have to crawl under the door.' "

For a man who had had depressions all his life, who had experienced a kind of persistent medium-level panic left from the childhood nights in New Orleans and a locked door which no time or success could open and no persona outlive, for Capote at the age of fifty-six, the postnatal *tristesse* was the deepest. He was as rich and famous as he had meant to be; his prayers had been answered. But the wizard man had finally got him. He took more drinks. He took more pills, graduating from Valium to Tuinal, a virtual sleeping pill. He took different lovers now, men of a rougher ilk, simpler, taking them with him now when he went to parties or abroad, a bit of him, he said, finally tired of his own good taste about that part of his life. One, a former prison guard turned air-conditioning installer, again married with children, he took with him to a dinner Princess Grace gave at the palace in Monaco. "He looked cute but he was so dumb," Capote said laughing. "At dinner a man sitting next to me said, 'Oh, is this your first time in Europe?' And he said, 'Yes it is, except for that time in Vietnam.' "

Then came the man who brought him down still further. Another Irish-Catholic family man—it was his white-clad family Capote had carried to the horse show—a clerk whom Capote carried into a world for which he was not equipped, scaring his friends, scaring the man probably, a man who turned mean and rank. And Capote drank with him. As if to stay afloat. His vanity failed him; he got fat, all the while wooing the man's family, consoling the wife for the loss of her husband, holding onto that family when he, in his turn, lost the man. "I have no ill feeling toward Truman," said the wife. "Maybe I'm supposed to feel differently. He's been wonderful to my family. If the kids want anything, he's the first one they call. We've had good times together; I've met wonderful people. No door is closed to Truman." Capote's drinking turned into a despair that became suicidal. "He had grown this thing up in him," Jack Dunphy said, "like a Thurber dog." In his diary entry of May 13, 1974, Sandy Campbell wrote:

A weekend at the house in Fire Island Pines. Me, Don [Windham], Truman and Truman's latest friend. It is the first time I've spent time—more than a meal or drinks or an evening—with Truman since 1964, and, alas, a depressing time it was. Truman is as sweet and considerate as ever, but something has gone bad in his life in the last couple of years. I always thought of Truman's enjoyment of his success in contrast to Monty's [Clift] and Tennessee's misery, but now they are three of a kind.

To jolt himself out of his sadness, Capote decided to publish the sections of *Answered Prayers*. He was in California when the "Côte Basque" section appeared on the stands. Had he been home in New York, he might have more successfully defended his terrain, his talent, but he was not, and a feeling of betrayal swept through his friends, written about or not, and his phone calls went unanswered. He could hear doors shut, long distance. He had thought they would be amused, charmed, and he was in total shock. The stories he had told had been told countless times before, he said, forgetting, of course—how he could forget is hard to imagine—that the world to which he had a passkey was based, above all, on discretion. Gossiping among themselves was not the same as seeing that gossip in print. How could he had not have known? He did not, or he had forgotten.

Joanne Carson, with whom Capote was staying California at the time, said Capote looked like a baby who had been slapped. He didn't say anything to her, but she would find him in his bedroom reading and rereading the section. For the public record, he was feisty at first, saying things like, "Wait till they see the rest: they'll have to go live in glossed in the North Pole." Then he was brave, saying things like, "They always knew I was a writer: What did they expect?" Then he was sad, oh so sad, when he realized that he and Babe Paley were no longer to be friends. He had included a story that people assumed to be about her husband. Babe Paley, according to Capote and all who knew her, had the most style—hence virtue—the most grace, the most natural loveliness, inside and out, of all the women in that world. She was simply the best of it, managing houses and children and dinner parties and "good works" with consummate ease, part of her held back, Capote said, tucked away somewhere, a part she was able to share with him. "She was my best friend," Capote said. "I really loved her. One of the saddest things is that while she was sick I couldn't go to her." Babe Paley died ten days ago after a long illness.

Capote says the piece cost him only three friends: the Paleys and Nancy (Slim) Keith (Lady Keith, once married to director Howard Hawks and to agent-producer Leland Hayward), but there were other casualties near enough to the same line. The Gore Vidal lawsuit centered around a story Capote had been told, in part, by Lee Radziwill about Vidal being asked to leave a fancy White House dinner for insulting Jackie Kennedy. Vidal sued Capote for repeating the story in *Playgirl* magazine and Lee Radziwill did not want to give a deposition, though Capote says they are still friends. Lawyers for Capote and Vidal are trying to work out an amicable resolution.

Then, too, there was not only social fallout over *Answered Prayers* but critical fallout as well, rumblings about it not being Capote's best work, or near. When *Esquire*, with much fanfare, published the first section, "Mojave," in June 1975, Arnold Gingrich, publisher of the magazine, was heard to say: "We gave the impression the mountains were paturiating and out came this little mouse." "LA COTE 65," as art, did not engender much more praise than it did as gossip. With the third section, "Unspoiled Monsters," in May 1976, there was critical recovery. People unmoved by the first pieces found the third, a long, spinning story about atrocities committed in the name of love, full, again, of the narrative skill they associated with Capote. Of course, all the criticisms are premature; the work should be judged as a whole; judged against the whole, against Capote's previous writings, there is a sense that the people he was trying to write about, the people he was trying to live among, did not, could not, could never engage his imagination or his sympathy the way a Miss Sook or a Perry Smith had.

"Abandonment, the theme of so much of his earlier work, had become too difficult a subject to handle; he had become ashamed of it, afraid of his own sentimentality," said writer-critic Alfred Kazin. "He forced himself to have a biting edge, a sophistication that was false. But Truman's very, very good, a natural writer, his authenticity comes through. The obvious jumping around in his career reflects the confusion of American writers as a whole rather than his own confusion."

By June of 1976, Capote was in great pain. He says he saw five psychiatrists, each for no more than two months. He went into Silver Hill hospital in Connecticut for month to get off pills and alcohol, fighting very hard, losing ground again and landing in September of 1977 in the fortress-like Smithers Alcohol Rehabilitation Center in New York City. "the night I took him to Smithers," said Alan Schwartz, Capote's lawyer and major custodial friend, "he turned to me as we were leaving his apartment—he was so frightened—but he turned to me and said, 'Alan, don't forget to water the flowers.' " He broke the tranquilizer habit finally, Capote said, coming out to find his current "friend" had moved out. He then went to Towson State University, near Baltimore, to make a speech, not continuing, announcing instead that he was an alcoholic and that he would not be back, in public, until he was well.

The Truman Capote one meets today is, when he does not drink, when he takes Antabuse, which he does every few months for some days, like the magic, slightly wicked boy he must have been the first days in New York, as if all the years, good then bad, had not mattered. There is still about him an optimism that is only somewhat weary. He kisses me when we meet and he kisses me when we part. He holds my hand when we cross the street and gives me money one late night for cab fare. He asks me always if I like what he's wearing. He puts on his black beret and dark glasses and takes me to a gay bar, just a normal one first, and, finding no spectacle, takes me to a gay prostitute's bar where he tells me who does what to whom and for how much. It is dark inside; commuters in their pinstripe suits eye the pretty big boys. Capote tells me he has never picked up anybody for a one-night stand. "I'd sooner," he says, "jump off the Brooklyn Bridge." He tells me, too, that he has been with women whose names I'd know, that they were always the aggressors and that he doesn't pretend to be bisexual and that he doesn't think there is such a thing. In this bar, we are voyeurs, both of us, just as Capote is a voyeur, I now understand, at a place like Studio 54 where he goes maybe twice a month. He watches, dancing, enchanting when he must, but mostly content to look. Looking, he is a lot of fun. He sees everything and can make stories out of everyone. After a few days together, he says: "I know a lot more about other people than I know about myself."

His days in New York are much alike. He sleeps late, lunches out, often with what his older friends call "his back-up girls," one of whom, socialite Jan Cushing, young, blond, said, "Lucky for me that I met Truman at his down point; in his up point he wouldn't have even noticed me. I was with him one day at Quo Vadis where Slim Keith was lunching with some other women. I was happy to be there with him. It's like you want someone there to protect you when you run into an old beau."

After lunch, he goes to a gym for an hour's workout, then home to try to write for three of four hours. He says he has finished another section of *Answered Prayers* called "A Severe Insult to the Brain," which he explains is the official phrase for death by alcoholism, and that the book is two-thirds done. He has told Random House that he will deliver the entire book by August of next year. His close friends say he will finish the book if he does not drink, but between Antabuse periods he is drinking. Capote says that living with the book is like having an illness, like being in chains. If he has lost faith in any way with it, he does not say so. It is the one fence he puts up, even with friends, that one around his work. He won't look back, say what are his favorites of his books, won't compare any of his writing, part of a writer's prerogative, and, perhaps, sanity.

The one thing he will say is that he thinks he writes as good a sentence as anyone writing. Most critics agree. "Capote," said

Malcolm Cowley, "is a writer of real talent. *In Cold Blood* was a very good job, but it was an act of research, not an act of the imagination. We had hope for something else from Capote."

"Basically deep down I don't give a damn what any of them think about my writing, even Jack," Capote said. "If *Answered Prayers* is as good as I want, I'll have nothing further to prove ... it's not necessary. I really have nothing to prove now."

Evenings, he reads, has dinner with a friend and occasionally goes to parties, only fine, fancy ones—"I like to do it big if I'm going to do it," he said. He is planning another big party of his own, a day of reckoning, he calls it, for, again, about 540 of his friends. Scheduled for December of this year, it is to be a night in Arabian tents set up in some warehouse in the city. He is having the tents made now, blue and khaki. They are to wear black caftans, the women with veils till midnight. Capote's will be half street urchin, half sheik, he says, eyes glowing as he describes his costume. "I will be all in white, a white galabia with appliqued butterflies and a white turban, on the side of which will be one large emerald. I will be barefoot and will carry a fabulous Fabergé walking cane. I will be the prince of all Araby and you will all kiss my ring when you come in."

Postscript:

"Capote suggested to the *New York Times Magazine* that a piece should be done about him," says Fleming. "They asked if he'd been drinking, and he assured them he was sober. Capote and his people were spinning the *Times*. So, I arrive, a California blond with hair below my waist."

"First day we met at La Côte Basque. I had this little old crummy tape recorder and he said, 'You don't use that do you? Why?' He said, 'If you're going to be a good reporter all you have to do is listen, put that away.' I put it away. Part of it was a game. Putting me on notice. A challenge. It gives him freedom. So, I listened with all the fiber I had. I never used a tape recorder on this story. I did later, and certainly in a litigious world you have to.

"Capote was generous with his time. But his seduction, which had been so apparent, and so ahead of his time in its complicated allure, had changed. He was just so weary of his own performance. The effort to be Truman Capote and to have had the talent he had and not looked after it the way he should have, was there in his eyes. There was a real sweetness to him. He was drinking. He hid it from me, but I know what it looked like."

Capote wrote one of the most memorable hit pieces ever—the 1957 *New Yorker* profile of Marlon Brando—but Fleming had no interest in that kind of story.

"A savage review can decimate your career. I was not built that way. To make smart-ass comments would be the farthest thing from my mind. It would be dumb, irresponsible and very bad storytelling. Let people make their own decision."

She didn't hear from Capote after the pieces ran. "Somebody said to me he didn't expect you to see what you saw," says Fleming. "I think he thought I was nice and charming, but the portrait was poignant and pointed because of the place he was in his life. He was miffed that I'd gotten as much as I'd gotten. But he let me get it.

"Capote was a writer I wanted to be and that upped the ante. I come from Hollywood people, I knew the fame game, but with a writer of talent to have done that and engaged in that was something else—with Capote it hit the max pitch. The persona had cost him everything. It was revenge on himself. He knew what he'd done. He knew he'd sold his soul for fame. It was a cautionary tale."

It's a fair bet that Helen Dudar's (1924-2002) first encounter with Lauren Bacall happened in the pages of a movie magazine, back when Dudar was a bobby-soxer helping out in her family's candy store on Long Island, and fanzines were what there was to read. But by the time she met the real Bacall in 1979, the starstruck teen in the candy store had grown up to be a star in her own right—a journalist of penetrating vision and a near matchless way with words. She'd covered presidential campaigns and murder trials. She'd profiled a long list of people with boldface names, from Jimmy Carter to John Updike to Nelson Rockefeller to Robert Rauschenberg to Malcolm X, and, over the years, more showbiz stars than those enshrined in Hollywood's Walk of Fame. And she always got through the shrink-wrap encasing them because she never came unprepared. Bacall had agreed to an interview to plug her newly published and visibly homemade memoir. Dudar read it, twice. She devoured every print source she could find. She walked around the block to her neighborhood video shop, rented every Bacall movie on their shelves, watched them all, and checked what the critics had said about them. On the morning of the interview, she sat at her kitchen table with a second cup of espresso and wrote out the questions she meant to ask, as always including some she guessed her subject had never confronted before. (A recurring favorite: "Do you think of your childhood as having been happy?") It's another fair bet that Bacall had never confronted anyone like Dudar before.—Peter Goldman

LAUREN BACALL REMEMBRANCES OF BOGIE AND OTHER THINGS PAST

Writer's Bloc, 1979

Given the nature of movie imagery, which is strong, persistent, and sometimes indelible, we may be pardoned if we think of Lauren Bacall as a woman who combines steely independence with a sassy, unflinching social ease. Except, of course, she won't pardon us because, dammit, we really should know better than to confuse the real person with the performing persona.

The one up there is Lauren Bacall, a Hollywood invention whose presence, a critic once observed, lends new meaning to the term Bitch Goddess. The one down here thinks of herself as Betty Bacall, gets the shakes making an entrance alone in a room full of people, turns to jelly at the sight of such sentimental monuments as the Arch of Triumph, longs for a man to lean on, and assesses her temperament as vulnerable and romantic. Also, she's scared.

All but the last detail has been gleaned from her forthcoming book, which, naturally enough is the source of her apprehension. Mind you, it is not the critics who worry her. Convinced that film and stage critics don't know beans about the art of acting, Bacall is nearly as certain that book reviewers are equally at sea about the craft of writing.

In any event, she plans to avoid the reviews, having found that praise and blame are usually bestowed for equally invalid reasons. But what is she going to do about this feeling that she is, metaphorically speaking, naked to the world? Her long, bony fingers carving arabesques in the air, little gold rings glinting in the lights of lamps lit against the violent dusk, she tries to explain:

"When I turned the book in, I really did have postpartum depression. I really felt I had given up my child. Certainly, I'd given up my *life*. Now suddenly a lot of people are going to know much more about me than I ever thought they would. And I'm not going to know which ones know.

"And there are people who are not going to like what I say and people who don't think I can write and people who still aren't convinced that I did it myself and people who are not going to approve of things that I've written about various people. I know that's going to happen." There is scarcely a beat between this fit of uncertainty and a classic Bacallian method of dealing with opinions she does not value. "Well, what the hell. I can't do anything about that."

The book is called *Lauren Bacall By Myself*, and even a casual prowl of its pages can leave no doubt that Bacall had hardly any help. She wrote it between acting engagements over a three-year period, by hand on yellow legal pads, mostly in a series of temporarily empty offices at Alfred A. Knopf that proved to be the only distraction-free place she could find. It is all Bacall, including the sentences that don't parse, the feverish dashes that replace conventional punctuation, and the tendency to describe emotion in terms that echo the movie clichés of yesteryear: "When we looked at each other, trumpets sounded, rockets went off."

She tells us about Betty Jane Perske, a nice, sheltered Jewish girl from New York who cried at movies, who worshiped Bette Davis, and who, at twenty, was transformed into a movie siren in her very first film, *To Have and Have Not*. She tells us about the near-idyllic marriage to Humphrey Bogart, cruelly ended by cancer. She tells us about the near-marriage to Frank Sinatra, aborted by Sinatra's mercurial disposition and his apparent incapacity to deal with any human relationship as a grownup. ("Don't tell me," he would demand. "Suggest.") She tells us of the eight-year union with Jason Robards, done in by drink and his need to wander. She tells us she was spoiled, selfish, and self-absorbed. She tells us nothing more piercing than a single line memorializing her young Hollywood days and her twelve years with Bogart: "Whenever I hear the word *happy* now, I think of then."

When the sentence is read back to Bacall, she looks suspicious and faintly menacing. She is under the impression that she has been especially revealing and is wary about questions that seem designed to carry any point out of the shallows where much of her book dwells. Finally, she says: "I have not been happy in the full sense of happy. Number one, I think that anyone who has any brain at all—how can anyone be happy in this world? You have to be an idiot to be happy.

"But I think certainly then I had the world by the tail. I was nineteen years old. I was in love with a wonderful man who was in love with me. I had made a big hit in a film. I had everything anyone could possibly dream of, more than I ever dreamed I would have at once.

"I certainly have not had anything comparable to that feeling since. I've had rewarding moments. I love my kids. I have terrific friends. I have a lot of pluses in my life. But to say that I myself have been happy? I've had moments of feeling happy, but that's all. I've had nothing for *long*."

Publishers have been trying for years to put Bacall in print. "I've been asked to write books about myself and Bogie, which I always said I would never do, and books with pictures and coffee-table books and blah-blah-blah." Knopf's editor-in-chief, Robert Gottlieb, succeeded where others had failed for a number of reasons. Chief among them, says Bacall, is that "he did not want anything cheap. He did not want anything sensational. And he wanted it to be about *me*. Bogie was part of my life, but he was not all of my life. Most people wanted only that. I said I would not do it. I'm not out to make a buck on my marriage and my first husband and on his fame and on his legend. That was twelve years of my life. I've lived a few more than twelve years."

Bacall will make a bounteous buck indeed out of her life story, but it's no use asking her for details. At Knopf, which ordered up a handsome first printing of 100,000 copies, it is already seen as "a million-dollar book" based on sales of reprint rights. The English, the Swedes, the French, and the Italians have bought it; *Family Circle* here and *The Daily Telegraph* in London each paid better than $100,000 for excerpts. a nice piece of change for a woman who is no stranger to thrift. An inquiry about profits brings from her a frosty reply: "It's been sold in many places. I don't intend to discuss figures. I haven't gotten rich from the book yet. I hope I will, but I haven't."

Her blue eyes have turned cool, glacially neutral. She fingers one of several gold chains on her brown sweater and glances at the dog sprawled across her skirt in blissful sleep. He is Blenheim, a Cavalier King Charles spaniel, and they love one another. Outside the tall, uncurtained windows lies Central Park, a stretch of sere and wintry brown, and beyond that the silhouetted skyline of New York's Upper East Side. For eighteen years, Bacall has owned an apartment in the Dakota, a prestigious, venerable West Side building with soaring ceilings, three-inch-thick mahogany doors, and immense rooms, each with a brilliantly embellished fireplace.

We are in the library, perfumed by the narcissus growing in a bowl on the coffee table and artfully cluttered. The place is a tribute to decades of exploring the world's antique shops. Bacall doesn't collect things, she collects collections: little brass boxes, oil paintings of cats and dogs, Ashanti gold weights, pearl-inlaid furniture. Lately seized with a passion for early American quilts, she has acquired enough to cover all the beds in four bedrooms, to change them seasonally, and to decorate the rooms of the weekend place she acquired a year ago in Amagansett, on the eastern end of Long Island. She buys them compulsively and in quantity and won't even guess how many she owns. Genuinely appalled, she begins to enumerate the objects she can't resist: "Faience, pewter, good old furniture—you name it, I buy it. It's awful."

When she is not worried that an effort is underway to extract information that she's not prepared to surrender, Bacall is a quite cozy, likable woman with a modest gift for self-mockery and a tendency to offer up details no one has thought of soliciting.

Cracking and consuming walnuts out of a silver bowl, she glumly reveals that she is struggling with eight unwanted pounds. Not readily apparent under the folds of her gathered brown skirt, the extra weight arrived after a successful course with Smokenders during which she cured her addiction to nicotine and took up candy bars. For the first time in her life as a naturally slender person, she is having trouble slimming down.

Then there is the matter of the natural erosions of time and the way in which Americans culturally deal with them. Bacall has strong opinions on the subject, and they come roaring out:

"This country drives me up the wall with that attitude about age. That everyone has got to have a facelift is so depressing. One must not have a line. To see those pictures of Betty Ford side by side, you just want to cut your throat. I mean—what is it? We're all convinced we must look young. Madness. Sad.

"I can see where my face could be improved. But I also feel your life is in your face. Now, I'm going to sound awfully silly if two years from now I go and have a facelift. I'm fighting it. I may lose, but I'm fighting it. People tell me, 'Why not it's part of your business. You should have a little thing done here and a little thing there.' Half the people I meet think I've had one anyway. After thirty-two, if you look good, you have got to have had cosmetic surgery."

Lauren Bacall is fifty-four and she looks good. There's little point in asking her about the rewards of maturity—she has no talent for introspection. If anything, the years have given her more things to be indignant about. She is angry about a movie business that in general has no interest in stories that might reflect the lives of women who are no longer young. She doesn't think much of the new Hollywood, deploring the disappearance of the old studio system—"the good times," which she devoutly believed fostered an unmatchable range of talented stars and creative people. As for many of the new performers now rated as stars, "Ten years from now they will never be heard of again. Everyone is a star for two minutes."

Since Bacall's great long-running hit in the 1970 Broadway musical *Applause*, she has worked less than she would have liked. She has a role as a fanatic nutrition expert in the new Robert Altman film *Health*, to be shot in Florida this winter, and the prospect genuinely excites her. But opportunities of that sort are rare. She turns down scripts regularly. "I've been sent an average of two or three plays a year lately—one worse than the other. They're awful. It's all well and good to do things for money if occasionally you have to, but not a film that's going to come back to haunt you and certainly not a play that you have to do eight times a week. I couldn't bear it."

Work is important to her, perhaps, she muses, the most important thing in her life. She is not ruling out other essentials. Bacall is a woman who likes and needs male companionship, but the possibilities for permanence seem dim. During a two-year stay in England, for the London run of *Applause* and then the filming of *Murder on the Orient Express*, she fell in love with a married Englishman. They had a "happy" six-month relationship that came to a "devastating" end. And that's all anybody needs to know about that affair.

Now she leans back in her chair and calmly confronts a future alone. "I think it is very possible that I will spend the rest of my life by myself, just because the averages are not necessarily in my favor. I had it terrific once and that's it. How many chances do you get?

"I'm not desperate about it at all. I just feel that I don't want to waste my time and that I really want to spend my life doing what I want to do. I don't want to give myself away. I don't want to go to cocktail parties anymore. I could spend all of my time going out, because the whole world would have you decorating their living rooms."

Actually, as a resident and available star, Bacall is on everybody's party list, and her face or name seems to turn up in the columns for at least one big New York event a week. But she insists she avoids most of the big bashes. "I don't want to dissipate my energies. I would like to focus on my friends, my work, my children."

There are three children—two Bogarts and one Robards. Bacall is pleased with them. "I think they have all turned into very good people. I don't take credit for that. I think you can give your kids everything, and they can turn out badly. I think they must finally take some of the responsibility."

Steven Bogart, married and the father of a son, went back to school after six years as a dropout—"a late bloomer like his father"; he is graduating from the University of Hartford in May, and will work in some aspect of television news. Her daughter, Leslie, is a nurse. Her youngest, Sam, is seventeen and in his last year in high school, and with any luck will be the third generation of Robardses in the acting profession.

"He's been around Jason a lot in rehearsal, he's been on tour with Jason and with me, so he knows an actor's life is hard work. I would never point any kid of mine in that direction because I just think it's too tough a life. But, by God, in Sam's case, I just know he'll make it."

She took Sam off for a Christmas visit in London, a little breather for her before a bone-crushing, fifteen-city tour on behalf of *By Myself*. London has special appeal for her, and she looks back on her two-year stay with something like longing. "It is quieter, it is cleaner; it has more to do with yesterday than with today. There's no question that it's easier there. And that's why I left." There were, after all, today and tomorrow to be faced. Besides, she knows very well it's not supposed to be easy.

Postscript:

Here's how Nora Ephron remembered Dudar in *The Attentive Eye*, a collection of Dudar's work self-published by her husband, Peter Goldman, shortly before Dudar passed away in 2002:

"The first time I heard about Helen Dudar, I was working at *Newsweek* magazine as a fact-checker in the National Affairs department. A new writer named Peter Goldman had just arrived at the magazine from St. Louis, and he was good. He was really good. Everyone was buzzing around about how good, how really good, Peter Goldman was, and someone finally buzzed it right at Peter

Goldman himself, who replied—at least this is how I remember it—that he just wished he could write as well as his wife.

"I had no idea who his wife was, but I soon found out. She was Helen Dudar of the *New York Post*. And she was, according to my friend Nan, brilliant. Nan had a way of saying the word *brilliant* that was completely terrifying, and I believed virtually everything she ever said to me for quite a long time. From Nan I learned not just about Helen but also about Brie and vitello tonnato and the omelet place, and she was right about Helen and Brie although not really about vitello tonnato or the omelet place. Anyway, I began to read Helen Dudar in the *New York Post*, and she was as good as I'd been told.

"And then, within a few weeks, I was there, too—a reporter on tryout at the paper, and met the now legendary-to-me Tiny Helen, as Peter called her, and got to watch her do her thing. And she could do anything. She could write a lyrical feature piece, she could write hard news, and she was—in a city room full of world-class rewrite men—the greatest rewrite man of all. I can see her at the rewrite desk in the center of the newsroom on November 22, 1963, as page after page of wire copy mounted up, reporters phoned in from the street, and she sat at the typewriter, with a phone set on her head, writing the lead piece on the Kennedy assassination. Flawlessly. Calmly. One paragraph at a time of clean, clear prose.

"She was grace under pressure, she was the epitome of unself-conscious professionalism, she was simply great. I idolized her, and then, as I got to know her, I found more and more things to admire. My eventual theory about her was that Helen wrote the way Ella Fitzgerald sang. They both made it look easy when it wasn't. They both avoided anything extraneous, or self-serving, or self-aggrandizing, or forced, or strained; what Helen and Ella both managed to bring off was the equivalent of the purest, clearest spring water. For years, I tried to figure out how she did it—at the *Post* and later, when she became a wonderful magazine writer—but eventually I gave up and simply enjoyed it all.

"I was also, happily, the beneficiary of her wisdom on a great many subjects. Unlike Nan, Helen was right about everything: fish soup with *rouille,* exercise as an antidote to depression, copper pots, the Bridge company, Sonia Rykiel, Fairway, and the South of France, to name just a few of the things I know something about because of her.

"She is a writer's writer, a journalist's journalist, a reporter's reporter. She's a generalist in the most flattering sense of the word—there's no subject she can't write about with intelligence. Well, not mere intelligence—a 'demanding, sinewy intelligence,' to quote one of Helen's more felicitous phrases, which happens to be quoted in *Webster's Dictionary*, no less. After she left the *Post*, she became at ease writing about Cezanne, Arthur Miller, Jack Nicholson, and Rome. 'Helen Dudar frequently writes about the theater,' it would say at the bottom of her articles. Or: 'Helen Dudar frequently writes about art.' Or: 'Helen Dudar frequently writes about publishing.' The truth is that Helen Dudar frequently writes about everything and does it better than just about anyone else."

ACKNOWLEDGMENTS

Our first debt of gratitude goes to the writers, editors, and craftspeople involved in the making of these stories—the magazine industry or culture as a whole, as it were.

Big love goes to Mike Sager without whom you would not be reading this. Mike hasn't just enjoyed a long career as a top-flight magazine writer, he's a true believer. At The Sager Group, he's put his money where his mouth is, publishing numerous volumes of classic longform journalism, including The Stacks Reader series. He's our poobah as well as our biggest cheerleader and we're honored to be part of The Sager Group collective.

In addition to thanking all of the authors who appear in this collection, I'd also like to extend my appreciation to Leigh Hubbard, Kate Tarlow Morgan, Alison Brower, Johanna Lawrenson, Ken Norwick, Gay Daly, John Goldsmith, Jane Krupp, Jere Herzenberg, Nick Pileggi, JJ Sacha for all of their help and goodwill.

Let's give a hand to John Schulian, Malcolm Jones, Peter Goldman, James Wolcott, Fred Schruers, and Will Blythe for contributing author head notes, and encouraging the project for the beginning. And special thanks to the ever-hilarious Joyce Wadler for her savvy, and hilarious, foreword.

So many people touched this project along the way. In no particular order, huge thanks to Rob O'Hare, Steve Randall, Jay Lovinger, John Ed Bradley, Rob Fleder, John Kenney, Rae Lewis, Alex Wolff, Jenny Allen, Richard Johnson, Steve Oney, Mary Bahr, Thomas Hayes, Paul Slansky, Rob Cohen, Shawn Nuzzo, and the late, great, Bill Zehme.

On the home front, love to my friends and family. And especially to the love of my life, Emily Joy. —Alex Belth

PERMISSIONS

"A Comedian of Guilt" (also titled "Portnoy's Complaint by Philip Roth Looms as a Wild-Blue Shocker and the American Novel of the Sixties") by Albert Goldman, first published by *Life*, February 7, 1969. Reprinted with permission of the author's estate.

"La Dolce Viva" by Barbara L. Goldsmith, first published by *New York*, April 29, 1968. Reprinted with permission of the author's estate.

"Sex Goddess of the Seventies" by Mark Jacobson, first published by *New York Magazine*, May 1975. Reprinted with permission of the author.

"Warren Beatty Has Been Wronged!" by Helen Lawrenson, first published by *Cosmopolitan*, May 1967. Reprinted with permission of the author's estate.

"What Makes Sammy Jr. Run?" by Thomas B. Morgan, first published by *Esquire*, October 1959. Reprinted with permission of the author's estate.

"Not Only Is He Beautiful, but He Can Dance Too" by Sally Quinn , first published by *The Washington Post*, June 1, 1974. Reprinted with permission of the author.

"Ava: Life in the Afternoon" by Rex Reed, first published by *Esquire*, May 1967. Reprinted with permission of the author.

"Donna Summer: Intimate and Untouchable, Trying to Cool Her Image" by Jacqueline Trescott , first published by *The Washington Post*, April 3, 1978. Reprinted with permission of the author.

"Reggie Jackson in No-Man's Land" by Robert Ward, first published by *Sport*, June 1977. Reprinted with permission of the author.

ABOUT THE EDITOR

Alex Belth is the editor of Esquire Classic, the magazine's digital archive, as well as the editor of The Stacks Reader, a website dedicated to preserving great journalism from the golden age of magazines. He is also imprint editor of The Stacks Reader Series, published by The Sager Group LLC and sponsored by NeoText. Belth has been a contributor to *Esquire*, *Sports Illustrated*, Deadspin, and The Daily Beast, and created BronxBanter, one of the original New York Yankees blogs, which the *Village Voice* called a "New York City treasure." In a previous life, Belth worked in film postproduction for Ken Burns, the Coen brothers, and others.

ABOUT THE PUBLISHER

The Sager Group was founded in 1984. In 2012 it was chartered as a multimedia content brand, with the intent of empowering those who create art—an umbrella beneath which makers can pursue, and profit from, their craft directly, without gatekeepers. TSG publishes books; ministers to artists and provides modest grants; and produces documentary, feature, and commercial films. By harnessing the means of production, The Sager Group helps artists help themselves. For more information, please see TheSagerGroup.net.

ABOUT THE STACKS READER SERIES

The Stacks Reader Series highlights classic literary nonfiction and short fiction by great journalists that would otherwise be lost to history—a living archive of memorable storytelling by notable authors. Sponsored in part by NeoText, it is curated by Alex Belth and brought to you by The Sager Group.

MORE BOOKS FROM THE SAGER GROUP

The Stacks Reader Series

The Cheerleaders: A True Story by E. Jean Carroll

An American Family: A True Story by Daniel Voll

Flesh and Blood: A True Story by Peter Richmond

An Accidental Martyr: A True Story by Chip Brown

Death of a Playmate: A True Story by Teresa Carpenter

The Detective: And Other True Stories by Walt Harrington

Soldiers in the Army of God: A True Story by Daniel Voll

Original Gangster: A True Story by Paul Solotaroff

The Dreamer Deceiver: A True Story by Ivan Solotaroff

Mary in the Lavender Pumps: A True Story about Love,
Murder and Gender Identity by Joyce Wadler

Not Guilty by Reason of Afghanistan:
And Other True Stories
by John H. Richardson

The Strange and Mysterious Death of Mrs. Jerry Lee Lewis
by Richard Ben Cramer

Love and Death in Vermont by Marguerite Del Giudice

Growing up Stoned by Elizabeth Kaye

General Interest

The Stories We Tell: Classic True Tales
by America's Greatest Women Journalists

New Stories We Tell: True Tales
by America's New Generation of Great Women Journalists

Newswomen: Twenty-Five Years of Front-Page Journalism

Next Wave: America's New Generation of Literary Journalists

The Devil & John Holmes: And Other True Stories by Mike Sager

Lifeboat No. 8: Surviving the Titanic by Elizabeth Kaye

Hunting Marlon Brando: A True Story by Mike Sager

Notes from the Road: A Filmmaker's Journey through American Music
by Robert Mugge

The Living and the Dead by Brian Mockenhaupt

See our entire collection @ TheSagerGroup.net

THE SAGER GROUP
Artifex Te Adiuva